It's Another Quality Book from CGP

This book is for anyone doing GCSE Spanish.

We've stuck in the _new syllabus changes_ and all the
really important stuff you need to do well in GCSE Spanish.
And we've unravelled the mysteries of Spanish Grammar.

Then we've had a really good stab at
making it funny — so you'll _actually use it_.

Simple as that.

What CGP is All About

Our sole aim here at CGP is to produce the highest quality books
— carefully written, immaculately presented, and dangerously
close to being funny.

Then we work our socks off to get them out to you
— at the cheapest possible prices.

Contents

Numbers and Amounts

Here we go! Here we go! Here we go!

Uno, dos, tres — One, two, three...

① 11 to 15 all end in '<u>ce</u>'. But 16, 17, 18 and 19 are '<u>ten and six</u>' etc.

② All <u>twenty-something</u> numbers are rolled into one — "<u>veintiuno</u>" etc.

0	cero
1	uno (un), una
2	dos
3	tres
4	cuatro
5	cinco
6	seis
7	siete
8	ocho
9	nueve
10	diez

11	once
12	doce
13	trece
14	catorce
15	quince
16	dieciséis
17	diecisiete
18	dieciocho
19	diecinueve

21	veintiuno
22	veintidós
23	veintitrés

31 treinta y uno

20	veinte	60	sesenta
30	treinta	70	setenta
40	cuarenta	80	ochenta
50	cincuenta	90	noventa

After <u>30</u>, numbers are joined by "<u>y</u>" (and), but written <u>separately</u> — "<u>treinta y uno</u>" etc.

When you want to put "<u>one</u>" in front of a <u>masculine</u> word, "<u>uno</u>" <u>drops</u> the "<u>o</u>" — eg *Treinta y un discos* = 31 discs. ...And before a <u>feminine</u> word, the "<u>o</u>" changes to "<u>a</u>" — eg *veintiuna pesetas*.

③ Most 'ten-type' numbers end in 'nta' (except '<u>veinte</u>').

④ When you get to hundreds and thousands, just put ciento, doscientos, mil (etc) before the number. A date is written like an ordinary number.

mil novecientos cuarenta y siete = 1947

1900   40   7

100	ciento (cien)
101	ciento uno
200	doscientos
500	quinientos
923	novecientos veintitrés
1000	mil
1,000,000	un millón

Ciento becomes "<u>cien</u>" unless it's followed by a number.

First, second, third — they're a bit different...

These always end in "o" for masculine things or "a" for feminine things.

1st	primero, primera		
2nd	segundo/a		
3rd	tercero/a	7th	séptimo/a
4th	cuarto/a	8th	octavo/a
5th	quinto/a	9th	noveno/a
6th	sexto/a	10th	décimo/a

NB When "<u>primero</u>" or "<u>tercero</u>" appear in front of a masculine word, they always drop the "<u>o</u>" — "el <u>primer</u> baile" = the first dance.

Tome la segunda *calle a la izquierda.*

= Take the second street on the left.

1st is written 1°, or 1ᵉʳᵃ. 2nd is written 2° or 2ª, etc.

¿Cuánto? — How much?

These tasty words for how many or how much are <u>important</u>. There are a fair few to learn down there, but write each one out in different sentences — make sure you don't cheat and skip <u>any</u>.

Tengo todas las *manzanas.*

= I have all the apples.

Cada *manzana es verde.*

= <u>Every/each</u> apple is green.

all the *(masc. plural):* todos los
other: otros/as
some: unos/as

several: varios/as
many: muchos/as
few: pocos/as

all the *(singular):* todo el / toda la

Your days are numbered — today's the 20th...

You're bound to know a bit about numbers already — which is cool. And it means you can spend more time checking that you know the rest of the page. Learn <u>all</u> of these words about amounts. The <u>best</u> way to check is to cover up the page, and then try to write them down — right now.

Times and Dates

Time — it's one of the most precious things... especially if you want to do well in your Spanish.

¿Qué hora es? — What time is it?

There are <u>loads</u> of ways of saying the time in English, and there are in Spanish too.

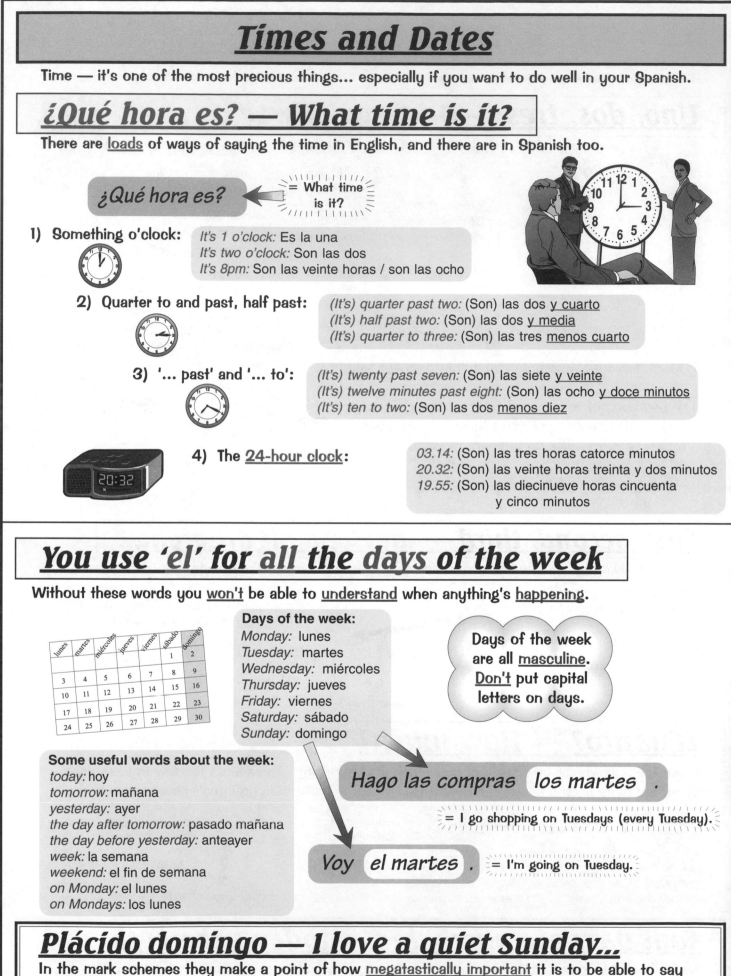

> ¿Qué hora es?   ← = What time is it?

1) **Something o'clock:**

    It's 1 o'clock: Es la una
    It's two o'clock: Son las dos
    It's 8pm: Son las veinte horas / son las ocho

2) **Quarter to and past, half past:**

    (It's) quarter past two: (Son) las dos <u>y cuarto</u>
    (It's) half past two: (Son) las dos <u>y media</u>
    (It's) quarter to three: (Son) las tres <u>menos cuarto</u>

3) **'... past' and '... to':**

    (It's) twenty past seven: (Son) las siete <u>y veinte</u>
    (It's) twelve minutes past eight: (Son) las ocho <u>y doce minutos</u>
    (It's) ten to two: (Son) las dos <u>menos diez</u>

4) **The <u>24-hour clock</u>:**

    03.14: (Son) las tres horas catorce minutos
    20.32: (Son) las veinte horas treinta y dos minutos
    19.55: (Son) las diecinueve horas cincuenta
    y cinco minutos

You use 'el' for all the days of the week

Without these words you <u>won't</u> be able to <u>understand</u> when anything's <u>happening</u>.

lunes	martes	miércoles	jueves	viernes	sábado	domingo
					1	2
3	4	5	6	7	8	9
10	11	12	13	14	15	16
17	18	19	20	21	22	23
24	25	26	27	28	29	30

Days of the week:
Monday: lunes
Tuesday: martes
Wednesday: miércoles
Thursday: jueves
Friday: viernes
Saturday: sábado
Sunday: domingo

> Days of the week are all <u>masculine</u>. <u>Don't</u> put capital letters on days.

Some useful words about the week:
today: hoy
tomorrow: mañana
yesterday: ayer
the day after tomorrow: pasado mañana
the day before yesterday: anteayer
week: la semana
weekend: el fin de semana
on Monday: el lunes
on Mondays: los lunes

Hago las compras [los martes] .

= I go shopping on Tuesdays (every Tuesday).

Voy [el martes] . = I'm going on Tuesday.

Plácido domingo — I love a quiet Sunday...

In the mark schemes they make a point of how <u>megatastically important</u> it is to be able to say <u>when</u> you do things. So you absolutely have to know how to say the <u>days of the week</u> and things like '<u>tomorrow</u>' or '<u>weekend</u>'. So find the time... and <u>get down to it</u>.

Times and Dates

You can <u>bet</u> your bottom dollar they'll ask you something needing a date in the Exam. When you're going on holiday, when your birthday is... something like that.

Enero, febrero, marzo, abril...

Spanish month names bear a striking resemblance to the English ones
— make sure you learn what's different.

January: enero   *July:* julio
February: febrero   *August:* agosto
March: marzo   *September:* se(p)tiembre
April: abril   *October:* octubre
May: mayo   *November:* noviembre
June: junio   *December:* diciembre

Se va en julio.

= He's leaving in July.

Months are all <u>masculine</u>.
<u>Don't</u> put capital letters on them.

You say "the 3 of May" instead of "the 3rd of May"

Here's how you say <u>the date</u>. This is <u>bound to come up</u> in your <u>Speaking Exam</u> — and the examiners won't be impressed if you can't tell them what the date is.

Check out page 1 for help with the numbers.

1) In Spanish, they don't say "the <u>third of</u> May" — they say "the <u>three</u> of May". Weird, huh.

Llego el tres de octubre. = I am coming / I arrive on the 3rd of October.

2) And this is how you <u>write the date</u> in a letter:

Londres, 5 de marzo de 2001. = London, 5th March 2001.

See pages 66-7 for letters.

3) And here are some other useful bits:

in the year 2000: en el año dos mil
in 2001: en el dos mil uno ← NOT 'dos mil y uno'

Mañana — Tomorrow... Ayer — Yesterday

Use these with the <u>stuff</u> on <u>page 2</u> — great for sorting out your <u>social life</u>.

Voy a esquiar a menudo. = I often go skiing.

always: siempre
often: a menudo
seldom: pocas veces
sometimes: a veces

See <u>page 97</u> for how to say you <u>never</u> do something.

¿Qué haces esta noche? = What are you doing tonight?

tomorrow: mañana
yesterday: ayer
this morning: esta mañana
this afternoon/evening: esta tarde
tonight: esta noche
tomorrow morning: mañana por la mañana
this week: esta semana
next week: la semana próxima
last week: la semana pasada
every fortnight: cada quince días
every day: todos los días
at the weekend: el fin de semana

Dates — better at the cinema than in Spanish...

It doesn't come much more <u>crucial</u> than this. It <u>will</u> get you more marks — this stuff on timeframes is specifically mentioned in the <u>syllabus</u>. It's not that hard, either. You have to learn the phrase '<u>¿Qué haces esta noche?</u>', and the words you can slot in instead of 'esta noche'.

Being Polite

You'll lose marks (and sound <u>rude</u>) if you don't stay polite in the exam — it's <u>dead important</u>.

¿Qué tal? — How are you?

Learn these phrases — they're <u>crucial</u>. Nuff said.

How are you?: ¿Qué tal?
How are you? (to a friend): ¿Cómo estás?
How are you? (formal): ¿Cómo está usted?

Say this when you're introduced to someone:

Pleased to meet you: Encantado/a

Change the 'o' to an 'a' if you're female.

or: Mucho gusto

This one doesn't change.

Por favor — Please... Gracias — Thank you

Easy stuff — maybe the first Spanish words you ever learnt. Don't ever forget them.

por favor = please   **gracias** = thank you

It was nothing/ you're welcome: De nada

Quisiera — I would like

It's more polite to say '<u>quisiera</u>' (I would like) than '<u>quiero</u>' (I want).

Here's how to say you would like <u>a thing</u>:

Quisiera un zumo de naranja. = I would like some orange juice.

Here's how to say you would like <u>to do</u> something:

Quisiera hablar. = I would like to talk.

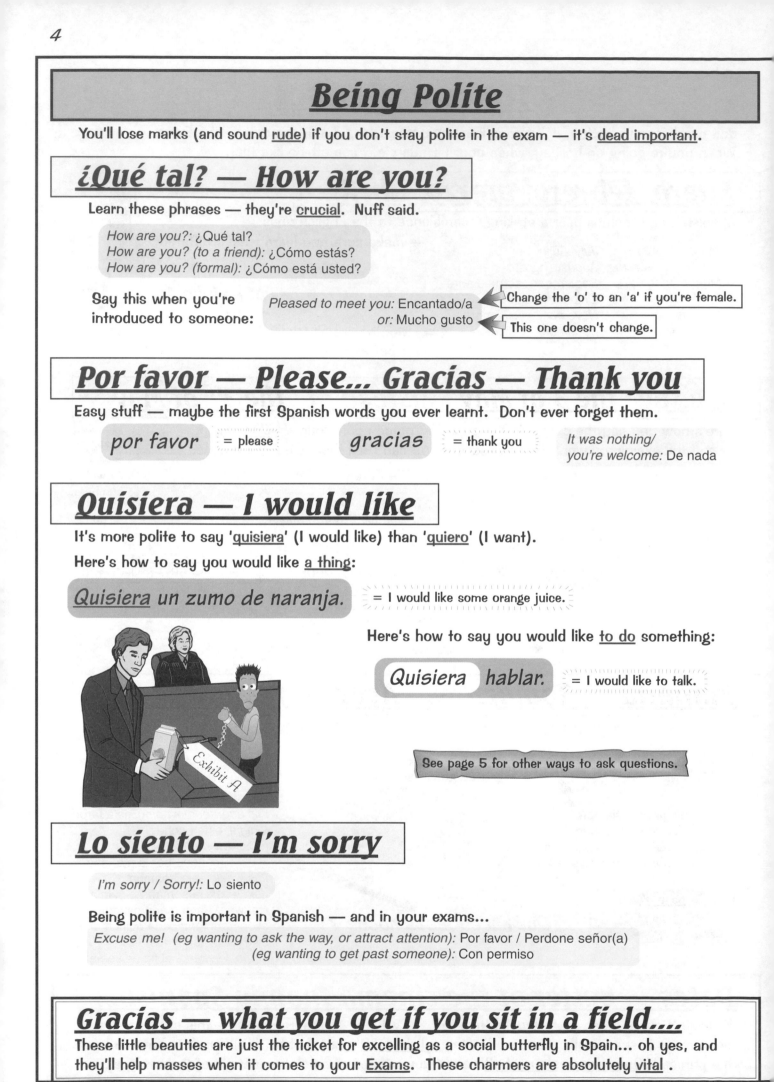

Exhibit A

See page 5 for other ways to ask questions.

Lo siento — I'm sorry

I'm sorry / Sorry!: Lo siento

Being polite is important in Spanish — and in your exams...

Excuse me! (eg wanting to ask the way, or attract attention): Por favor / Perdone señor(a)
(eg wanting to get past someone): Con permiso

Gracias — what you get if you sit in a field....

These little beauties are just the ticket for excelling as a social butterfly in Spain... oh yes, and they'll help masses when it comes to your <u>Exams</u>. These charmers are absolutely <u>vital</u>.

Asking Questions

Curiosity may have killed the cat, but you'll <u>have to</u> ask questions to score good marks... gulp...

1) Make it a question with ¿ ? or tone of voice

To turn a statement into a <u>question</u>, just add <u>question marks</u> to the beginning and the end.
When you're speaking, raise your voice at the end to show it's a question.

¿Tus plátanos son amarillos?

= Are your bananas yellow?
(Literally: Your bananas are yellow?)

See the grammar section
for more on endings.

¿Tienes un coche?

= Do you have a car?
(Literally: You have a car?)

2) 'What' questions — stick qué at the start

If your question starts with "<u>What</u>...", use "<u>¿Qué</u>...".

¿<u>Qué</u> comes por la mañana?

= What do you eat in the morning?

¿<u>Qué</u> quieres hacer?

= What do you want to do?

3) Cuándo – When... Por qué – Why... Dónde – Where

There are loads of other question words you can slot into a sentence at the start instead of '<u>qué</u>'.

Look at these question words — then cover 'em up and learn 'em.

when?:	¿cuándo?
why?:	¿por qué?
where?:	¿dónde?
how?:	¿cómo?
how much?:	¿cuánto?
how many?:	¿cuántos/as?
at what time...?	¿a qué hora?

¿ Cuándo vuelves a casa?

= When are you coming home?

who/whom?:	¿quién?
which...?:	¿cuál?

¿ Quién rompió la ventana?

= Who broke the window?

what?:	¿qué?
is...?:	¿es...?

... umop apisdn s,ti — siht daer t'nac I

This page is full of question words — start by <u>learning them all</u>. Shut the book and write down <u>all</u>
the <u>question</u> words. <u>Look back</u> for the ones you missed and <u>try again</u> till you get them <u>all</u>.

Opinions

It pays to have an opinion, in more ways than one. Learn how to say what you think, or stay dull.

¿Qué piensas de...? — What do you think of...?

All these nifty phrases mean the same thing — 'What do you think of ...?'. Look out for them.
If you can use all of them then your Spanish will be wildly fascinating — and that means more marks.

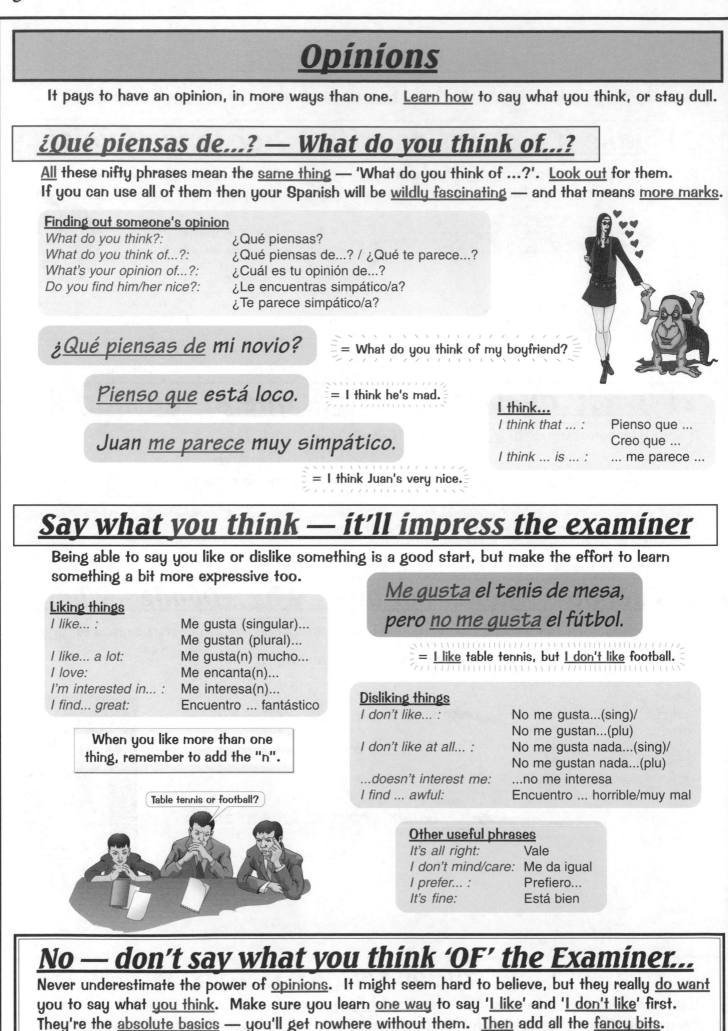

Finding out someone's opinion

What do you think?:	¿Qué piensas?
What do you think of...?:	¿Qué piensas de...? / ¿Qué te parece...?
What's your opinion of...?:	¿Cuál es tu opinión de...?
Do you find him/her nice?:	¿Le encuentras simpático/a?
	¿Te parece simpático/a?

¿Qué piensas de mi novio?

= What do you think of my boyfriend?

Pienso que está loco.

= I think he's mad.

Juan me parece muy simpático.

= I think Juan's very nice.

I think...

I think that ... :	Pienso que ...
	Creo que ...
I think ... is ... :	... me parece ...

Say what you think — it'll impress the examiner

Being able to say you like or dislike something is a good start, but make the effort to learn something a bit more expressive too.

Liking things

I like... :	Me gusta (singular)...
	Me gustan (plural)...
I like... a lot:	Me gusta(n) mucho...
I love:	Me encanta(n)...
I'm interested in... :	Me interesa(n)...
I find... great:	Encuentro ... fantástico

*Me gusta el tenis de mesa,
pero no me gusta el fútbol.*

= I like table tennis, but I don't like football.

> When you like more than one thing, remember to add the "n".

Table tennis or football?

Disliking things

I don't like... :	No me gusta...(sing)/
	No me gustan...(plu)
I don't like at all... :	No me gusta nada...(sing)/
	No me gustan nada...(plu)
...doesn't interest me:	...no me interesa
I find ... awful:	Encuentro ... horrible/muy mal

Other useful phrases

It's all right:	Vale
I don't mind/care:	Me da igual
I prefer... :	Prefiero...
It's fine:	Está bien

No — don't say what you think 'OF' the Examiner...

Never underestimate the power of opinions. It might seem hard to believe, but they really do want you to say what you think. Make sure you learn one way to say 'I like' and 'I don't like' first. They're the absolute basics — you'll get nowhere without them. Then add all the fancy bits.

Opinions

Don't <u>just</u> say that you like or hate something. Really blow those Examiners away by explaining <u>why</u> — er, well, you'll get good marks from them anyhow...

Use words like 'bueno' (good) to describe things

Here are a juicy bunch of words to describe things you <u>like</u> or <u>don't like</u>. They're rather easy to use, so it really is worth learning them.

good:	bueno/a	*fantastic:*	fantástico/a	*marvellous:*	maravilloso/a
great:	estupendo/a		magnífico/a	*bad:*	malo/a
great:	fenomenal	*fabulous:*	fabuloso/a	*awful:*	horrible
beautiful:	precioso/a	*interesting:*	interesante		
friendly:	amable	*nice (person):*	simpático/a		
excellent:	excelente	*nice / kind:*	agradable		

Owen es estupendo .

= Owen is great.

Los niños son horribles .

= The children are awful.

To say 'because' say 'porque'

Congratulations you have an opinion, so you're officially <u>undull</u>. But to reach the coveted rating of '<u>interesting</u>', you need to know how to back it up with '<u>porque</u>'.

'porque' is <u>ultra-important</u> — forget it at your peril.

Me gusta esta película <u>porque</u> los actores son muy buenos.

= I like this film, because the actors are very good.

Pienso que esta película es horrible <u>porque</u> la historia es aburrida.

= I think this film is awful, because the story is boring.

Don't mix up 'por qué', and 'porque'

Be careful not to <u>mix up</u> "why" and "because". They're almost the same — but not quite:

WHY = POR QUÉ   BECAUSE = PORQUE

Tell the truth — or tell a porque...

It's not much cop <u>only</u> knowing how to ask someone else's opinion, or how to say 'I think', without being able to say <u>what</u> and <u>why</u> you think. All these phrases are easy — just <u>stick them together</u> to get a sentence. Just make sure you don't say something <u>daft</u> like 'I hate it because it's lovely'.

Revision Summary

This section is all the absolute basics. You need to know all this backwards by the time you get into the exams. All the bits on your opinions, and on times (including today, tomorrow, every week, on Mondays etc.) can make a huge difference to your marks. The best way to check you know it all is to do all these questions — if you get stuck or get it wrong, go back over the section and have another try at the questions until you get them right every time.

1) Count out loud from 1 to 20 in Spanish.

2) How do you say these numbers in Spanish? a) 22 b) 35 c) 58 d) 71 e) 112 f) 2101

3) What are these in Spanish? a) 1st b) 2nd c) 5th d) 10th e) 25th f) 52nd

4) What do these words mean? a) cada b) unos

5) Ask 'What time is it?' in Spanish.
   Look at your watch, and say what time it is, out loud and in Spanish.

6) How would you say these times in Spanish? a) 5.00 b) 10.30 c) 13.22 d) 16.45

7) Say all the days of the week in Spanish, from Monday to Sunday.

8) How do you say these in Spanish? a) yesterday b) today c) tomorrow

9) Say all of the months of the year, from January to December.

10) How do you say the <u>date</u> of your birthday in Spanish?

11) '¿Qué haces <u>esta noche</u>?' means 'What are you doing <u>tonight</u>?'
    How would say 'What are you doing a) this morning?' b) this afternoon?' c) next week?'

12) 'Practico <u>pocas veces</u> el deporte' means 'I <u>seldom</u> do sport.'
    How would you say: a) 'I do sport every day.' b) 'I often do sport.'
    c) 'I sometimes do sport.'

13) How would you say: a) 'I would like some coffee.' b) 'May I have the coffee?'
    c) 'I'm sorry.' (give two ways)

14) How do you say these in Spanish? a) Please b) Thank you c) How are you?

15) 'Cantas' means 'You sing' or 'You are singing'. What do these questions mean?
    a) ¿Por qué cantas? b) ¿Dónde cantas? c) ¿Qué cantas?
    d) ¿Cantas bien? e) ¿Cuándo cantas? f) ¿Cantas?

16) How would you ask someone what they think of Elvis Presley? (In Spanish.)
    Give as many ways of asking it as you can.

17) How would you say these things in Spanish? Give at least one way to say each of them.
    a) I like Elvis Presley. b) I don't like Elvis Presley. c) I find Elvis Presley interesting.
    d) I love Elvis Presley. e) I find Elvis Presley awful. f) I think that Elvis Presley is fantastic.

18) To win this week's star prize, complete the following sentence in
    10 words or less (in Spanish): 'I like Elvis Presley because...'

19) To win last week's rotten eggs, complete the following sentence
    in 10 words or less (in Spanish): 'I don't like Elvis Presley because...'

Getting Through the Exam

These pages tell you how to <u>improve</u> your mark <u>without</u> learning <u>any more</u> Spanish — so read on...

Read the questions carefully

<u>Don't</u> lose <u>easy marks</u> that <u>everyone</u> should get — make <u>sure</u> you do these things:

1) <u>Read all the instructions</u> properly.

2) <u>Read the question</u> properly.

3) <u>Answer the question</u> — don't waffle on about something irrelevant.

4) <u>Write in paragraphs</u>, and use <u>correct English</u> in the Reading and Listening Tests.

5) Take time to <u>plan</u> your answer in the Writing Paper — don't just charge in.

Vocab and grammar make you look good

The more <u>correct grammar</u> and <u>vocab</u> you can cram into your Spanish, the better. <u>Really get your teeth into describing</u> things — don't just say the minimum (see page 73). But <u>don't</u> bite off more than you can chew — a <u>correct</u> simple sentence will get you <u>more marks</u> than a nonsensical <u>complicated</u> effort.

<u>Don't panic</u> if you say something and then realise that it wasn't quite right — your grammar doesn't have to be <u>perfect</u>. But the way to get the really <u>top marks</u> is to get your grammar <u>sorted</u> — see section 11.

Examiners like to travel through time

Big bonus marks will be yours if you can say when you did something. Learn the section on <u>time</u> and <u>dates</u> carefully (<u>pages 2–3</u>), and say <u>when</u> or <u>how often</u> you do things.

Reminiscing about <u>the past</u> or boasting about your plans for <u>the future</u> will impress the examiner no end (see <u>page 88</u> on tenses).

So, if I add one more drop we'll go back in time two hours...

...two hours later...

Examiners like to hear your opinions

Examiners also go weak at the knees for <u>opinions</u> — so learn the stuff in this book about opinions (<u>especially pages 6–7</u>) really well.

<u>Don't worry</u> if you have to make your opinions up — the important thing is that you have something nifty to <u>say</u> about the topic, and that you sound <u>interested</u> in talking about it.

Examiners travel through time — Yeah, right...

No surprises — the more <u>vocab</u> and <u>grammar</u> you have at your fingertips, the better. And using the stuff about times and opinions will get you off to a flying start. Don't think 'This page doesn't have any Spanish on it — I won't bother'. If you don't know this stuff you'll <u>lose marks</u>, and that's that.

How to Use Dictionaries

OK, so if you have a dictionary, you <u>don't</u> need to learn anything. WRONG. If you didn't learn things first you'd spend all exam looking them up, and you'd end up with the <u>wrong</u> words all the time. You have to be <u>ultra-careful</u> — these two pages will help stop you making a pig's ear of it.

Only use the dictionary when you HAVE TO

1) Don't have your nose <u>stuck</u> in a dictionary for the <u>whole Exam</u> — you won't have <u>time</u> to write any <u>answers</u>.

2) First try to do <u>all</u> the questions <u>without</u> using the dictionary — then with the time left at the end <u>go back</u> and do the rest.

Make sure you know how to check whether a word is <u>masculine</u> or <u>feminine</u> in your dictionary.

3) For goodness sake don't <u>waste time</u> checking how to <u>spell</u> Spanish words you're pretty sure you <u>know</u> — a few little mistakes <u>won't</u> lose you many marks.

The <u>VERB TABLES</u> at the back can be dead useful though — use 'em if you need to check your <u>past participles</u> (see page 92).

WARNING: DICTIONARY DOES NOT REPLACE BRAIN

Use the Spanish you know

<u>DON'T</u> try to use the dictionary to say huge <u>complicated</u> things — use your <u>brain</u> and stick to what you <u>know</u>.

LOOK AT THIS QUESTION:

¿Qué regalos recibiste para Navidad?

(What presents did you get for Christmas?)

<u>DON'T</u> launch into the dictionary to look for a <u>weird and exotic</u> present you actually got.

<u>Pretend</u> you got something <u>easy</u> that you <u>DO</u> know in Spanish — like a football or something.

Don't translate word for word — it DOESN'T work

If you turn each word of this phrase into English, you get <u>rubbish</u>.

¿Qué tal? → What such?

NO!

Do you like me? → ¿Hacer usted como me?

It's the <u>same</u> the other way round — turn English into Spanish word by word, and you get <u>balderdash</u> — <u>don't do it</u>.

Dictionaries — useful for holding doors open...*

'But everyone knows how to use a dictionary' — <u>wrong</u>. Every year, <u>loads</u> of people lose handfuls of <u>marks</u> because they <u>don't</u> know the stuff on these two pages. So get it stuck in your brain.

How to Use Dictionaries

Learn this <u>fact of life</u>: if it <u>doesn't make sense</u>, it <u>can't</u> be <u>right</u> — you're not Miss Marple or Poirot.

Finding the right Spanish word can be dead TRICKY

A dictionary is <u>no use</u> if you don't <u>know</u> anything to start with. An English word may mean loads of things and have loads of <u>different translations</u> — you have to have some idea of what is <u>right</u> before you go searching.

If it doesn't make sense, you've got it wrong

Some words have several meanings — don't just pick the first one you see. Look at the <u>meanings</u> listed and <u>suss out</u> which one is what you're looking for.

If you read this...   *Me duele el ojo derecho.*

...you might look up '<u>derecho</u>' and find this:

So the sentence could mean:

My straight eye hurts.   ✗

My right eye hurts.   ✔

My upright eye hurts.   ✗

This is the only one that sounds sensible.

derecho, a
<u>adj</u> upright; straight; right, right-hand
// <u>adv</u> straight // <u>nm</u> law; justice
<u>tener derecho a hacer algo</u>: to have the right to do something
<u>derecho de paso</u>: right of way
// derechos; rights; taxes, duties

It's straightforward really:

If it doesn't make sense — you've picked the wrong word.

Verbs change according to the person

When you look up a <u>verb</u> in the dictionary, you'll find the <u>infinitive</u> (the 'to' form, like '<u>to</u> run', '<u>to</u> sing' etc). But you may need to say '<u>I</u> run', or '<u>we</u> sing' — so you need to change the verb <u>ending</u>.

Say you need to say '<u>I work</u>'.

1) If you looked up '<u>work</u>', you'd find the word '<u>trabajar</u>', meaning 'to work'.
2) But '<u>trabajar</u>' is the <u>infinitive</u> — you can't put 'yo trabajar'.
3) You need the '<u>I</u>' (yo) form of the verb — '(yo) <u>trabajo</u>'.
4) Check the <u>tense</u> too — for the <u>past</u>, it could be '(yo) <u>trabajé</u>'.

For the low-down on verbs and all their different endings, see the grammar section.

The grammar section shows you how to get the 'yo' form from the infinitive and how to get your tenses right.

If you're looking up a <u>Spanish</u> word, look for its <u>infinitive</u> (it'll end in 'ar', 'er' or 'ir'). If you want to know what 'limpiamos' means, you'll find '<u>limpiar</u>' (to clean) in the dictionary. So 'limpiamos' must mean '<u>we clean</u>' or '<u>we are cleaning</u>'.

...also good for standing on to reach high shelves...

You've got to be 100% sure you've got the right word — if a dictionary gives more than one answer, use your <u>common sense</u> to work out what's right. <u>Don't</u> pick one without <u>thinking</u>.

The Weather

You may be asked about the <u>weather</u> in the <u>Speaking</u> Exam. Or you might have to listen to a <u>weather forecast</u> in your <u>Listening</u> Exam — or you may be in Spain planning a picnic...

¿Qué tiempo hace? — What's the weather like?

These <u>short sentences</u> are the ones you definitely <u>can't do without</u> — and they're <u>easy</u>.

Está lloviendo . ⌐ = It's raining.

It's snowing: Está nevando
The sky's clear: Está despejado
It's cloudy: Está nublado
It's foggy: Hay niebla
It's stormy: Hay tormenta

Of course, it doesn't <u>always</u> rain, so here are a few others you could use:

Hace frío . = It's cold.

warm: calor   *hot:* mucho calor
windy: viento   *nice:* buen tiempo
sunny: sol   *bad:* mal tiempo

You can use any of these words after 'Hace...'.

¿Qué tiempo hará mañana?
— What will the weather be like tomorrow?

This is quite easy, and it sounds <u>dead impressive</u>:

Mañana **lloverá / va a llover** .   = It will rain tomorrow.

next week:
la semana próxima
on Tuesday: el martes

It'll snow: nevará / va a nevar
It'll rain: lloverá / va a llover
It'll thunder: habrán truenos
It'll be hot: hará calor / va a hacer calor
It'll be cold: hará frío / va a hacer frío
It'll be windy: hará viento / va a hacer viento
It'll be cloudy: estará nublado / va a estar nublado

Tomorrow it'll be wet.

See pages 2–3 for more on times and dates, and page 91 for the future tense.

You only need to get the gist of a weather forecast

OK, here's a <u>real</u> weather forecast — time to show what you can do. You <u>won't know all the words</u>, but you don't need to. Look at the words you <u>do know</u> and work out the gist.

Work through this one, and see if you can <u>figure out</u> which bit means what. Look up any words you <u>don't</u> know in a <u>dictionary</u>. When you've figured it out as best you can, check it here to see if you got it all right.

today: hoy
in the south: en el sur
in the north: en el norte

<u>El tiempo de hoy</u>
Hoy hará calor en España. Mañana hará viento en el sur y estará nublado en el norte. Lloverá en la costa.

Today's Weather Forecast
Today it will be warm in Spain. Tomorrow it will be windy in the south and cloudy in the north. It will rain on the coast.

Albert Niño's got a lot to answer for...

This stuff on weather and forecasts nearly <u>always</u> comes up in the <u>Exams</u> — so you've got to do it. Still, all you need to do is <u>learn</u> the <u>main sentences</u> on this page and the <u>bits of vocab</u> — and you'll be working for the Met Office in no time. Well, maybe you'll just get a good mark in your GCSE.

Tricky Stuff   Tricky Stuff

Countries

You're a <u>foreigner</u> in Spain so you need to be able to say what country you're from and what your <u>nationality</u> is. It'll be handy to know some others too as they may well come up in your <u>Exams</u>.

¿De dónde eres? — Where do you come from?

Such a <u>useful pair</u> of wee phrases — and so easy to learn. There's <u>no excuse</u> to forget 'em, is there... If the country you're from isn't somewhere here, go look it up in a dictionary.

Soy **de Inglaterra** . Soy **inglés/inglesa** .

= I come from England.
I am English.

Wales: (del país) de Gales
Northern Ireland: de Irlanda del Norte
England: de Inglaterra
Scotland: de Escocia

Welsh: galés/galesa
Northern Irish: norirlandés/norirlandesa
English: inglés/inglesa
Scottish: escocés/escocesa

IMPORTANT BIT:
You must add '<u>a</u>' on the end and drop the accent for <u>women and girls</u> (see page 76).

Soy ingles<u>a</u>.

¿Dónde vives? *= Where do you live?*

Vivo en **Inglaterra** . *= I live in England.*

Learn these foreign countries

Names of <u>countries</u> come in handy all the time — for talking about holidays, future plans, current events, football... you get the picture.

France: Francia (fem.)
Germany: Alemania (fem.)
Italy: Italia (fem.)
Spain: España (fem.)
Austria: Austria (fem.)
Holland: Holanda (fem.)
America: América (fem.)
USA: los Estados Unidos (masc.)

French: francés/francesa
German: alemán/alemana
Italian: italiano/a
Spanish: español/a
Austrian: austríaco/a
Dutch: holandés/holandesa
American: americano/a
North American:
norteamericano/a

IMPORTANT: <u>Don't</u> use a capital letter for inglés, francés etc.

For extra <u>marks</u>, learn these places as well:

Belgium: Bélgica (fem.)
Denmark: Dinamarca (fem.)
Norway: Noruega (fem.)
Switzerland: Suiza (fem.)
Great Britain:
Gran Bretaña (fem.)

The United Kingdom:
el Reino Unido
Sweden: Suecia (fem.)
Russia: Rusia (fem.)
Europe: Europa (fem.)
Africa: África (fem.)

El país de Gales — no wonder it's so windy...

Knowing <u>countries</u> and <u>nationalities</u> in Spanish is a good idea even if you're pants at geography. Find an <u>atlas</u> and see <u>how many</u> of the countries you know in Spanish. With the ones where the Spanish word is <u>a bit like the English</u>, check you've got the <u>spelling</u> right — like <u>Holland</u> and <u>Holanda</u>.

Hotels and Hostels Vocab

Holidays are another Exam favourite. This page has all the words you need to know about hotels, hostels, and camping. GCSEs are always full of this sort of thing, so you'd better get learning...

Las vacaciones — Holidays

Booking the right kind of room in the right kind of hotel is darned important to Examiners — best learn how to do it...

General vocabulary.

holiday: las vacaciones
abroad: el extranjero
person: la persona
night: la noche

Verbs used in hotels.

to reserve: reservar
to stay: alojarse/quedarse
to cost: costar
to leave: irse

Things you might want to ask for.

room: la habitación
double room: la habitación doble
single room: la habitación individual

What kind of accommodation
(for more on meals see pages 50–52).

full board: la pensión completa
half board: la media pensión

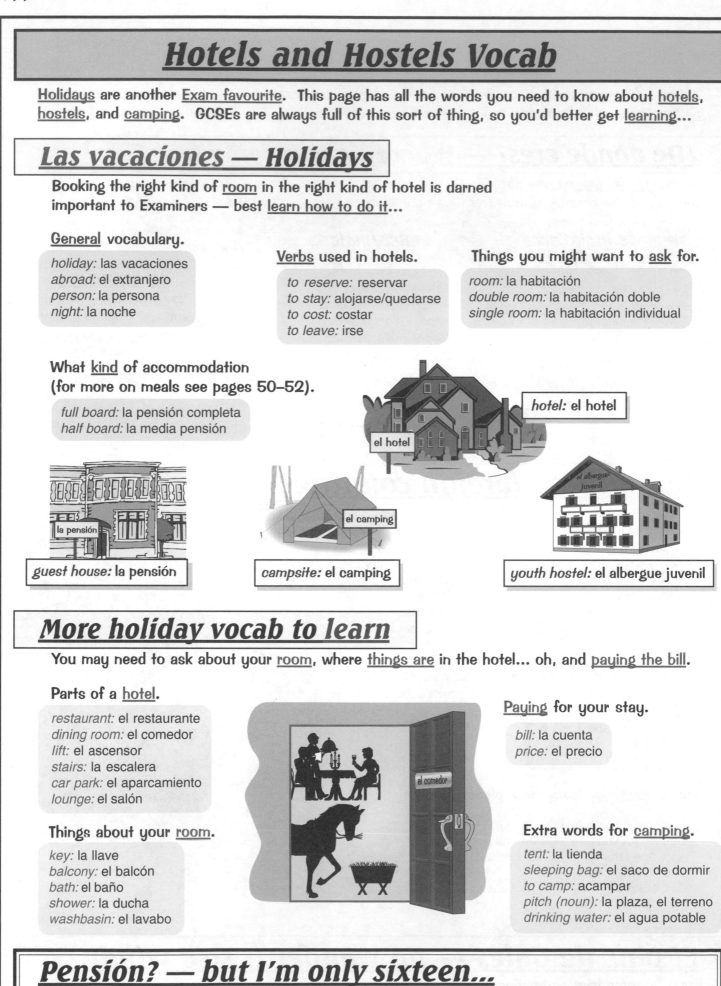

hotel: el hotel

el hotel

la pensión

el camping

el albergue juvenil

guest house: la pensión

campsite: el camping

youth hostel: el albergue juvenil

More holiday vocab to learn

You may need to ask about your room, where things are in the hotel... oh, and paying the bill.

Parts of a hotel.

restaurant: el restaurante
dining room: el comedor
lift: el ascensor
stairs: la escalera
car park: el aparcamiento
lounge: el salón

el comedor

Paying for your stay.

bill: la cuenta
price: el precio

Things about your room.

key: la llave
balcony: el balcón
bath: el baño
shower: la ducha
washbasin: el lavabo

Extra words for camping.

tent: la tienda
sleeping bag: el saco de dormir
to camp: acampar
pitch (noun): la plaza, el terreno
drinking water: el agua potable

Pensión? — but I'm only sixteen...

OK, I admit this is just a load of vocabulary. If you want to really learn how to use and understand these words you need to write out at least one sentence for each one. Get to it...

Booking a Room / Pitch

<u>Learn</u> this page if you don't want to end up sharing a room in Spain with two sweaty, cycling Swedes — or if you do. Oh and asking about <u>rooms</u> comes up loads in the Exams as well.

¿Tiene habitaciones libres?

— Do you have any rooms free?

Quisiera una habitación **individual** .   = I'd like a single room.

If you want to talk about different kinds of bookings, use the vocab you've just learned on <u>page 14</u>.

double room: doble

You could be a bit more specific and use these:

room with a bath: habitación con baño
room with a balcony: habitación con balcón

Quisiera quedarme aquí **dos noches** .   = I'd like to stay here for two nights.

Put the number of nights you want here. See <u>page 1</u> for more numbers.

IMPORTANT BIT:
If you're staying for one night, use una noche.

¿Cuánto es por noche para **una persona** ?   = How much is it per night for one person?

If there's more than one person, use dos persona**s**, tres persona**s** etc.

La tomo.   = I'll take it.   No la tomo.   = I won't take it.

¿Se puede acampar aquí? — Can I camp here?

Even if you're not into the <u>outdoor life</u> these phrases will be useful in your exams.

Quisiera **una plaza** para **una noche** .   = I'd like a pitch for one night.

Put how long you want to stay in here.

You might need these phrases too:

Is there drinking water here?: ¿Hay agua potable aquí?
Can I light a fire here?: ¿Puedo hacer un fuego aquí?
Where can I find...?: ¿Dónde hay…?

pitch (place for a tent): la plaza

tent: la tienda

caravan: la caravana

sleeping bag: el saco de dormir

You may have to book ahead. See page 67 for information on how to write a formal letter.

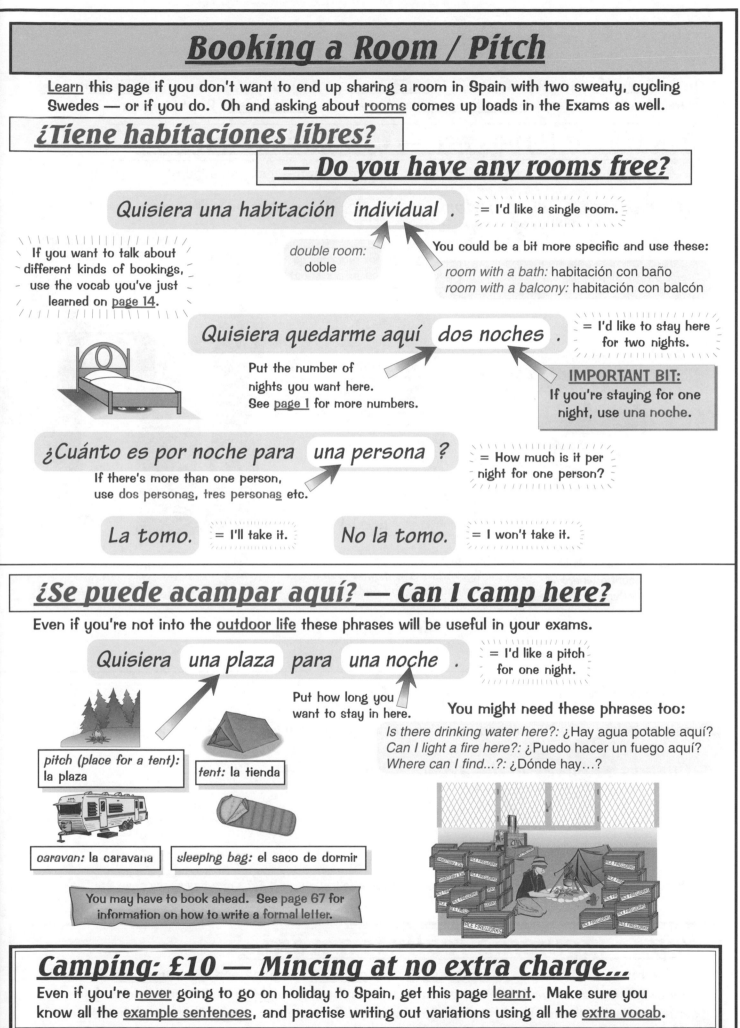

Camping: £10 — Mincing at no extra charge...

Even if you're <u>never</u> going to go on holiday to Spain, get this page <u>learnt</u>. Make sure you know all the <u>example sentences</u>, and practise writing out variations using all the <u>extra vocab</u>.

Where / When is...

In the <u>Exam</u>, they won't just get you to <u>book a room</u> — they can get you to do a <u>whole load more</u>. Here's how to <u>ask</u> people <u>where things are</u> and how to <u>get yourself fed</u>. Pretty important stuff.

Ask where things are — use '¿Dónde está... ?'

Knowing how to ask <u>where</u> things are is very important — get these <u>learnt</u>.

¿Dónde está el comedor , por favor?   = Where is the dining room, please?

car park: el aparcamiento
games room: la sala de juegos
telephone: el teléfono

See <u>page 14</u> for more things you might need to ask about.

Where are the loos?: ¿Dónde están los servicios?

Está en el tercer piso .   = It's on the third floor.

fourth floor: cuarto piso
second floor: segundo piso
first floor: primer piso
ground floor: la planta baja

For higher floor numbers, see <u>page 1</u>.

These are other words you might need when you describe where something is.

outside: fuera
on the left / right: a la izquierda/derecha
straight on: todo recto / derecho
upstairs: arriba
downstairs: abajo
at the end of the corridor: al final del pasillo

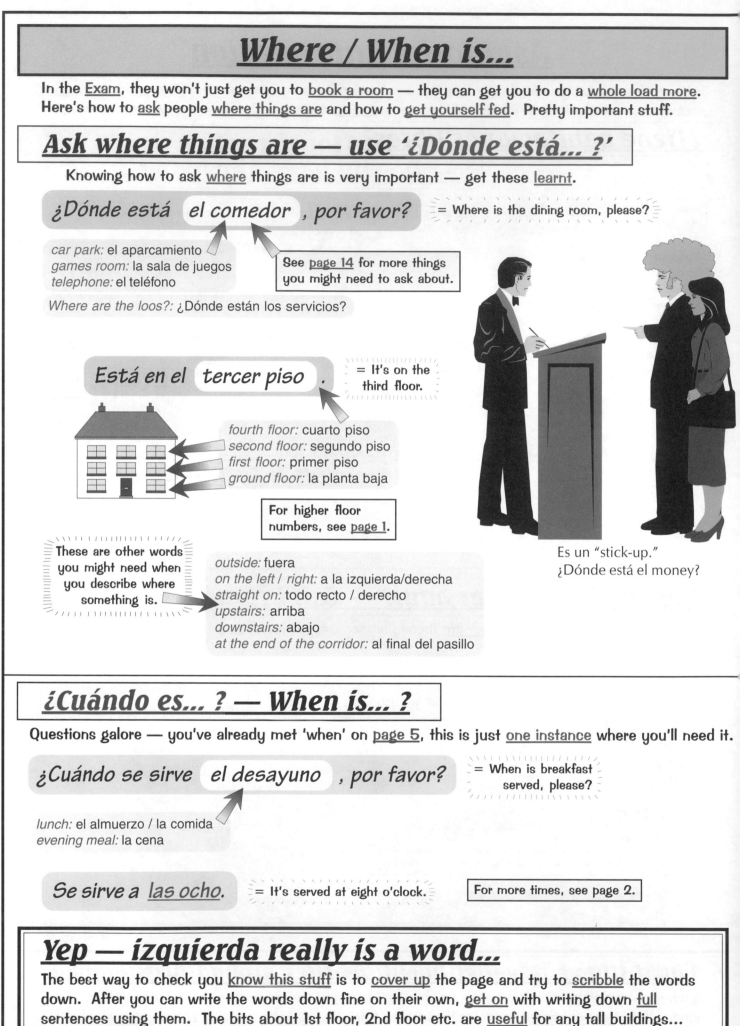

Es un "stick-up."
¿Dónde está el money?

¿Cuándo es... ? — When is... ?

Questions galore — you've already met 'when' on <u>page 5</u>, this is just <u>one instance</u> where you'll need it.

¿Cuándo se sirve el desayuno , por favor?   = When is breakfast served, please?

lunch: el almuerzo / la comida
evening meal: la cena

Se sirve a <u>las ocho</u>.   = It's served at eight o'clock.

For more times, see page 2.

Yep — izquierda really is a word...

The best way to check you <u>know this stuff</u> is to <u>cover up</u> the page and try to <u>scribble</u> the words down. After you can write the words down fine on their own, <u>get on</u> with writing down <u>full</u> sentences using them. The bits about 1st floor, 2nd floor etc. are <u>useful</u> for any tall buildings...

Asking for Information

In the <u>Speaking</u> Exam, they might want you to pretend you're in a tourist office <u>asking for leaflets</u> about excursions. Or you might have to <u>write a letter</u> to a tourist office in the <u>Writing</u> Exam.

La oficina de turismo — The tourist office

Here's how you <u>find out</u> what a town's got to offer.

¿Puede darme información sobre | el parque zoológico |, por favor?

= Can you give me information about the zoo, please?

the sights of Madrid: los monumentos de Madrid
the museum: el museo

tourist office: la oficina de turismo

For more things you could ask about, see pages 21, and 36.

¿Cuándo | abre | el museo | ?

= When does the museum open?

close: cierra

the exhibition: la exposición
the gallery: la galería

See page 22 about asking for directions.

Ask about las excursiones — you'll sound dead clever

¿Tiene unos folletos sobre | las excursiones por Sevilla | ?

= Do you have any leaflets about excursions around Sevilla?

the museums in Toledo: los museos de Toledo

The place you want leaflets about goes here.

¿Qué clase de excursión quiere hacer?

= What kind of excursion do you want to go on?

Quisiera | visitar Aranjuez |.

= I'd like to visit Aranjuez.

go to a museum: visitar un museo
see the castle: ver el castillo

¿Cuánto es? = How much is it?

Son mil pesetas por persona. = It costs 1000 pesetas per person.

Este autocar va a Aranjuez. | El autocar | sale | del ayuntamiento | a la una | y media |.

= This coach goes to Aranjuez. The coach leaves from the town hall at half past one.

from the church: de la iglesia
from the market: del mercado

the train: el tren

2 o'clock: a las dos
3.15: a las tres y cuarto

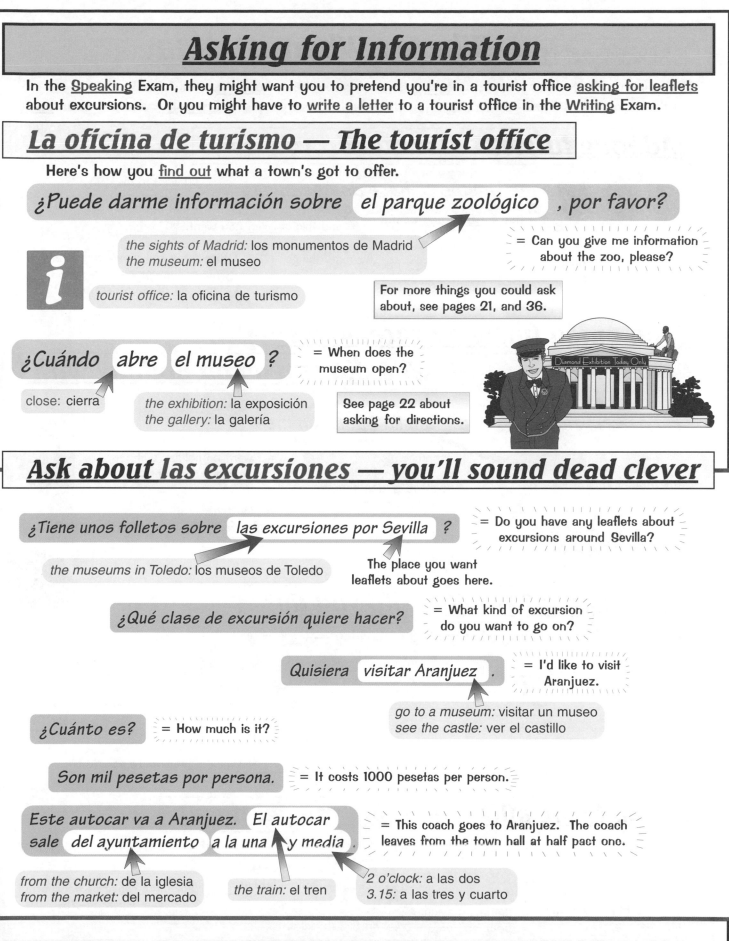

'Could I have a leaflet about beaches around Birmingham?'

<u>Examiners love</u> those "<u>pretend you're on holiday in Spain</u>" questions — that's where this stuff is handy. And the next time you go on holiday to Spain by mistake and don't know where you are...

Tricky Stuff   Tricky Stuff   Tricky Stuff   Tricky Stuff

Talking About Your Holiday

Everyone wants to bore people by <u>telling</u> them all about their <u>holidays</u>. Yes, you too...
By the time you've finished this page you'll be able to bore people in <u>Spanish</u>... and get good <u>marks</u>.

¿Adónde fuiste? — Where did you go?

Fui **a los Estados Unidos** **hace dos semanas** .

= I went to the USA two weeks ago.

This is <u>where</u> you went...

and this is <u>when</u> you went.

Spain: a España
France: a Francia
Ireland: a Irlanda

a week ago: hace una semana
a month ago: hace un mes
in July: en julio
in the summer: en el verano

- Other dates and times: pages 2–3.
- Points of the compass: page 23.
- A bigger list of countries: page 13.

¿Con quién fuiste de vacaciones?

<u>Answer</u> this question or there'll be all sorts of gossip.

— Who did you go on holiday with?

Fui de vacaciones con **mi familia** por **un mes** .

my brother: mi hermano
my friends: mis amigos/as

a fortnight: quince días
two weeks: dos semanas
a month: un mes

= I went on holiday with my family for a month.

For friends and family
— see page 55.

For past tenses, see
pages 92 to 95.

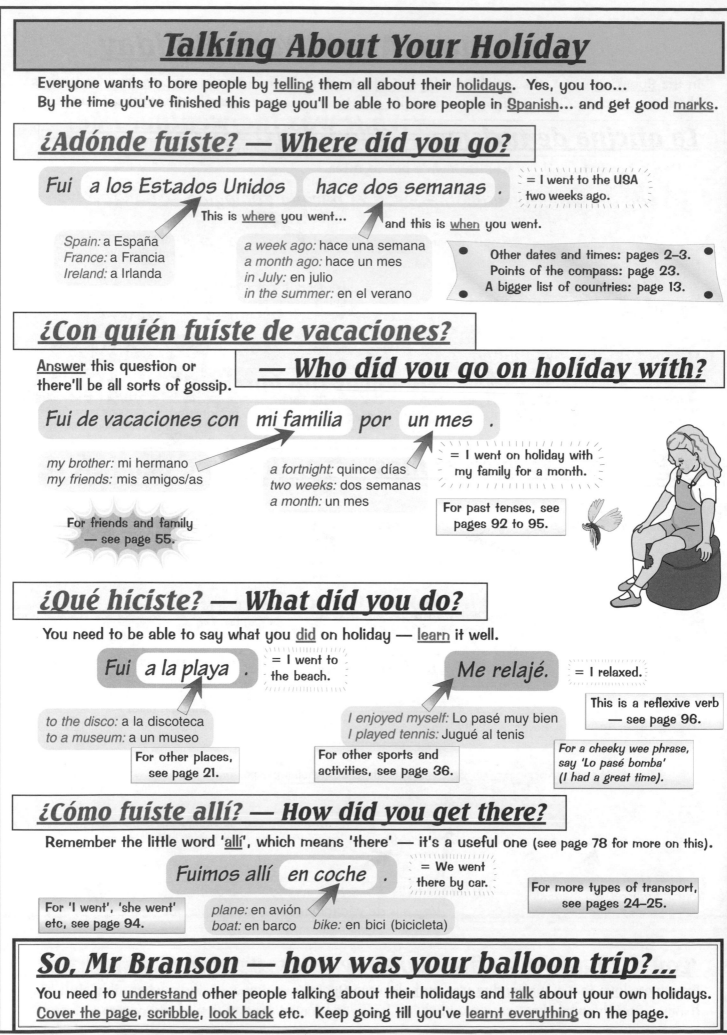

¿Qué hiciste? — What did you do?

You need to be able to say what you <u>did</u> on holiday — <u>learn</u> it well.

Fui **a la playa** .

= I went to the beach.

Me relajé.

= I relaxed.

to the disco: a la discoteca
to a museum: a un museo

I enjoyed myself: Lo pasé muy bien
I played tennis: Jugué al tenis

This is a reflexive verb
— see page 96.

For other places,
see page 21.

For other sports and
activities, see page 36.

For a cheeky wee phrase,
say 'Lo pasé bomba'
(I had a great time).

¿Cómo fuiste allí? — How did you get there?

Remember the little word '<u>allí</u>', which means 'there' — it's a useful one (see page 78 for more on this).

Fuimos allí **en coche** .

= We went there by car.

For 'I went', 'she went'
etc, see page 94.

plane: en avión
boat: en barco   *bike:* en bici (bicicleta)

For more types of transport,
see pages 24–25.

So, Mr Branson — how was your balloon trip?...

You need to <u>understand</u> other people talking about their holidays and <u>talk</u> about your own holidays.
<u>Cover the page</u>, <u>scribble</u>, <u>look back</u> etc. Keep going till you've <u>learnt everything</u> on the page.

Talking More About Your Holiday

Details — the Examiners love them. So plough on and learn this stuff as well...

¿Qué tiempo hacía? — What was the weather like?

No description of your holiday would be complete without giving a rundown of the weather.

Hacía sol y hacía calor .

= It was sunny and it was warm.

It was raining: Llovía
It was snowing: Nevaba

it was cold: hacía frío
it was windy: hacía viento

See page 12 for more ways of talking about the weather.

¿Cómo fue el viaje? — How was the journey?

You can never have too many opinions as far as Spanish GCSE is concerned.

Good news for motormouths like me.

¿Cómo fueron tus vacaciones?

= How was your holiday?

Me gustaron.   Así así.   No me gustaron.

= I liked it.   = So-so.   = I didn't like it.

¿Adónde irás? — Where will you go?

You've got to be able to talk about the future — things that you will be doing...

For more info about the future tense, see the grammar section — page 91.

Where will you go?
¿Adónde irás?

I'm going to go to America in two weeks.
Voy a ir a América dentro de dos semanas.

How will you get there?
¿Cómo irás?

I'm going to go by car.
Voy a ir en coche.

What will you do?
¿Qué harás?

I'm going to go to the beach.
Voy a ir a la playa.

Who will you go on holiday with?
¿Con quién irás de vacaciones?

I'm going to go on holiday for a month with my family.
Voy a ir de vacaciones con mi familia por un mes.

Exotic holidays — and all they talk about is the weather...

More details = more marks. Simple. You can always make up a holiday you didn't have, or invent things you did, as long as you know the Spanish words for it. Smile — it could be worse. Just.

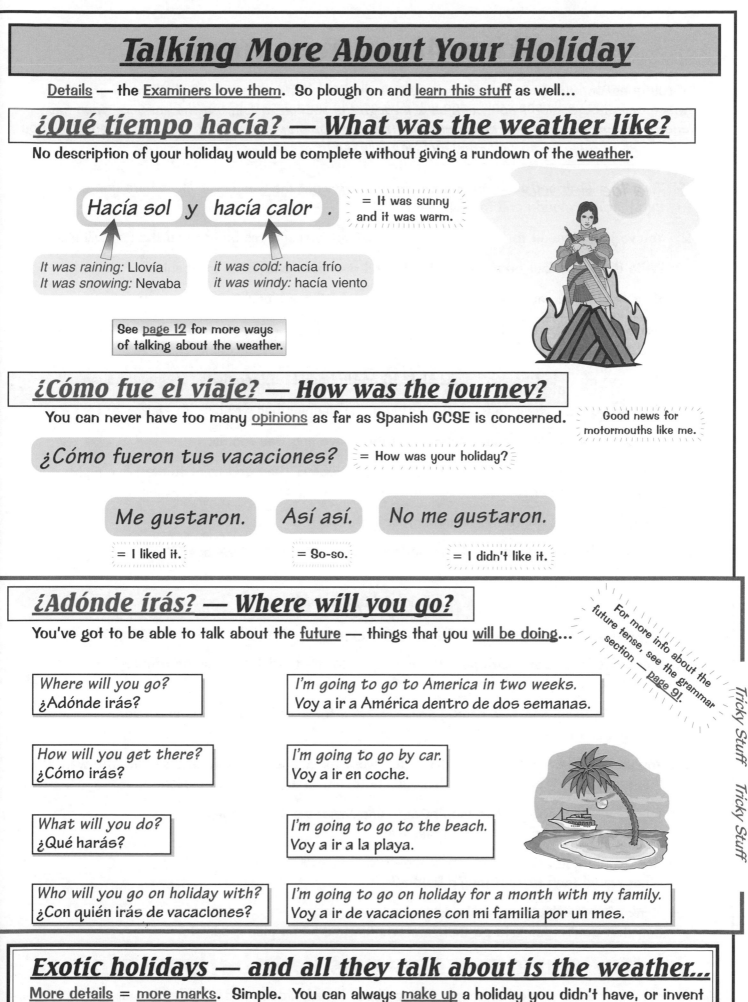

Tricky Stuff   Tricky Stuff

Revision Summary

These questions are here to make sure you know your stuff. Work through them all and check which ones you couldn't do. Look back through the section to find out the answers, then have another go at the ones you got stuck on. Then look up any you still can't do. Keep going till you can do all of them — so you know you've really learnt it.

1) Your Spanish friend Juan Antonio wants to know what the weather is like where you are. Say that it is cloudy and raining, and cold.

2) You've just listened to the forecast. Say that tomorrow it will be hot and the sun will shine.

3) Write down the four countries in the UK and five other countries, in Spanish.

4) How would you say that you come from each of these places?

5) Write down the nationality to go with each of the places — eg 'German', 'Welsh' or whatever (but in Spanish).

6) What are these in Spanish?   a) hotel   b) youth hostel   c) campsite   d) guest house

7) How do you say these in Spanish?   a) key   b) sleeping bag   c) bill   d) stairs   e) tent

8) You get to a hotel in Spain. Ask them if they have any free rooms.

9) Say you want one double room and two single rooms. Say you want to stay five nights. Say you'll take the rooms.

10) How do you ask where the restaurant is, in Spanish?

11) You're told: 'Gire a la izquierda y siga todo recto. Está al final del pasillo'. What does that mean?

12) Ask when breakfast is served, out loud and in Spanish.

13) You arrive at a campsite. Ask if there are any places. Ask if there is drinking water.

14) You arrive in Granada with your family and go to the tourist information office. How do you ask for information about the sights?

15) There's an excursion to a nearby museum. Ask for a leaflet about the excursion. Ask what time the bus leaves from the town hall.

16) You've just been on holiday to Italy. You went for two weeks with your sister. You went there by plane. You relaxed and enjoyed yourself. Say all that in Spanish.

17) Teresa went on holiday two months ago, and Javier went a year ago. How would they tell you that, in Spanish?

18) How would you ask someone how their holiday was? What would they reply if they'd liked it?

19) Think of somewhere you'd like to go next year. Say that you're going to go there and whether it'll be by plane, car etc.

Names of Buildings

If you're going to talk about your town, you need to know the names for buildings.
Yes, it's a bit dull, but you absolutely <u>have</u> to learn them.

Learn all these edificios — buildings

These are the basic, bog-standard '<u>learn-them-or-else</u>' buildings. (Building = el edificio.)
Don't go any further until you know <u>all</u> of them.

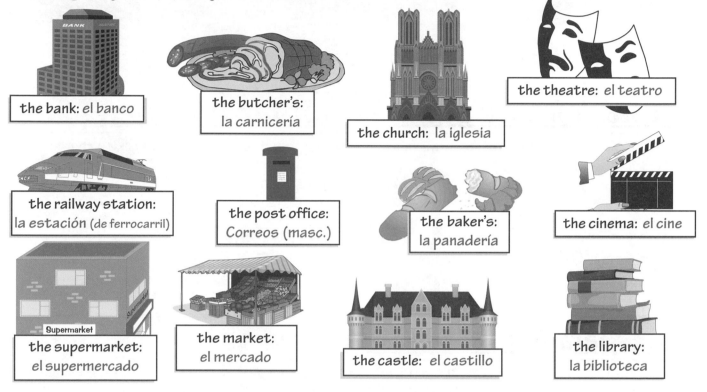

the bank: el banco

the butcher's:
la carnicería

the church: la iglesia

the theatre: el teatro

the railway station:
la estación (de ferrocarril)

the post office:
Correos (masc.)

the baker's:
la panadería

the cinema: el cine

the supermarket:
el supermercado

the market:
el mercado

the castle: el castillo

the library:
la biblioteca

Otros edificios — Other buildings

OK, I'll come clean. There are absolutely <u>loads</u> of buildings you need to <u>know</u>. Like these:

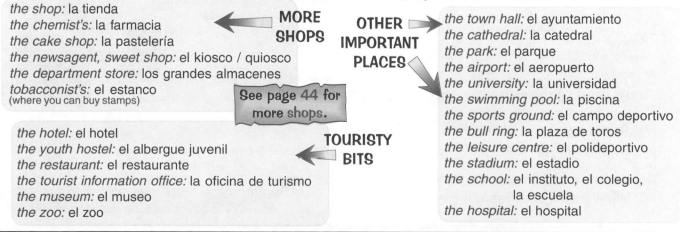

the shop: la tienda
the chemist's: la farmacia
the cake shop: la pastelería
the newsagent, sweet shop: el kiosco / quiosco
the department store: los grandes almacenes
tobacconist's: el estanco
(where you can buy stamps)

MORE SHOPS

OTHER IMPORTANT PLACES

See page 44 for more shops.

the hotel: el hotel
the youth hostel: el albergue juvenil
the restaurant: el restaurante
the tourist information office: la oficina de turismo
the museum: el museo
the zoo: el zoo

TOURISTY BITS

the town hall: el ayuntamiento
the cathedral: la catedral
the park: el parque
the airport: el aeropuerto
the university: la universidad
the swimming pool: la piscina
the sports ground: el campo deportivo
the bull ring: la plaza de toros
the leisure centre: el polideportivo
the stadium: el estadio
the school: el instituto, el colegio,
           la escuela
the hospital: el hospital

Edi Ficio — a Spanish builder perhaps...

Learning vocab is just such great fun, don't you think... OK, so it's pretty dull. The best way to learn it is to <u>turn over</u> the page and try to write all the words down. When you've sussed them <u>all</u>, start writing cunning <u>sentences</u> with them in. No <u>gain</u> without boredom, or summat...

Asking Directions

You're going to get at least <u>one</u> question about asking <u>directions</u> to get somewhere. Nothing too complicated — but worth getting straight in your mind now.

¿Dónde está... ? — Where is... ?

It's dead easy to ask <u>where</u> a place is — say '¿Dónde está...?' and stick the <u>place</u> on the end.

¿Dónde está la estación , por favor?

= Where is the station, please?

See page 21 for more buildings.

¿Hay una biblioteca por aquí?

= Is there a library near here?

¿Está lejos de aquí? — Is it far from here?

If the place you're looking for is miles away, you don't just want to set off walking there.

¿ Está el cine lejos de aquí?

= Is the cinema far from here?

the tourist office: la oficina de turismo
the park: el parque
the museum: el museo

Está a dos kilómetros .

= It's two kilometres away.

a hundred metres: a cien metros
near: cerca *far:* lejos

Use 'para ir a...?' to ask the way

You may need to ask directions in one of those little <u>role plays</u> that come up in the <u>Speaking</u> Exams.

¿Por favor, señor , para ir al banco ?

= Excuse me please, how do I get to the bank?

(to a woman): señora

Important bit:
Replace this with any place, using "al" for "el" words and "a la" for "la" words. See page 76.

to the station: a la estación
to the library: a la biblioteca
to the castle: al castillo

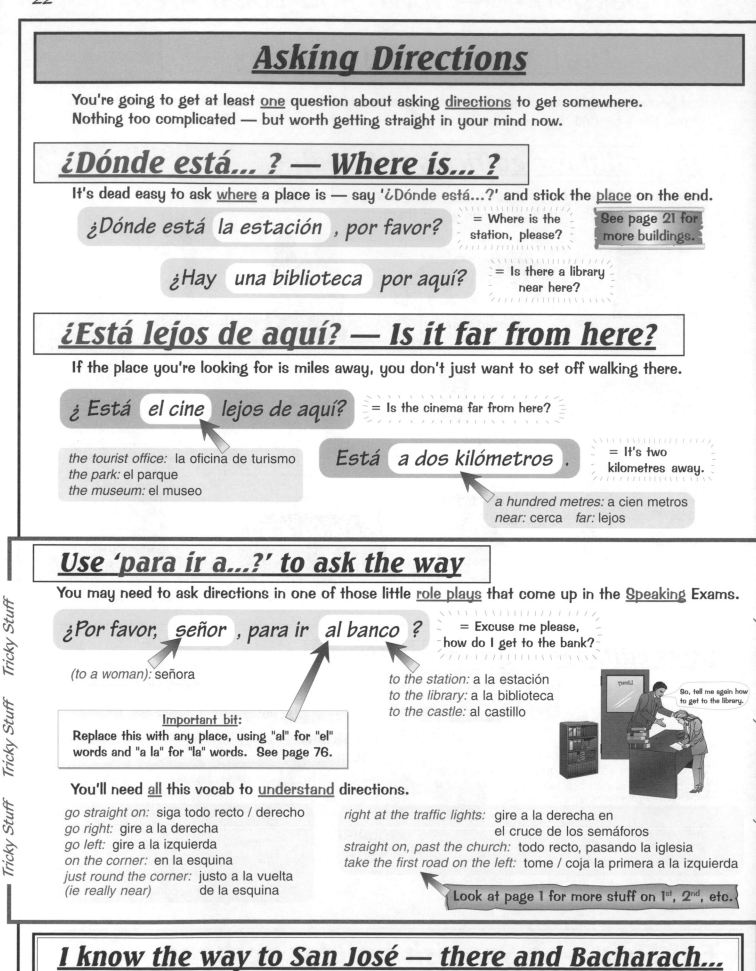

So, tell me again how to get to the library.

You'll need <u>all</u> this vocab to <u>understand</u> directions.

go straight on: siga todo recto / derecho
go right: gire a la derecha
go left: gire a la izquierda
on the corner: en la esquina
just round the corner: justo a la vuelta
(ie really near) de la esquina

right at the traffic lights: gire a la derecha en el cruce de los semáforos
straight on, past the church: todo recto, pasando la iglesia
take the first road on the left: tome / coja la primera a la izquierda

Look at page 1 for more stuff on 1st, 2nd, etc.

I know the way to San José — there and Bacharach...

Cover up, scribble it down, check what you got wrong, and try it again. That's the way to learn this stuff. Keep at it until you know it <u>all</u> — then you'll be really ready for the Exam. Just reading the page is <u>nowhere near</u> enough — you wouldn't remember it tomorrow, never mind in the Exam.

Tricky Stuff   Tricky Stuff   Tricky Stuff   Tricky Stuff

What You Think of Where You Live

Opinions, opinions, opinions — that's all the examiners are interested in.
They don't just want to know <u>where</u> you live, but what it's <u>like</u> there too.

¿Dónde vives? — Where do you live?

See page 13 for more countries.

Vivo en <u>Barrow.</u>   = I live in Barrow.

Barrow está en el noroeste de Inglaterra.   = Barrow's in the north-west of England.

north: el norte   *south:* el sur   *south-east:* el sureste
east: el este   *west:* el oeste   *in the north of Scotland:* en el norte de Escocia

You have to talk about life 'en tu ciudad' — 'in your town'

This is <u>another</u> question that comes up loads — practise your answers <u>before</u> the Exam.

¿Qué hay en tu ciudad?

Hay un mercado .   = There's a market.

= What is there in your town?

See page 21 for more buildings and places.

¿Te gusta vivir en Barrow?

Me gusta vivir en Barrow.   = I like living in Barrow.

= Do you like living in Barrow?

I don't like: No me gusta

¿Cómo es Barrow? — What is Barrow like?

If you want a <u>really good</u> mark, make sure you're ready to give more <u>details</u>.

If you live in a <u>village</u> or <u>small town</u> it's 'el pueblo' so any adjectives you use with it will need to <u>end in</u> an '<u>o</u>' not an 'a'.

La ciudad es muy interesante .   = The town is very interesting.

boring: aburrida
great: estupenda
dirty: sucia
clean: limpia
quiet / peaceful: tranquila

Hay mucho que hacer.   = There's lots to do.

See pages 6–7 for more on opinions.

there's not much: no hay mucho
there's always something: siempre hay algo

There's nothing to do: No hay nada que hacer

Put them all <u>together</u> and make <u>longer</u> sentences — you'll get <u>extra marks</u> if you get it right.

Me gusta vivir en Barrow , porque siempre hay algo que hacer.   = I like living in Barrow, because there's always something to do.

No me gusta vivir en Bogville , porque no hay nada que hacer.   = I don't like living in Bogville, because there's nothing to do.

Tricky Stuff   Tricky Stuff   Tricky Stuff

Barrow — paradise on earth...*

If you do come from a really dreary place which has <u>nothing</u> going for it, you can <u>make things up</u> (within reason) — but chances are there'll be <u>something</u> to say about a place near you. Start with <u>whereabouts</u> it is and see how much you can say about it <u>without</u> looking at the page.

* This page is not sponsored by the Barrow Tourist Board.
However, any used banknotes will be much appreciated.

Section 4 — Town and Local Area

Catching the Train

Trains, planes and automobiles... Well, just <u>trains</u> for now. Vehicle vocab is a must for speaking work. Learn how to <u>talk about trains</u> — not like a parrot, but so you can actually <u>use</u> the vocab.

Quisiera tomar el tren — I'd like to take the train

Here's how to buy a <u>ticket</u>.

¿Hay un tren para Madrid ? = Is there a train to Madrid?

to Toledo: para Toledo
to Malaga: para Málaga

Un billete sencillo para Madrid, de primera clase . = One single to Madrid, first class.

two: dos   *single(s):* billete(s) sencillo(s) / billete(s) de ida   *first class:* de primera clase
three: tres   *return(s):* billete(s) de ida y vuelta   *second class:* de segunda clase

Un billete de ida y vuelta para Madrid, por favor. = One return ticket to Madrid, please.

¿Cuándo va a viajar? — When are you travelling?

This is more <u>complicated</u>, but <u>important</u>. You won't <u>get far</u> (in Spain or your Exam) without it.

Quisiera ir a Santander el sábado . = I would like to go to Santander on Saturday.

today: hoy   *next Monday:* el lunes próximo   *on the tenth of June:* el diez de junio

¿Cuándo sale el tren para Santander? = When does the train leave for Santander?

¿Cuándo llega el tren a Santander? = When does the train arrive in Santander?

¿De qué andén sale el tren? = Which platform does the train leave from?

More <u>vocab</u>... Yes, it's as <u>dull</u> as a big dull thing, but it's also <u>vital</u> to know as <u>much</u> as you <u>can</u>.

to depart: salir	*to arrive:* llegar	*to change (trains):* hacer transbordo, cambiar
departure: la salida	*arrival:* la llegada	*platform / line:* el andén / la vía
the waiting room: la sala de espera	*ticket:* el billete	*ticket window:* la taquilla
timetable: el horario	*to get on:* subir a	*to get off:* bajar de
Spanish rail network: RENFE	*smoking:* fumadores	*non-smoking:* no fumadores
the railway: el ferrocarril	*delay:* retraso (masc.)	*left luggage:* la consigna

I'd catch the train — but it's a bit too heavy... *

You'd better make sure you can answer <u>all</u> the questions on travelling that could be thrown at you in an Exam. If you find this really boring now, when it gets to the Exam, you'll be wishing you'd bothered. And <u>don't just</u> learn the words, learn <u>how</u> to use them in <u>sentences</u>.

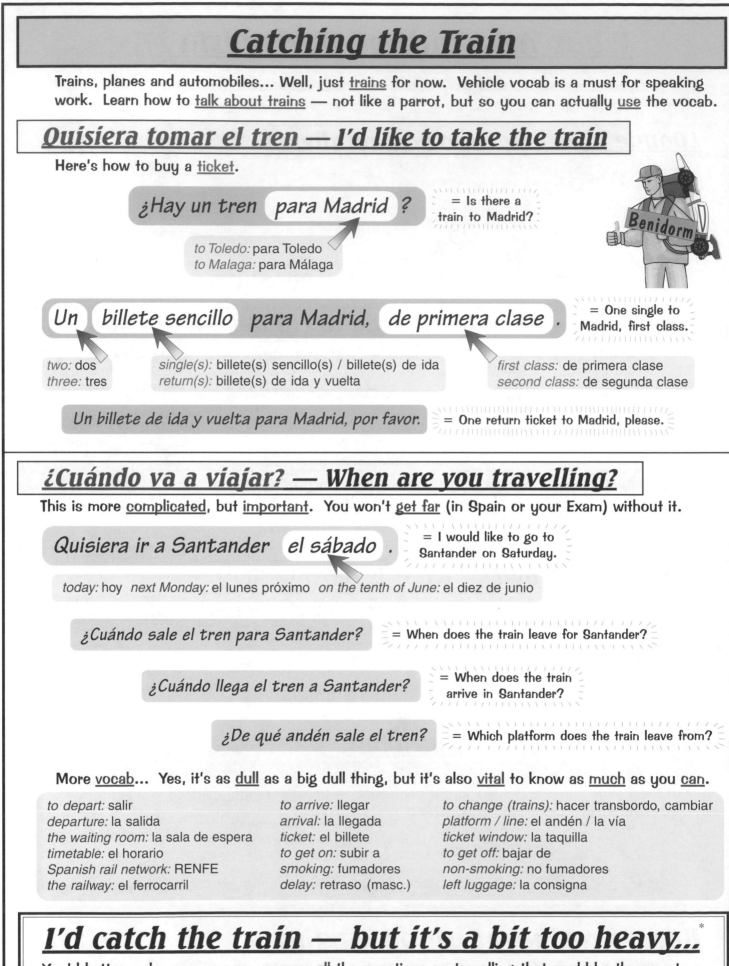

All Kinds of Transport

Here's what you need to <u>know</u> about other forms of <u>transport</u>. This is another of those topics that you'll need to know <u>really well</u> — and you need to know loads of <u>vocab</u> for it too.

¿Cómo vas? — How do you get there?

You'll need to say how you <u>get about</u>. For '<u>by</u>' (eg by car), use '<u>en</u>' — unless you're going by foot.

Voy a pie. = I go on foot.

Normalmente voy a la ciudad en autobús . = I normally go into town by bus.

by bus: en autobús
on the underground: en el metro
by bike: en bici (bicicleta)
by car: en coche
by motorbike: en moto (motocicleta)
by coach: en autocar
by boat: en barco
by plane: en avión

Voy en tren . = I go by train.

La salida y la llegada — Departure and arrival

You really do <u>need</u> these kinda questions when you're travelling.

¿Hay un autobús para <u>Córdoba</u>? = Is there a bus to Córdoba?

a plane: un avión
a coach: un autocar   a boat: un barco

I really had to use this phrase in Mexico — at least after using it in an Exam you won't have a 10 hour journey on a non-airconditioned bus to look forward to. Phew.

¿A qué hora sale el próximo autobús para Almería? = When does the next bus to Almería leave?

the (next) coach: el (próximo) autocar   the (next) boat: el (próximo) barco

¿Cuándo llega el avión a Barcelona? = When does the plane arrive in Barcelona?

¿Qué autobús...? — Which bus...?

No doubt about it — you need to be able to ask <u>which bus</u> or <u>train</u> goes <u>where</u>. Just learn <u>this</u>.

¿ Qué autobús va al centro , por favor? = Which bus goes to the town centre, please?

Which train... : ¿Qué tren...   to the bus stop: a la parada (de autobuses)
to the airport: al aeropuerto
to the harbour / port: al puerto

I can't walk — I ate all the pies...

A doddle. Well, it will be if you bother to <u>learn it now</u>. This stuff's straightforward, really. All of the words and phrases <u>behave themselves</u> — none of those weird ones that change depending on where you're going or anything like that. "I go..." is "Voy..." and that's that. Thank heavens...

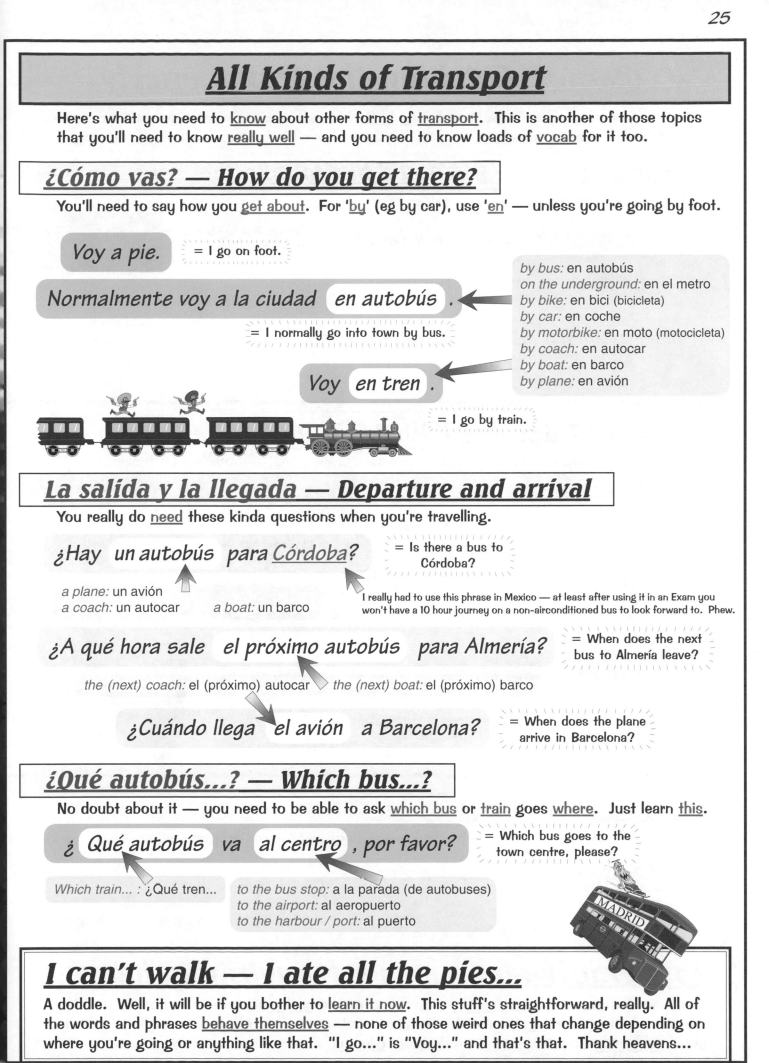

Changing Money and Lost Property

We all hope everything's gonna go <u>without a hitch</u>, but just in case, prepare yourself for the worst case scenario. <u>Losing something</u> in Spain crops up a fair bit in <u>Exams</u>. Learn this for <u>peace of mind</u>.

El cambio — The bureau de change

This comes up all the time in the <u>Speaking Test</u>.

Quisiera cambiar dinero , por favor.

= I would like to change some money, please.

> Look at pages 45 & 1 for more on money and numbers.

some English money: dinero inglés
£50: cincuenta libras esterlinas

Quisiera cambiar este cheque de viaje , por favor.

= I would like to cash this traveller's cheque, please.

these traveller's cheques: estos cheques de viaje

La comisaría — The police station

Here's another situation likely to come up in the <u>Speaking Test</u> — but it's a bit trickier.

He perdido mi bolso . = I've lost my bag.

¿Dónde perdió su bolso ? = Where did you lose your bag?

Perdí mi bolso   en la estación . = I lost my bag at the station.

my bag: mi bolso
my passport: mi pasaporte
my purse: mi monedero

my money: mi dinero
my key: mi llave

> For more buildings & places, see page 21.

Alguien me ha robado el bolso . = Someone has stolen my bag.

Me robaron el bolso   hace una hora . = My bag was stolen an hour ago.

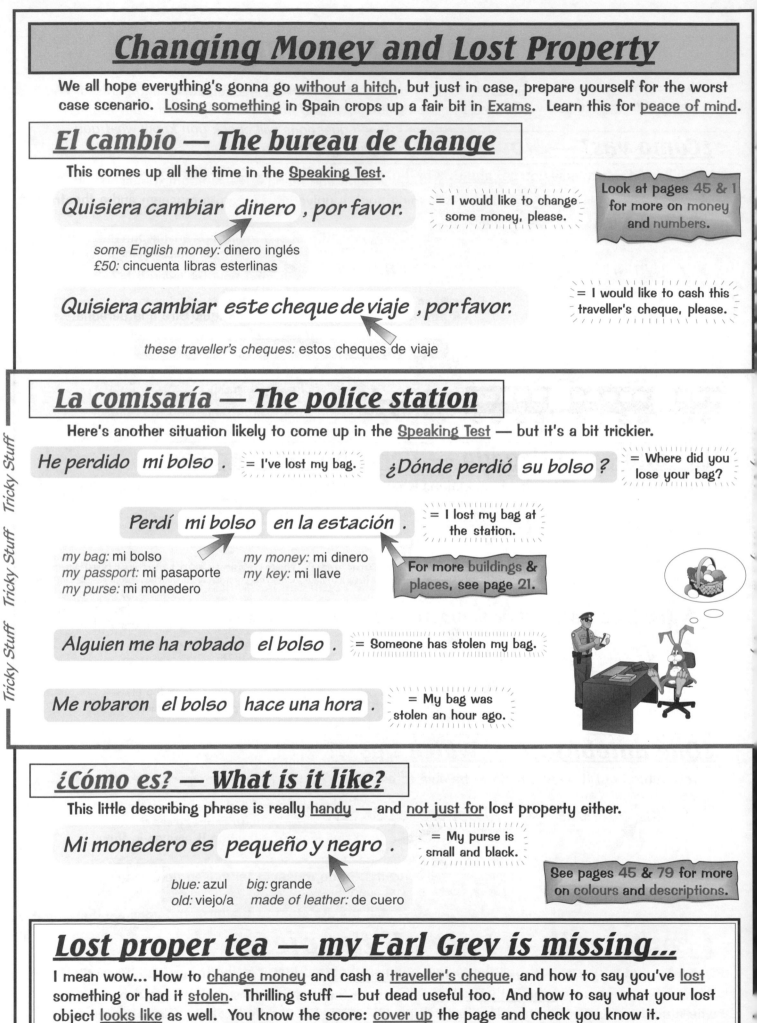

¿Cómo es? — What is it like?

This little describing phrase is really <u>handy</u> — and <u>not just for</u> lost property either.

Mi monedero es pequeño y negro . = My purse is small and black.

blue: azul   *big:* grande
old: viejo/a   *made of leather:* de cuero

> See pages 45 & 79 for more on colours and descriptions.

Lost proper tea — my Earl Grey is missing...

I mean wow... How to <u>change money</u> and cash a <u>traveller's cheque</u>, and how to say you've <u>lost</u> something or had it <u>stolen</u>. Thrilling stuff — but dead useful too. And how to say what your lost object <u>looks like</u> as well. You know the score: <u>cover up</u> the page and check you know it.

Tricky Stuff Tricky Stuff Tricky Stuff

Revision Summary

The thing with doing GCSE Spanish is that it's mainly about learning the key vocab and phrases, and being able to adapt them to different questions. Do that, and you're onto a winner. But if you don't know the phrases, you've got a problem. These questions will check you know what you need to know from this section. Keep trying them until you can do them all.

1) You've arrived in Sevilla and are writing to your penfriend María Eugenia about the sights. How do you say that there's a castle, a swimming pool, a university, a zoo, a museum and a theatre?

2) Write down five shops and five other buildings you might find in a town (apart from the ones above).

3) You need to go to the chemist's. How do you ask where it is, and how far away it is?

4) What do these directions mean: "La farmacia está a un kilómetro de aquí. Gire a la derecha, tome la primera calle a la izquierda, siga todo recto hasta la iglesia. La farmacia está a la derecha."

5) A Spanish tourist has come to see your home town and is looking for the youth hostel. Tell him to go straight on, turn left at the traffic lights and the youth hostel is on the right.

6) Tell your Spanish penfriend José María where you live and whereabouts it is (which city or town and whether it's in the north-east etc).

7) Say that you like living in your town, there's loads to do and it's quite clean. Say there's a sports centre and a cinema.

8) Julio doesn't like the town because it's very big and dirty. María Pilar doesn't like the country because it's boring and too quiet. What would they both say in Spanish?

9) You're at a Spanish train station. How would you do these in Spanish?
a) Say that you'd like to travel to Bilbao on Sunday.   b) Ask if there are any trains.

10) How do you say these in Spanish?
a) the platform   b) the waiting room   c) the timetable   d) non-smoking   e) the departure

11) Ask for three return tickets to Pontevedra, second class. Ask what platform the train leaves from and where the waiting room is. Ask if you have to change trains.

12) Say that you go to school by car, but your friend walks.

13) You've missed the bus to Vigo. Ask when the next bus leaves and when it arrives in Vigo.

14) You're lost in Madrid. Ask which bus goes to the Prado museum (el museo del Prado).

15) You've arrived in Spain without any pesetas. Tell the assistant at the bureau de change that you want to change 50 pounds and a traveller's cheque.

16) You've lost your purse — tell the police, and say that you lost it in the bakery, an hour ago.

17) They ask for a description — say the purse is red and made of leather.

School Subjects

There's no way to avoid school and jobs however much they stress you out.
Great news though — learn all this really well for your Exams and you'll have less to stress about.

¿Qué asignaturas estudias?

What school subjects do you do?

Write out your timetable in Spanish and learn it all.

Estudio **español** . = I do Spanish.

Languages
French: el francés
German: el alemán
Spanish: el español
Italian: el italiano
English: el inglés

Physical Education
P.E.: la educación física

Humanities
history: la historia
geography: la geografía
philosophy: la filosofía
religious studies:
　　　　la religión

Numbers and Stuff
maths: las matemáticas
IT: la informática
business studies:
　　las ciencias empresariales

Sciences
science: las ciencias
physics: la física
chemistry: la química
biology: la biología

Arts and Crafts
art: el arte
drawing: el dibujo
music: la música

¿Cuál es tu asignatura favorita?

What's your favourite subject?

Or your least unfavourite subject if that's how you feel about it all...

¿Cuál es tu asignatura favorita / preferida? = What is your favourite subject?

Mi asignatura preferida es el español. = Spanish is my favourite subject.

Prefiero la biología. = I prefer biology.

> There's more on how to say what you like and don't like on pages 6–7.

Me gustan las matemáticas. = I like maths.

Odio el deporte. = I hate sport.

Frank Sinatra — what subjects did he doobeedoobeedoo...

Play around with this page until you've got it firmly lodged in your brain. Make sure you can say all the subjects you do, and at least understand the ones you don't do when you hear them.

The School Routine

Not the most exciting of pages ever, but it's worth all the effort when you get tricky questions on school routine. Go for short snappy sentences — that way they're easier to remember.

¿Cómo vas al instituto?

Practise saying the sentence you're going to use in the Speaking Exam.

How do you get to school?

Voy al instituto en coche .   = I go to school by car.

on foot: a pie
by bus: en autobús
by bike: en bicicleta

Use "al instituto" for "to school". Use "en" with the form of transport, but "a" for "pie" (on foot).

Don't stop there though — any of the other variations could come up in the Reading or Writing Exams, so learn the lot of them.

Una clase — A lesson

Write out all these sentences and practise slotting in the right times and numbers for your school.

Las clases comienzan a <u>las nueve</u>.   = School begins at 9.00.

Las clases terminan a <u>las tres y cuarto</u>.   = School ends at 3.15.

Tenemos <u>ocho</u> clases por día.   = We have 8 lessons per day.

Cada clase dura <u>cuarenta minutos</u>.   = Each lesson lasts forty minutes.

Tenemos el recreo a las once .   = Break is at 11.00.

For more on times, see page 2 in 'General Stuff'.

break: el recreo
lunch break: la hora de comer

Hacemos una hora de <u>deberes</u> por día.   = We do one hour of homework every day.

Una clase — let that be a lesson to you...

Don't forget the phrases for your exciting school routine, and the sentences for saying how you go to school. Remember the handy phrase 'por día' — you can stick it in loads of sentences.

School Rules and Activities

School is still about 99% of your life so it makes sense that you're gonna be expected to talk about it in Spanish. Reading this page out loud is a great way of practising for your Speaking Exam.

¿Qué haces en tus ratos libres?

Time to admit to all your weird extra-curricular activities — or pretend you do something that's easy to say.

For more on hobbies, see page 36 in 'Free-time and Hobbies'.

What do you do in your free time?

Hago deporte . = I do sport.

I play in a band.: Toco en un grupo.
I collect stamps.: Colecciono sellos.

¿Cuánto tiempo hace que...? — How long...?

This isn't here because I like it. It's here because it could be in your Exam. So learn it.

¿Cuánto tiempo hace que aprendes español? = How long have you been learning Spanish?

Be careful to use the present tense — you don't say 'I have been' as in English. See page 89.

For more on numbers, see page 1 in 'General Stuff'.

Aprendo español desde hace tres años. = I've been learning Spanish for three years.

El horario etc. — The timetable etc.

This is all a bit more tricky and also fairly random, but if you want a top mark, you need to learn it.

Tenemos seis semanas de vacaciones en el verano . = We have six weeks' holiday in the summer.

eight weeks: ocho semanas
five days: cinco días

at Christmas: en Navidad
at Easter: en Semana Santa

Hay tres trimestres. = There are three terms.

See page 45 for more on colours and page 47 for more clothes.

Las reglas son estrictas. = The rules are strict.

Llevamos uniforme en el instituto. = We wear a uniform at school.

You're right, this timetable is a bit much.

Nuestro uniforme es un jersey rojo, pantalones grises, una camisa blanca y una corbata verde. = Our uniform is a red jumper, grey trousers, a white shirt and a green tie.

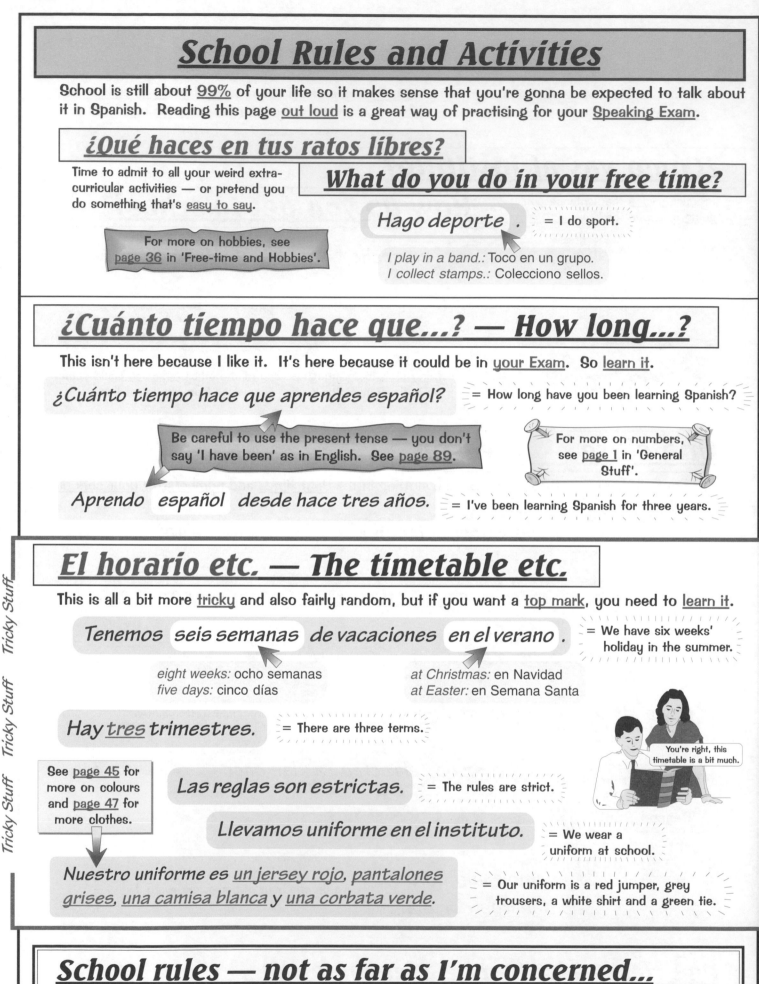

School rules — not as far as I'm concerned...

Spanish numbers are vital for this section. Close the book and see how much of it all you can remember — the more you can reel off about your school, the better.

Tricky Stuff Tricky Stuff Tricky Stuff Tricky Stuff

Classroom Language

We all have our 'off' days, so it's really <u>useful</u> to be able to ask someone to <u>repeat</u> something, or <u>spell out</u> a word you're not sure about. The stuff at the top of the page is useful, too.

¡Siéntese! — Sit down!

<u>Learn</u> these three short phases to avoid the wrath of a scary teacher.

¡Levántese! = Stand up!   ¡Siéntese! = Sit down!   ¡Silencio! = Be quiet!

¿Habla usted español? — Do you speak Spanish?

We all make <u>mistakes</u> and <u>misunderstand</u> things sometimes, but if you can ask for help, you just might never make the same mistake twice. So this stuff can <u>help</u> you <u>understand</u> better, nuff said.

¿Entiendes? = Do you understand?   ¿Cómo se escribe? = How do you spell that?

(No) entiendo/comprendo. = I (don't) understand.

¿Cómo se pronuncia? = How do you pronounce that?

¿Cómo se dice en español? = How do you say that in Spanish?

If you don't understand say "No entiendo"

These phrases can be <u>vital</u> in your <u>Speaking Exam</u>. Even if the worst happens, it's far better to say 'I don't understand' <u>in Spanish</u> than to shrug, give a cheesy smile and mumble something in English.

¿Me puedes explicar esta palabra? = Can you (informal) explain this word?

Can you (formal): puede

¿Qué quiere decir eso? = What does that mean?

¿No es correcto? = Is that wrong?

No es correcto. = That's wrong.   No lo sé. = I don't know that.

¿<u>Puede</u> repetir eso, por favor? = Can you repeat that, please?   Eso es. = That's right.

Classroom language — teacher, blackboard...

You can <u>save</u> yourself from an embarrassing silence and get <u>credit</u> for asking the Examiner to repeat something at the same time — all you have to do is learn <u>all</u> these <u>dead useful</u> phrases. Just remember, bouts of forgetfulness happen to everyone — <u>DON'T PANIC</u>.

Types of Job

There are more jobs here than you can shake a stick at — and <u>any</u> of them could pop up in your Spanish <u>Exams</u>. The jobs you and your family do are <u>extra</u> important.

The gender of a job depends on who is doing it

You'll need to be able to <u>say</u> and <u>write</u> any of the jobs you and your family do — and <u>recognise</u> the rest when you see or hear them.

I've been soliciting for 20 years now, and it hasn't got me anywhere.

> The gender of the job is always <u>masculine</u> for a man and <u>feminine</u> for a woman, although sometimes the only thing that changes is the article - "el turista" or "la turista".

Grey-suit-type jobs
accountant: el/la contable
secretary: el/la secretario/a
engineer: el/la ingeniero/a

Arty jobs
actor/actress: el actor, la actriz
musician: el/la músico/a

Get-your-hands-dirty jobs
mechanic: el/la mecánico/a
electrician: el/la electricista
plumber: el/la fontanero/a
chef: el/la cocinero/a
baker: el/la panadero/a
butcher: el/la carnicero/a

A load more jobs
salesperson: el/la dependiente/a
journalist: el/la periodista
teacher: el profesor, la profesora
hairdresser: el/la peluquero/a
policeman/woman: el policía, la mujer policía
postman/woman: el cartero, la mujer cartero
estate agent: el/la agente inmobiliario/a

Medical jobs
dentist: el/la dentista
chemist: el farmacéutico/a
nurse: el/la enfermero/a
doctor: el doctor, la doctora / el médico, la médica

Being a student or having a part-time job
student: el/la estudiante
part-time worker: trabajador a tiempo parcial / trabajadora a tiempo parcial

Female versions of jobs can be tricky

There <u>are</u> hard and fast <u>rules</u> to how the female version of a job is formed, <u>but</u> there are also <u>exceptions</u> to every rule. The <u>only</u> way to be sure you get the female version right is to <u>learn it</u>.

> This table shows how <u>most</u> names for female jobs are formed, it's a good <u>guide</u>, but <u>won't work</u> for <u>every</u> job.

Masculine	Feminine
el ingenier<u>o</u> ⟹	la ingenier<u>a</u> (an "o" ending becomes "a")
el doct<u>or</u> ⟹	la doct<u>ora</u> ("or" becomes "ora")
el contabl<u>e</u> ⟹	la contabl<u>e</u> ("e" just stays the same)

Good job you've learnt all this...

None too nice, but start with the jobs you find the <u>easiest</u> — then <u>learn</u> the rest. Remember, the jobs people in your family do are the <u>most important</u> — but you should <u>understand</u> the others too. <u>Female</u> versions of each job need learning — so do those tricky <u>odd</u> ones.

Jobs You and Your Parents Do

Don't get tripped up in the Exams by trying to talk about your mum's <u>inverse-polarity-dynamo maintenance job</u>. Pretend she's a teacher or something — it'll make the Exams much easier.

Mi padre — My father, Mi madre — My mother

Pick easy-to-say jobs from page 32 to put in these sentences for your whole family — then learn them.

For more stuff about families, see page 55. For more about numbers, see page 1.

Mi padre **es** vendedor .

= My father is a salesman.

My brother: Mi hermano
My sister: Mi hermana

a chef: cocinero
doctor: médico

Remember: <u>don't</u> put 'un' or 'una' before the job description. Just put 'es' and the job.

five days: cinco días

Mi madre trabaja treinta y cinco horas por semana.

= My mother works 35 hours a week.

Tengo trabajo a tiempo parcial — I have a part-time job

Make these easier by choosing <u>easy</u> jobs and <u>simple</u> values — if only the rest of life was like that.

Tengo trabajo a tiempo parcial .

= I've got a part time job.

You can find plenty of jobs to put into this white box on page 32.

Soy carnicero/a .

= I am a butcher.

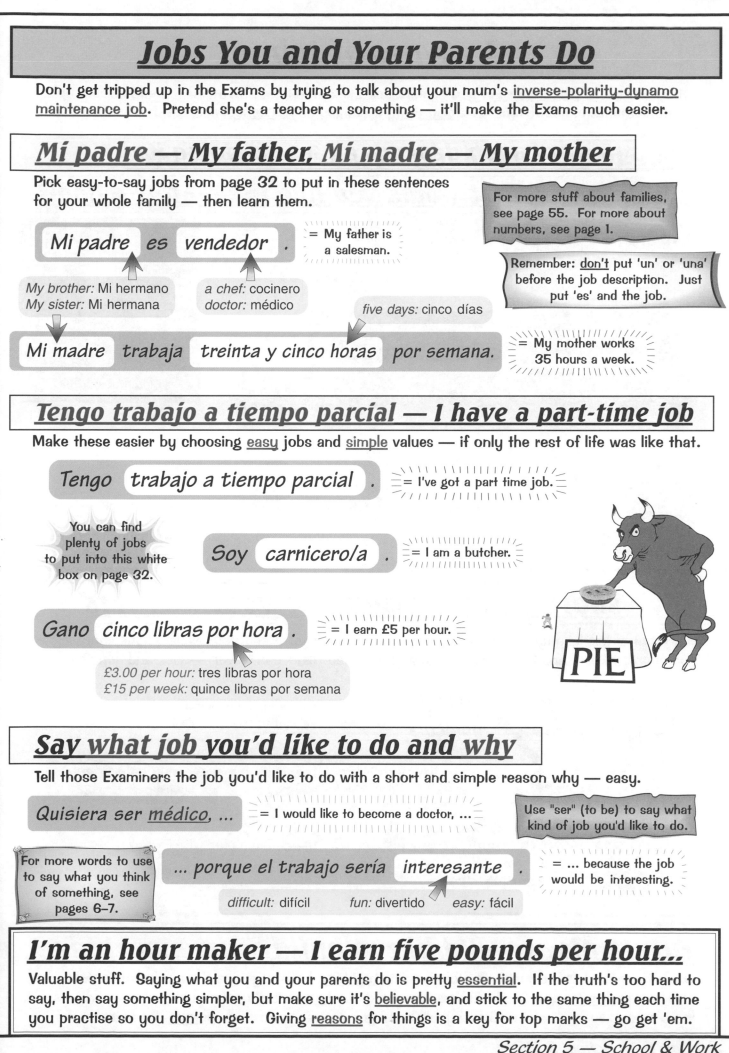

Gano cinco libras por hora .

= I earn £5 per hour.

£3.00 per hour: tres libras por hora
£15 per week: quince libras por semana

Say what job you'd like to do and why

Tell those Examiners the job you'd like to do with a short and simple reason why — easy.

Quisiera ser <u>médico</u>, ...

= I would like to become a doctor, ...

Use "ser" (to be) to say what kind of job you'd like to do.

For more words to use to say what you think of something, see pages 6–7.

... porque el trabajo sería interesante .

= ... because the job would be interesting.

difficult: difícil   fun: divertido   easy: fácil

I'm an hour maker — I earn five pounds per hour...

Valuable stuff. Saying what you and your parents do is pretty <u>essential</u>. If the truth's too hard to say, then say something simpler, but make sure it's <u>believable</u>, and stick to the same thing each time you practise so you don't forget. Giving <u>reasons</u> for things is a key for top marks — go get 'em.

Plans for the Future

If your idea of <u>future plans</u> is what you're doing next weekend, then you'll need to come up with some ideas about what you <u>plan to do</u> when you've <u>left school</u> pronto. It's an Exam fave.

¿Qué te gustaría hacer después del instituto?

Think of a <u>reason</u> why you want to do it too.

— What would you like to do after school?

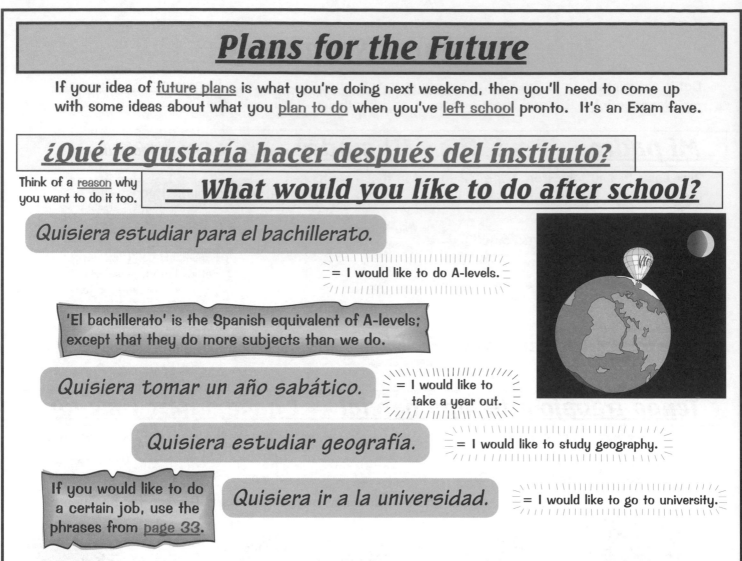

Quisiera estudiar para el bachillerato.

= I would like to do A-levels.

'El bachillerato' is the Spanish equivalent of A-levels; except that they do more subjects than we do.

Quisiera tomar un año sabático.

= I would like to take a year out.

Quisiera estudiar geografía.

= I would like to study geography.

If you would like to do a certain job, use the phrases from <u>page 33</u>.

Quisiera ir a la universidad.

= I would like to go to university.

Give short, sharp reasons for your answers

Work out an explanation for the answer you've given above. Keep your explanations <u>short</u>, <u>clear</u> and <u>simple</u>. For example 'I want to take a year out so that I can travel' — nice and concise.

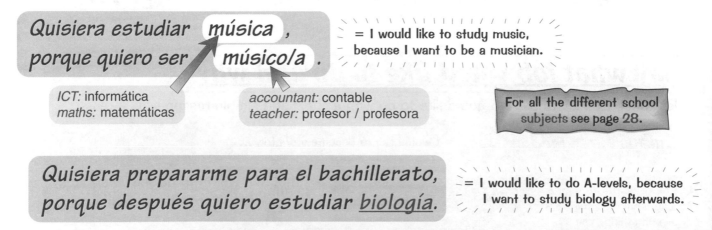

Quisiera estudiar música , porque quiero ser músico/a .

= I would like to study music, because I want to be a musician.

ICT: informática
maths: matemáticas

accountant: contable
teacher: profesor / profesora

For all the different school subjects see page 28.

Quisiera prepararme para el bachillerato, porque después quiero estudiar <u>biología</u>.

= I would like to do A-levels, because I want to study biology afterwards.

Future plans — I'd like to build a time machine...

Sometimes the Exam seems like a big looming <u>mystery</u>, but things like the stuff on this page come up <u>year after year</u> in the Exams. You basically <u>know</u> what's gonna be in your exam — so there's no excuse. Learn it all and you'll be laughing. Use words like '<u>porque</u>' for extra marks.

Tricky Stuff   Tricky Stuff

Revision Summary

You really need to know this stuff. Go through these questions — if you can answer them all without looking anything up, then give yourself a pat on the back and smile widely. If there are some you can't do, look them up. Then try again. And again. Until you can do them all with no problems. It might take a while, but let's face it, you can't expect to learn it all in one day.

1) Say what all your GCSE subjects are in Spanish (or as many as possible). I guess one of them will be 'el español'...

2) What is your favourite subject? What subject(s) don't you like? Answer in Spanish.

3) María goes to school by bike, but Carlos goes by car.
   How would each of them say how they get to school?

4) How would you say that your lunch break begins at 12:45pm and that you have one hour?

5) How do you say that you have six lessons every day, each lesson lasts fifty minutes and you have to do homework?

6) John is describing his school to his Spanish penfriend Miguel. How would he say that there are three terms, that he wears a school uniform and that the rules are very strict?

7) How do you say that you've been learning Spanish for five years and German for four years?

8) Your teacher has just said a long sentence in Spanish and you don't understand.
   How would you ask him or her to repeat it?

9) You still don't understand. What could you say now?
   How do you ask the spelling of the word that is confusing you?

10) How do you say these jobs in Spanish? (Give both the male and female versions if they're different.)
    a) engineer   b) actor   c) policeman   d) hairdresser   e) accountant   f) doctor

11) Say what jobs your parents do.

12) You have a part-time job as a salesperson in a shop.
    You work for three hours on Saturday and you earn £4.50 an hour.
    Write down how you'd tell your Spanish penfriend José all about it.

13) Susana wants to study physics. How does she say that she wants to do the 'bachillerato' so that she can go to university? How does she say her favourite subjects are maths, physics and chemistry?

14) Pablo wants to take a year out after school and study later. How does he say this?

15) Write down the Spanish names of four jobs that you might possibly do in the future and four that you wouldn't be caught dead doing. For the one you like best and the one you like least, give reasons.

Sports and Hobbies

I was never much cop at sport — I could never remember the vocab. OK, maybe you <u>don't</u> need to know it <u>perfectly</u>, but you've gotta be able to <u>recognise</u> these words if they turn up.

¿Practicas algún deporte? — Do you do any sport?

Names of sports

badminton: el bádminton
football: el fútbol
match: el partido
game: el juego
tennis: el tenis
table tennis: el tenis de mesa, el ping pong
squash: el squash
hockey: el hockey

Verbs for outdoor sports

to go fishing: ir de pesca
to go out: salir
to run: correr
to cycle: hacer ciclismo
to swim: nadar
to ski: esquiar, hacer esquí
to go for a walk: dar un paseo
to play: jugar
to walk, hike: hacer senderismo
to jog: hacer footing/futing

Places you can do sports

sports centre, leisure centre: el polideportivo, el centro de deportes
swimming pool: la piscina
sports field: el campo de deportes
gymnasium: el gimnasio
park: el parque
ice rink: la pista de hielo

¿Tienes un pasatiempo? — Do you have a hobby?

Strewth — more flippin' lists. This time it's <u>hobbies</u>. Same thing applies — you <u>won't</u> need them all, but <u>any one</u> of them <u>could</u> turn up... But first off <u>learn</u> the ones that apply to hobbies <u>you do</u>.

General but vital

hobby: el pasatiempo
interest: el interés
club: un club (de...)
member: el/la miembro/a

Other important nouns

chess: el ajedrez
film: la película
performance: la sesión
play (in a theatre): la obra de teatro

Musical instruments

violin: el violín
flute: la flauta
drum kit: la batería
clarinet: el clarinete
guitar: la guitarra
trumpet: la trompeta
piano: el piano
cello: el violoncelo

Verbs for indoor activities

to dance: bailar
to sing: cantar
to collect: coleccionar
to read: leer

To see how to use verbs with different people, see pages 88-94.

Musical words

band, group: el grupo
CD: el CD, el disco compacto
instrument: el instrumento
cassette: el casete, la cinta
concert: el concierto
record: el disco
hi-fi: el equipo de música

Racy Spanish books — give us a quick leer...

<u>Sport</u> and <u>hobbies</u> are common enough topics — you need a good <u>spread</u> of vocab, especially for anything <u>you're involved with</u>. If you <u>aren't</u> into any of this stuff, <u>say so</u> or <u>pretend you are</u> — don't expect to sit in stony silence in your Speaking exam. <u>Practise</u> thinking of <u>something</u> to say.

Sports and Hobbies

What you do in your <u>free time</u> comes up in the Exams <u>every year</u>. You have to be able to say what <u>you</u> get up to, and give <u>opinions</u> on other hobbies. It's <u>must-learn</u> stuff.

¿Qué haces en tus ratos libres?

— What do you do in your free time?

Practise <u>writing</u> some of <u>your own</u> sentences about your free time.

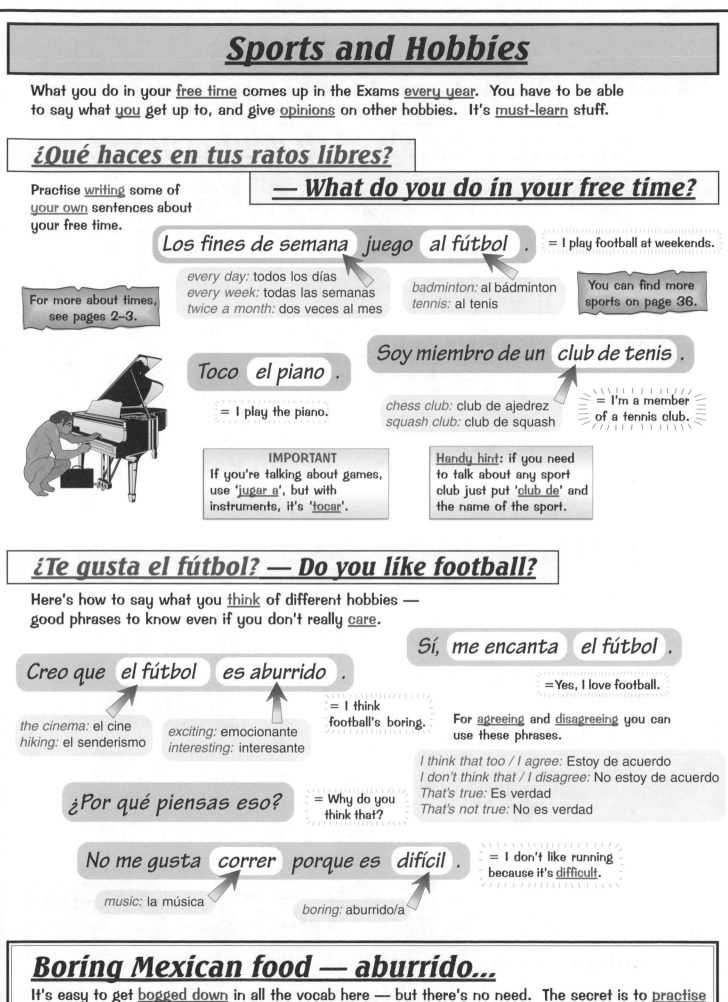

Los fines de semana juego **al fútbol** . ≈ I play football at weekends.

every day: todos los días
every week: todas las semanas
twice a month: dos veces al mes

For more about times, see pages 2–3.

badminton: al bádminton
tennis: al tenis

You can find more sports on page 36.

Toco el piano .

= I play the piano.

Soy miembro de un club de tenis .

chess club: club de ajedrez
squash club: club de squash

= I'm a member of a tennis club.

IMPORTANT
If you're talking about games, use 'jugar a', but with instruments, it's 'tocar'.

<u>Handy hint</u>: if you need to talk about any sport club just put '<u>club de</u>' and the name of the sport.

¿Te gusta el fútbol? — Do you like football?

Here's how to say what you <u>think</u> of different hobbies — good phrases to know even if you don't really <u>care</u>.

Sí, me encanta **el fútbol** .

=Yes, I love football.

Creo que el fútbol **es aburrido** .

= I think football's boring.

the cinema: el cine
hiking: el senderismo

exciting: emocionante
interesting: interesante

For <u>agreeing</u> and <u>disagreeing</u> you can use these phrases.

I think that too / I agree: Estoy de acuerdo
I don't think that / I disagree: No estoy de acuerdo
That's true: Es verdad
That's not true: No es verdad

¿Por qué piensas eso?

= Why do you think that?

No me gusta correr **porque es** difícil .

music: la música

boring: aburrido/a

= I don't like running because it's <u>difficult</u>.

Boring Mexican food — aburrido...

It's easy to get <u>bogged down</u> in all the vocab here — but there's no need. The secret is to <u>practise using</u> it in <u>sentences</u> — the sort of thing you'd stick in a letter or say in a Speaking exam.

Going Out

Heading out? — then <u>buying tickets</u>, <u>opening times</u> and finding <u>where things are</u> is essential stuff.

Ask how much it costs — '¿Cuánto cuesta?'

¿Cuánto cuesta una sesión de natación ?

= How much does it cost to go swimming?

tennis: de tenis
cycling: de ciclismo

Cuesta cien pesetas .

Cuesta cien pesetas la hora.

= It costs 100 pesetas per hour.

= It costs 100 pesetas.

¿Cuándo está abierta la piscina?
— When is the swimming pool open?

¿Cuándo está abierta   la piscina ?

= When is the swimming pool open?

closed: cerrado/a
open: abierto/a

sports centre: el polideportivo
ice rink: la pista de hielo

Abre a las nueve y media
y cierra a las cinco .

= It opens at half past nine and closes at five o'clock.

Quisiera una entrada , por favor.

= I'd like one entrance ticket, please.

two entrance tickets: dos entradas

For more info on times and numbers <u>see pages 1–3</u>.

...por aquí? — ...near here?

¿Hay un teatro por aquí?

= Is there a theatre near here?

a sports field: un campo deportivo
a bowling alley: una bolera

play tennis: jugar al tenis
go for walks: pasear

¿Se puede nadar por aquí?

= Can people swim near here?

For hobbies & more places, <u>see pages 21 & 36</u>.

Spanish candles are rubbish — always going out...

Nothing too problematic here — provided you <u>learn</u> your stuff that is... A lot of this vocab will turn up in <u>different situations</u> — going out, asking for directions, buying tickets. It's <u>worth</u> learning.

Inviting People Out

A brief guide to having fun: 1) get someone to <u>agree</u> to do some <u>fun stuff</u>, 2) decide <u>when</u> and <u>where</u> to meet. The tricky bit is you <u>have</u> to do it in <u>Spanish</u>...

¡Salimos! — Let's go out

Here's <u>one way</u> to <u>suggest</u> a trip out:

Vamos a la piscina . = Let's go to the swimming pool.

to the theatre: al teatro
to the park: al parque

¡Me encantaría!

Your mate might <u>answer</u>:

Sí, me encantaría .   ...OR...   **No, gracias.**   = No, thank you.

= Yes, I'd love to.

Good idea: Buena idea.
Great!: ¡Estupendo!

It's always good to give a <u>reason</u> if you say no:

I'm sorry: Lo siento.
Unfortunately I can't: Desafortunadamente no puedo.
I don't have enough money: No tengo bastante dinero.

You'll pick up <u>extra marks</u> if you use 'preferiría' to say what you'd <u>prefer</u> to do:

Preferiría jugar al fútbol . = I'd prefer to play football.

¿Dónde nos encontramos? — Where shall we meet?

You <u>might decide</u> to meet in front of the town hall:

Nos vemos delante del ayuntamiento . = Let's meet in front of the town hall.

Meet me at the ...
burger bar.

at your house: en tu casa
beside the church: al lado de la iglesia

For other places, see pages 21, 36 and 44.

Your friend might ask <u>what time</u>:

¿A qué hora nos encontramos? = What time shall we meet?

You'd reply:

Nos encontramos a las diez . = We'll meet at 10 o'clock.

For more about times, <u>see pages 2–3.</u>

two thirty: las dos y media
half past three: las tres y media

I'm going on the town — Well, wipe it off then...

<u>Arranging a meeting</u> looks like a tricky topic. There's quite a bit of vocab to get to grips with. Then it's <u>practising sentences</u>, I'm afraid. Remember to <u>give reasons</u> and say what you'd <u>prefer</u>.

Cinema, Concerts, Plays

Blimey — lots of vocab here about <u>going to the cinema</u> or a <u>play</u> or <u>concert</u>. Some of it's a bit <u>dull</u>, I'm afraid, but that's the price you have to pay if you wanna <u>do well</u>. S'up to you, really.

¡Vamos al cine! — Let's go to the cinema!

It's a good move to <u>check the price</u> first:

¿Cuánto cuesta una entrada ? = How much does one ticket cost?

How much do two tickets cost?:
¿Cuánto cuestan dos entradas?

Watch out — you need <u>plural</u> endings for <u>more than one</u> ticket.

You should get a reply something like this:

Una entrada cuesta trescientas pesetas.

= One ticket costs 300 pesetas.

Here's your bog-standard '<u>give us a ticket</u>' phrase:

Quisiera dos entradas , por favor. = I'd like two tickets, please.

Finding out when things <u>start</u> and <u>end</u> is a good plan too:

¿A qué hora empieza la sesión ?

¿A qué hora termina la película ?

el espectáculo = show, performance
el concierto = concert
la película = film
la obra de teatro = play
la sesión = performance
empezar = start/begin
comenzar = start/begin
terminar = finish

Comienza a las ocho y termina a las diez y media . = It starts at 8 o'clock and finishes at half past ten.

¿Fue buena la película? — Was the film good?

Yep, <u>opinions</u> again — you've <u>got</u> to be able to give your thoughts.

¿Qué piensas de la película ? = What do you think of the film?

Fue bastante buena . = It was quite good.

very good: muy buena
bad: mala
boring: aburrida

If you're talking about '<u>el</u> concierto' or '<u>el</u> espectáculo' you'll need 'buen<u>o</u>'/ 'mal<u>o</u>'/ 'aburrid<u>o</u>' etc.

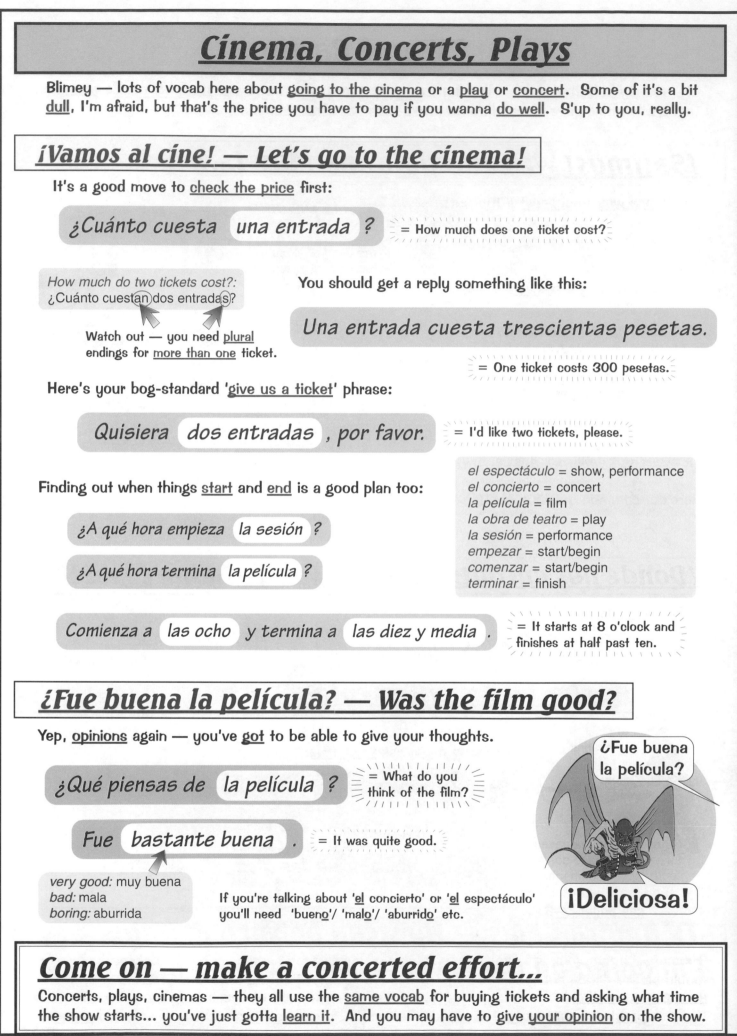

¿Fue buena la película?

¡Deliciosa!

Come on — make a concerted effort...

Concerts, plays, cinemas — they all use the <u>same vocab</u> for buying tickets and asking what time the show starts... you've just gotta <u>learn it</u>. And you may have to give <u>your opinion</u> on the show.

TV and Radio

OK, you can have <u>too much</u> of a host family — you may just prefer to <u>watch the box</u> instead. That's where this page comes into its own — it's got a lot of useful <u>conversational phrases</u>.

Ask politely: ¿Puedo...? — May I...?

Sometimes you may just want <u>mindless entertainment</u>:

¿Puedo **ver la televisión** , por favor?

= May I watch TV, please?

listen to the radio: escuchar la radio
use the telephone: hacer una llamada telefónica

At other times there may be a <u>particular show</u> you want to catch:

¿A qué hora empieza el programa?

= What time does the programme start?

El programa empieza a **las ocho** y termina a **las nueve y media.**

= The programme starts at eight and finishes at half nine.

Here's a common question about <u>what you like to watch</u>:

¿Qué programas te gusta ver?

= What programmes do you like to watch?

WATCH OUT — it's <u>el</u> programa <u>NOT</u> la... <u>Don't</u> get it wrong.

And here's how to <u>answer</u> it:

Me gusta **ver** **Westenders** .

= I like to watch Westenders.

¿Qué has hecho recientemente?

— What have you done recently?

Half the fun of going to the pictures or hearing a new song is <u>telling your mates</u> about it:

Hace poco vi 'Gladiator'.

= I saw 'Gladiator' recently.

last week: la semana pasada
two weeks ago: hace dos semanas
a month ago: hace un mes

heard: escuché
read: leí

the new song by Stairs: la nueva canción de Stairs
the new novel by Martin Amis: la nueva novela de Martin Amis

TV programmes — they can be such a drag...

Hmmm — it may look like a random selection of media-type sentences but that's what your exam could be like. They could ask you <u>any</u> of this stuff — not just the easy bits. There's <u>no point</u> learning set answers — you might <u>not</u> get asked the right question. The only way to do well is to <u>learn the vocab</u> and <u>practise</u> answering <u>different</u> questions <u>using</u> it. A <u>bit of effort</u>'s all you need.

What Do You Think of...?

Giving <u>opinions</u> is one of those things the examiners are <u>especially</u> looking out for. It's popped up in a few places with specific topics, but it's worth getting this <u>general vocab</u> sussed too.

Use 'creo que...' or 'pienso que...' to give your opinion

I think it's safe...

Creo que **este grupo** es **bueno** .

= I think this band is good.

this team: este equipo
this magazine: esta revista
this music: esta música

bad: malo/a
excellent: excelente
boring: aburrido/a
quite good: bastante bueno/a
fantastic: fantástico/a

Opinion words

¿Te gusta...? — Do you like...?

Sometimes you may also have to <u>ask</u> about <u>somebody else's opinions</u>.

¿Te gusta **este grupo** ?

= Do you like this band?

this film: esta película
this newspaper: este periódico
this book: este libro

Here's an answer:

No me gusta **este grupo** . Creo que es **malo** .

These are <u>linked</u>. If the <u>first bit</u> is <u>masculine</u>, then the <u>second bit</u> must be masculine too.

You may want to check the other person <u>agrees</u> with what you've just said:

¿Estás de acuerdo?

= Do you agree?

...or...

Creo que este periódico es aburrido. ¿<u>Y tú</u>?

= I think this newspaper is boring. And you?

And in reply:

Estoy de acuerdo.

= OK / I agree.

Creo que — it's my favourite sport, actually...

Giving your <u>opinion</u> about things gets you <u>big marks</u> in the Exam. It's all a matter of having the vocab at your fingertips, ready to use. And the best way to have that is, yep, lots of <u>practice</u>.

Revision Summary

These questions really do check what you know and don't know — which means you can spend your time learning the bits you're shaky on. But it's not a good idea to do this one day, then forget about it. Come back to these a day later and try them again. And then a week later...

1) What is the Spanish for each of these sports, and for the place where you would do them?
a) football   b) swimming   c) squash   d) skating

2) Escribe cinco pasatiempos que te gustan, y cinco que no te gustan.

3) Write down as many words as you can to do with playing or listening to music.

4) Juan Martín asks Marisol if she has a hobby. She says that she plays the guitar, goes cycling and reads books. Write down their conversation in Spanish.

5) Francisco and Anne are having an argument. Francisco says that he likes tennis because it's exciting. Anne finds tennis boring and difficult. Write down their conversation in Spanish.

6) Say you go for walks at the weekend and you're a member of a table tennis club.

7) You want to play squash. Ask when the sports centre is open and how much it costs to play squash. Ask for two tickets.

8) How would you ask a) if there's a sports centre near here?
b) if you can play badminton near here?

9) Dave wants to see 'Don Quijote' at the cinema, but Isabel says she wants to see 'Como Agua Para Chocolate'. They arrange to meet in front of the cinema at 8pm. Write down their conversation in Spanish.

10) Say that you'd like to go to the cinema, but unfortunately you haven't got enough money. Suggest going for a walk instead.

11) Quieres ir a un concierto. El concierto empieza a las nueve y media y termina a las diez y media. Una entrada cuesta trescientas pesetas. ¿Cómo se dice eso en inglés?

12) What questions would you have to ask to find out the information in Q.11?

13) You're at your penfriend's home. Ask if you can listen to the radio. Say that you also like watching TV.

14) Think of a film you saw recently and one you saw a month ago, and say this in Spanish. (You don't have to translate the film title into Spanish.)

15) You like the group 'The Sheep Shearers', but you think 'Desmond and the Dreamboats' are excellent. How would you tell someone that in Spanish?

16) How would you ask your penfriend if he/she agrees? (There are two ways.)

Where and When

This section gives you all the <u>key stuff</u> you need to know about <u>shopping</u> and <u>eating</u> — at last, a section after my own heart... Bring on the vocab...

¿Dónde está...? — Where is...?

A <u>dead handy</u> question, this one.

¿Dónde está | el supermercado | , por favor?

butcher's: la carnicería
baker's: la panadería
grocer's: la tienda de comestibles

= Where is the supermarket, please?

The word order's the same in English and Spanish.

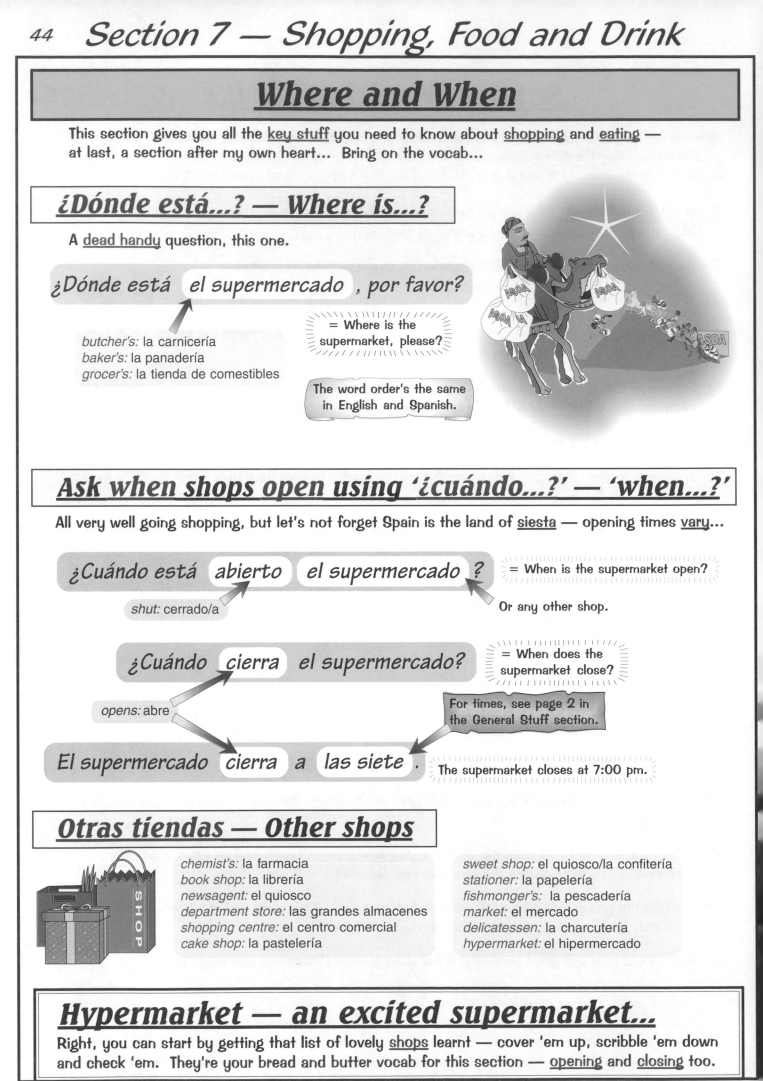

Ask when shops open using '¿cuándo...?' — 'when...?'

All very well going shopping, but let's not forget Spain is the land of <u>siesta</u> — opening times <u>vary</u>...

¿Cuándo está | abierto | el supermercado | ?

shut: cerrado/a

= When is the supermarket open?

Or any other shop.

¿Cuándo | cierra | el supermercado?

opens: abre

= When does the supermarket close?

For times, see page 2 in the General Stuff section.

El supermercado | cierra | a | las siete .

The supermarket closes at 7:00 pm.

Otras tiendas — Other shops

chemist's: la farmacia
book shop: la librería
newsagent: el quiosco
department store: las grandes almacenes
shopping centre: el centro comercial
cake shop: la pastelería

sweet shop: el quiosco/la confitería
stationer: la papelería
fishmonger's: la pescadería
market: el mercado
delicatessen: la charcutería
hypermarket: el hipermercado

Hypermarket — an excited supermarket...

Right, you can start by getting that list of lovely <u>shops</u> learnt — cover 'em up, scribble 'em down and check 'em. They're your bread and butter vocab for this section — <u>opening</u> and <u>closing</u> too.

Saying What You'd Like

OK, this is a page to get you started with the vocab for <u>buying things</u> — especially <u>saying what you want</u>. It's pretty darn <u>essential</u>, if you ask me.

El dinero español — Spanish money

Spanish money's really easy — <u>everything</u> is counted in pesetas.

This is what you'd <u>see</u> on a Spanish <u>price tag</u>: → *100ptas*

This is how you <u>say</u> the price: → 'Cien pesetas' = one hundred pesetas

For <u>numbers</u>, see <u>page 1</u>.

Quisiera... — I would like...

Quisiera is ultra polite — it's <u>more formal</u> than 'quiero' (I want), and it's <u>more common</u> in Spain.

Quisiera una barra de pan , por favor. = I'd like a loaf of bread, please.

Quisiera unos pantalones ; mi talla es la cuarenta y seis . = I'd like a pair of trousers. I'm size 46.

For clothing, see page 47.

Important Bit:
Another good way to say 'I would like' is 'Me gustaría (mucho)...'

Continental Sizes
size: la talla   shoe size: el número de pie
dress size 10 / 12 / 14 / 16: 38 / 40 / 42 / 44
shoe size 5 / 6 / 7 / 8 / 9 / 10: 38 / 39 / 40 / 41 / 42 / 43

They might ask what colour you want — ¿de qué color...?

<u>Colours</u> go <u>after</u> the noun, and have to <u>agree</u> with it (most change to end in 'a' if the noun's feminine and 's' or 'es' if it's plural).

Quisiera unos pantalones azul<u>es</u> . = I'd like a pair of blue trousers.

Colours: los colores
black: negro/a	green: verde	pink: rosa
white: blanco/a	blue: azul	purple: púrpura / morado/a
red: rojo/a	brown: marrón	light blue: azul claro
yellow: amarillo/a	orange: naranja	dark blue: azul oscuro

For adjective endings, see page 79.

153

Quisiera una falda roj<u>a</u> . = I'd like a red skirt.

Quiero vs quisiera — 'I want' doesn't get...

Saying what you want is an absolutely <u>vital</u> thing to learn. Spend some time on <u>colours</u> too, especially getting the <u>right ending</u>. If the noun's <u>feminine</u> or <u>plural</u> the colour word will <u>change</u>.

Shopping: The Basics

Ah the roar of the crowds, the push of the queues — we all have to shop sometime... often in the exams. Yep, shopping is one of those essential topics you'd be advised to get under your belt.

¿En qué puedo servirle? — Can I help you?

First you've got to be able to ask if the shop has what you want.

¿Tiene pan , por favor? = Excuse me, do you have any bread?

You'd expect a reply like: Sí, allí está. ...or... No, no tenemos.

= Yes, there it is. = No, we don't have any.

You can say what you'd like using 'Quisiera...':

Quisiera quinientos gramos de azúcar, por favor. = I'd like 500g of sugar, please.

1kg: un kilo
2kg: dos kilos

The shop assistant might say:

¿Algo más? = Anything else? ...or... ¿Eso es todo? = Is that everything?

You could reply: No, gracias. = No, thank you.

Sí, por favor, también quisiera una patata . = Yes, I'd like a potato as well, please.

¿Lo quiere? — Do you want it?

To buy or not to buy — that is the question...
and here are the answers...

Lo/La quiero. = I'll take it. (Literally = I want it)

No lo quiero. No me gusta el color.

It's too small: Es demasiado pequeño.
It's too expensive: Es demasiado caro.

= I don't want it.
I don't like the colour.

lo = masculine things, la = feminine

Will you be taking that? — no, I was going to pay...

The trick with shopping is knowing the basic vocab first — it's a nightmare trying to bluff your way through an exam if you don't know the words. Practising these phrases with different vocab helps.

Tricky Stuff

Section 7 — Shopping, Food and Drink

Clothes and Pocket Money

More lists of vocab, I'm afraid — but it's all everyday stuff that turns up frequently. Apart from clothes, there's a bit of vocab for pocket money and sales... Oh the thrills...

La ropa — Clothing

el sombrero

Me gusta este zapato . = I like this shoe.

No me gustan estos zapatos . = I don't like these shoes.

el niki

la falda

shirt: la camisa
trousers:
   los pantalones
skirt: la falda
jumper:
   el jersey, el suéter
socks: los calcetines
shoe: el zapato
shoes: los zapatos
dress: el vestido

coat: el abrigo
hat: el sombrero
T-shirt: la camiseta,
            el niki
suit: el traje
jacket: la chaqueta
tie: la corbata
glove: el guante
gloves: los guantes

pair of tights: las medias
shorts: los pantalones cortos
raincoat: el impermeable
a pair of socks:
      un par de calcetines
jeans: los vaqueros, los tejanos
tracksuit: el chandal

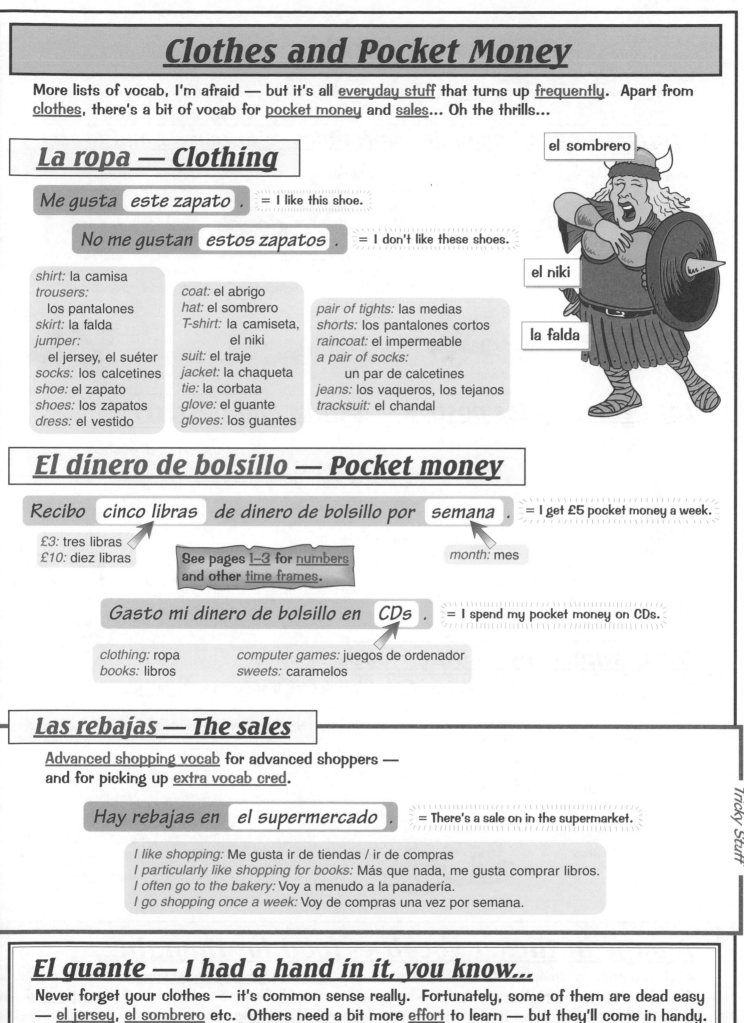

El dinero de bolsillo — Pocket money

Recibo cinco libras de dinero de bolsillo por semana . = I get £5 pocket money a week.

£3: tres libras
£10: diez libras

See pages 1–3 for numbers
and other time frames.

month: mes

Gasto mi dinero de bolsillo en CDs . = I spend my pocket money on CDs.

clothing: ropa
books: libros

computer games: juegos de ordenador
sweets: caramelos

Las rebajas — The sales

Advanced shopping vocab for advanced shoppers —
and for picking up extra vocab cred.

Hay rebajas en el supermercado . = There's a sale on in the supermarket.

I like shopping: Me gusta ir de tiendas / ir de compras
I particularly like shopping for books: Más que nada, me gusta comprar libros.
I often go to the bakery: Voy a menudo a la panadería.
I go shopping once a week: Voy de compras una vez por semana.

Tricky Stuff

El guante — I had a hand in it, you know...

Never forget your clothes — it's common sense really. Fortunately, some of them are dead easy
— el jersey, el sombrero etc. Others need a bit more effort to learn — but they'll come in handy.

Food

Woah — scary vocab page... <u>Any</u> of this stuff could come up, so you need to be on your toes.

La carnicería y la tienda de comestibles — Butcher's and Grocer's

Vegetables: las legumbres
potato: la patata
carrot: la zanahoria
tomato: el tomate
cucumber: el pepino
onion: la cebolla
cauliflower: la coliflor
French bean: la judía
mushroom: el champiñon
cabbage: la col
lettuce: la lechuga
pea: el guisante

Meats: la carne
beef: la carne de vaca
pork: la carne de cerdo
chicken: el pollo
lamb: el cordero
sausage: la salchicha
dry sausage: el chorizo,
           el salchichón
ham: el jamón
steak: el filete
fish: el pescado
seafood: los mariscos

Fruits: la fruta
apple: la manzana
banana: el plátano
strawberry: la fresa
lemon: el limón
orange: la naranja
raspberry: la frambuesa
peach: el melocotón
pear: la pera

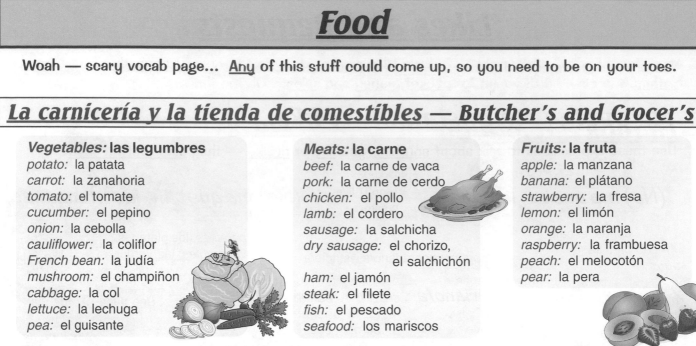

Las bebidas y los postres — Drinks and Desserts

Mmm, my favourite vocab — this is more like it...

Drinks: las bebidas
beer: la cerveza
tea: el té
coffee: el café
white coffee: el café con leche
wine: el vino
red/white wine: el vino tinto/blanco
orange juice: el zumo / jugo de naranja
mineral water: el agua mineral

Desserts: los postres
cake: la tarta / el pastel
biscuit: la galleta
ice cream: el helado
chocolate: el chocolate
sugar: el azúcar
cream: la nata
pancake: el crep
yogurt: el yogur
honey: la miel
jam: la mermelada

Otros alimentos — Other foods

Some <u>absolute basics</u> here — and some Spanish specialities that could just <u>pop up</u>.

bread: el pan
milk: la leche
butter: la mantequilla
cheese: el queso
bread roll: el panecillo
soup: la sopa
breakfast cereals: los cereales
chips: las patatas fritas
crisps: las patatas

egg: el huevo
salt: la sal
pepper: la pimienta
rice: el arroz
pasta: las pastas

Spanish Specialities: las especialidades españolas

olives: las olivas, las aceitunas

Spicy cold tomato soup: el gazpacho

small snacks eaten in cafés and bars: las tapas

Rice dish with chicken, seafood and vegetables: la paella
chocolate and churros (deep-fried fritters that are dipped into hot chocolate): chocolate y churros

A bar made of sweet almonds and various flavours: el turrón

A page of tucker vocab — food for thought...

A lot of foods are similar to the English words — like <u>el café</u>, <u>el chocolate</u>, <u>el limón</u>, but a lot aren't. You'll just have to <u>learn them</u> — but make sure you can <u>spell</u> them as well, or you'll be <u>scuppered</u> in the Writing Exam. Have a <u>good</u> look at those <u>Spanish specialities</u> too — they may turn up.

Likes and Requests

You probably have some foods you <u>can't stand</u>, and others you <u>love</u> — well, here's <u>how to say so</u>.

Me gusta / Me gustan... — I like...

Use these expressions to talk about <u>anything</u> you <u>like</u> or <u>dislike</u> — they <u>ain't just for food</u>.

(No) me gusta la nata .   = I (don't) like cream.

coffee: el café

vegan: vegetariano/a estricto/a

Soy vegetariano/a .   = I'm a vegetarian.

(No) me gustan las manzanas .   = I (don't) like apples.

bananas: los plátanos
vegetables: las verduras

See page 48 for the names of foods.

¿Puede...? — Can you...?

Here's a <u>dead nifty</u> phrase to <u>learn</u>.
Use it <u>properly</u> and you'll be the essence of politeness.

¿Puede pasarme la sal , por favor?   = Can you pass me the salt, please?

a napkin: una servilleta
the sugar: el azúcar
the cream: la nata
the milk: la leche
the pepper: la pimienta

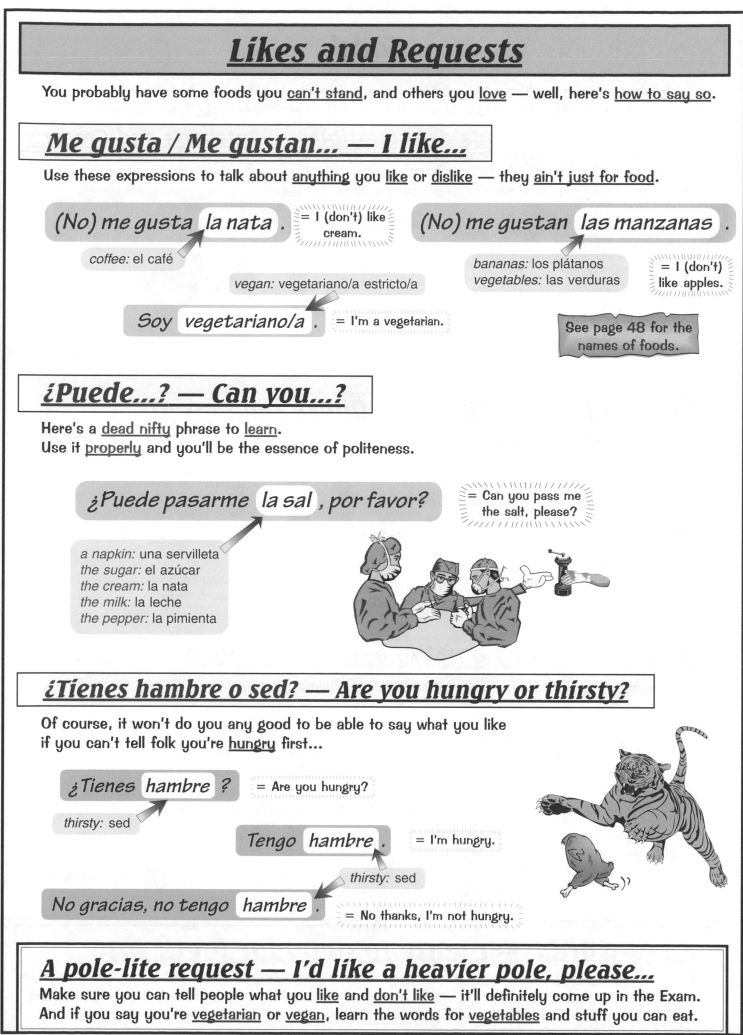

¿Tienes hambre o sed? — Are you hungry or thirsty?

Of course, it won't do you any good to be able to say what you like
if you can't tell folk you're <u>hungry</u> first...

¿Tienes hambre ?   = Are you hungry?

thirsty: sed

Tengo hambre .   = I'm hungry.

thirsty: sed

No gracias, no tengo hambre .   = No thanks, I'm not hungry.

A pole-lite request — I'd like a heavier pole, please...

Make sure you can tell people what you <u>like</u> and <u>don't like</u> — it'll definitely come up in the Exam.
And if you say you're <u>vegetarian</u> or <u>vegan</u>, learn the words for <u>vegetables</u> and stuff you can eat.

Dinner

A lot of this is useful in <u>different</u> situations — <u>not just</u> in conversations at the dinner table. It almost always comes up in the exams — it's the sort of stuff you <u>really need to know</u>.

¿Te gusta la cena? — Do you like the dinner?

You'd get asked for an opinion in <u>most restaurants</u>.

La comida estaba **buena** .

very good: muy rico/a
bad: malo/a
very bad: muy malo/a

= The meal was good.

La comida no estaba buena.

= The meal wasn't good.

El desayuno estaba **delicioso** , gracias.

= Breakfast was delicious, thanks.

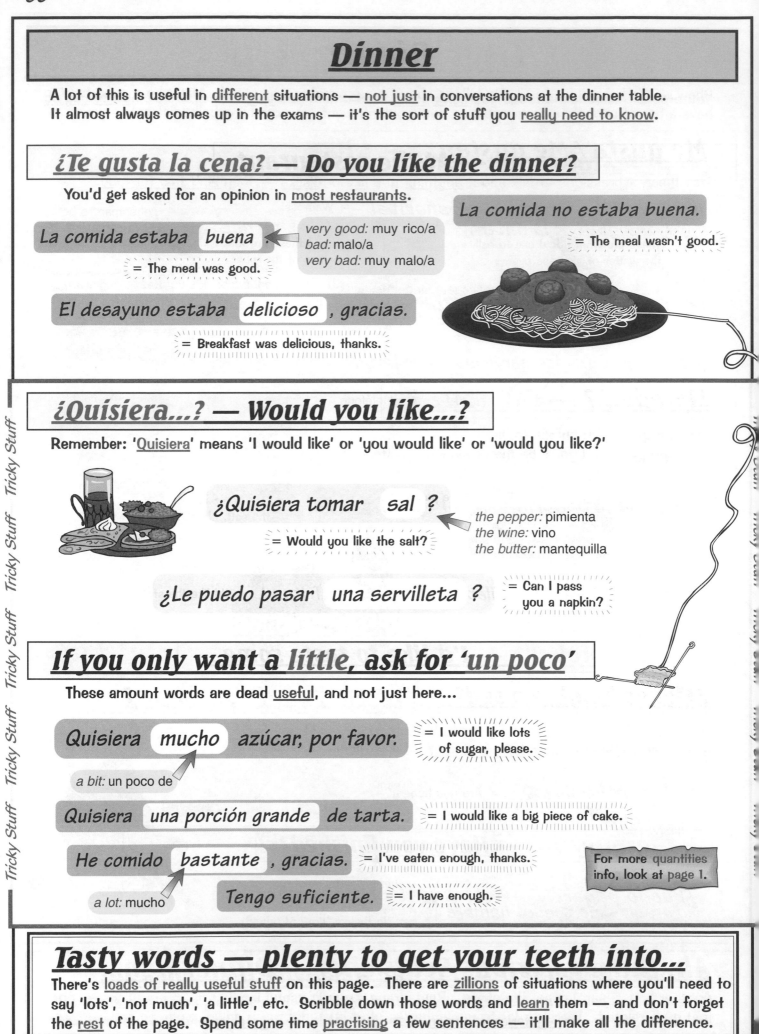

¿Quisiera...? — Would you like...?

Remember: '<u>Quisiera</u>' means 'I would like' or 'you would like' or 'would you like?'

¿Quisiera tomar **sal** ?

= Would you like the salt?

the pepper: pimienta
the wine: vino
the butter: mantequilla

¿Le puedo pasar **una servilleta** ?

= Can I pass you a napkin?

If you only want a little, ask for 'un poco'

These amount words are dead <u>useful</u>, and not just here...

Quisiera **mucho** azúcar, por favor.

= I would like lots of sugar, please.

a bit: un poco de

Quisiera **una porción grande** de tarta.

= I would like a big piece of cake.

He comido **bastante** , gracias.

= I've eaten enough, thanks.

a lot: mucho

Tengo suficiente.

= I have enough.

For more quantities info, look at page 1.

Tasty words — plenty to get your teeth into...

There's <u>loads of really useful stuff</u> on this page. There are <u>zillions</u> of situations where you'll need to say 'lots', 'not much', 'a little', etc. Scribble down those words and <u>learn</u> them — and don't forget the <u>rest</u> of the page. Spend some time <u>practising</u> a few sentences — it'll make all the difference.

Tricky Stuff Tricky Stuff Tricky Stuff Tricky Stuff Tricky Stuff Tricky Stuff Tricky Stuff

Dinner

Phew — it's <u>hungry work</u>, all this talking about <u>dinners</u> and <u>restaurants</u>... Might be a good time to have a bar of chocolate or an apple... You wouldn't want your rumbling belly distracting you.

En el restaurante — At the restaurant

¡Camarero! = Waiter!

¡Señorita! = Waitress!

These are what you'd use to call the waiter or waitress over...

...and these are the names of the jobs.

waiter: el camarero
waitress: la camarera

¿Me trae el menú, por favor? = May I have the menu, please?

See page 16 on 'hotels' for asking where things are.

¿Dónde están los servicios, por favor? = Where are the toilets, please?

is: está

the phone: el teléfono

Quisiera... — I'd like...

See page 48 for food vocab.

¿Tiene paella? = Do you have paella?

bread: pan
bananas: plátanos

the omelette: la tortilla
the dish of the day: el plato del día

salad: ensalada
rice: arroz
carrots: zanahorias

Quisiera / Para mí el filete con patatas fritas. = I'd like the steak with chips.

Quisiera probar... — I'd like to taste some...

You'd never learn <u>all</u> the different types of food — there are squillions.
So here's a handy sentence for when you've forgotten what something tastes like.

¿A qué sabe el turrón? = What does 'turrón' taste like?

(turrón = nougat)

rabbit: el conejo

¿Ha terminado? — Have you finished?

¿Puedo pagar? = May I pay?

La cuenta, por favor. = The bill, please.

Ah, the mysterious Scots chef — Dinner Ken...

Another '<u>must-learn</u>' page, I'm afraid. Restaurant vocab is useful in <u>all sorts of situations</u> — not just grub-related. There's a lot to remember — start by <u>scribbling</u> it down, <u>covering</u> and <u>learning</u>.

At a Restaurant

Restaurant role-plays <u>aren't</u> just about <u>ordering grub</u> — this vocab'll <u>win you marks</u> too...

¿Tiene una mesa libre?

Don't forget — it's all about being <u>polite</u>.

— Do you have a table free?

Una mesa para **cuatro**, por favor.

= A table for four, please.

See page 1 for more about numbers.

two: dos
three: tres

Somos **cuatro**.

= There are four of us.

two: dos
three: tres

Quisiéramos sentarnos **fuera**.

= We'd like to sit outside.

on the terrace: en la terraza

No estoy satisfecho/a — I'm not satisfied

If you want to <u>complain</u> about something...

Quisiera quejarme.

... remember to say what you're complaining about:

= I'd like to make a complaint.

La carne de ternera está **poco hecha**.

= The veal is underdone.

The steak: El filete
The pork: La carne de cerdo
The coffee: El café

too hot: demasiado caliente
too cold: demasiado frío/a

See page 48 for food vocab.

El servicio — Service charge

Remember the <u>service charge</u> — you'll be the waiter's friend forever...

¿Está incluido el servicio?

= Is service included?

Some useful words you might see on a menu:

Servicio incluido (= Service included)
El cubierto (= The cover charge)
El precio fijo (= Fixed price)

Zumo de naranja
Servicio incluido

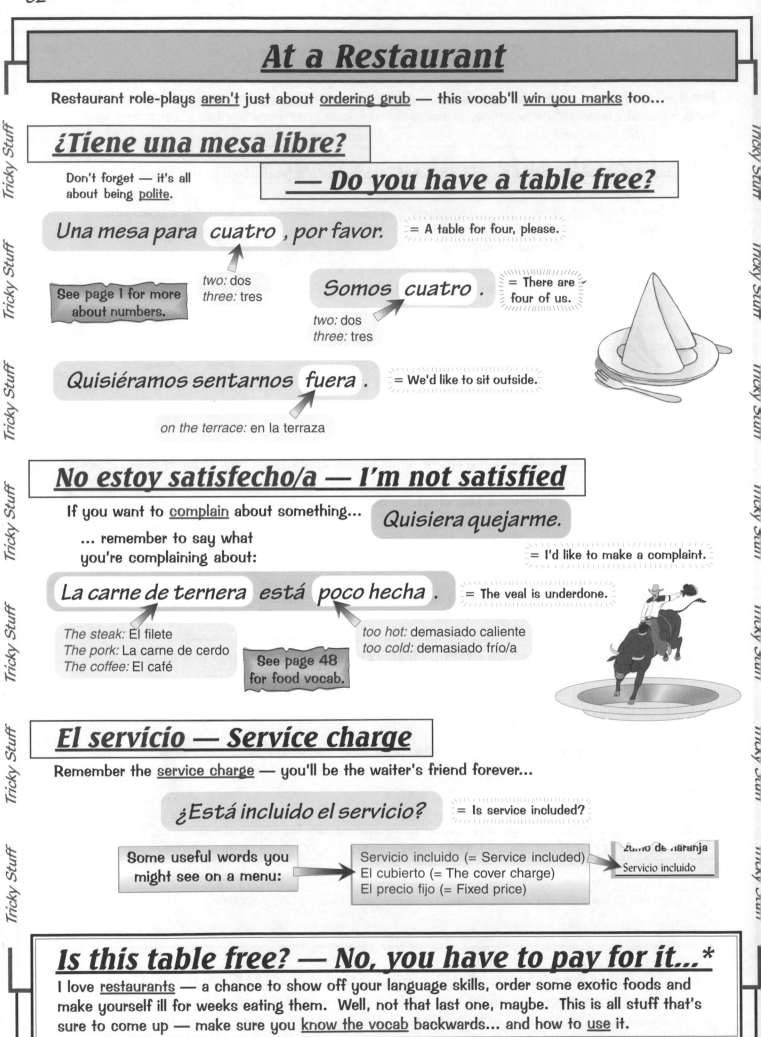

Is this table free? — No, you have to pay for it...*

I love <u>restaurants</u> — a chance to show off your language skills, order some exotic foods and make yourself ill for weeks eating them. Well, not that last one, maybe. This is all stuff that's sure to come up — make sure you <u>know the vocab</u> backwards... and how to <u>use</u> it.

(side margin, repeated) Tricky Stuff

Revision Summary

This kind of thing always comes up in exam papers, so make sure you know all the vocab for shopping and meals. You know how it works — do these questions, then look up the ones you get stuck on, THEN go back over them and check you really can do them.

1) You're out of bread. How do you ask where the baker's is and whether it is open?

2) You have a splitting headache. Ask where the nearest chemist's is, and if it's open now. Ask what the chemist's opening hours are.

3) What are the Spanish names for   a) a stationer's   b) a cake shop   c) a butcher's   d) a book shop   e) a sweet shop   f) a supermarket?

4) You've been looking at jeans, but decided not to buy any. A shop assistant asks '¿En qué puedo ayudarle?' What do you reply?

5) You want to buy a brown jumper, size 48, and three pairs of socks. How do you say this to the shop assistant?

6) Your penfriend asks if you like their new coat. Say you don't like it, you like big red or small yellow coats. Ask how much it cost.

7) How would you ask if there's a sale on at the supermarket?

8) Ask for 1 kilo of apples. The shop assistant says: '¿Quiere algo más?' What does he mean?

9) You're telling your penfriend Claudio about your shopping habits. Say you get £5 pocket money a week, you like to buy chocolate but you don't like shopping.

10) You're making a fruit salad for a party. Think of as many fruits as you can to put in it — at least 5. Make a list of 5 drinks you could offer people at the party.

11) Write down how you'd say that you like vegetables but don't like sausages. Also that you're hungry.

12) Thank your hosts for the meal, say you enjoyed it and it was delicious. Offer to pass your hostess the milk.

13) You're going out for a meal. Ask if you can have a table for two and ask where the toilet is.

14) Order steak and chips and an orange juice for you, and chicken with potatoes and carrots for your friend.

15) Attract the waitress's attention and say that you'd like the bill. Tell her that the meal was nice but the potatoes were cold. Ask if the service charge is included.

About Yourself

Talking about yourself — well, it's my favourite subject. There are <u>all sorts of things</u> they could ask about — it's a good idea to have a think about <u>how to answer</u> some of these questions <u>now</u>.

Háblame de ti — Tell me about yourself

What are you called?: ¿Cómo te llamas?

Me llamo **Angela** . = I'm called Angela.

How old are you?: ¿Cuántos años tienes?

Tengo **quince años** . = I'm 15 years old.

When is your birthday?: ¿Cuándo es tu cumpleaños?

Mi cumpleaños es el **doce de diciembre** . = My birthday is on the 12th December.

See pages 23 & 56 for where you live, page 1 for more numbers and page 2 for more dates.

Where do you live?: ¿Dónde vives?

Vivo en **Lancaster** . = I live in Lancaster.

What do you like?: ¿Qué te gusta?

Me gusta **el fútbol** . = I like football.

¿Cómo eres? — What are you like?

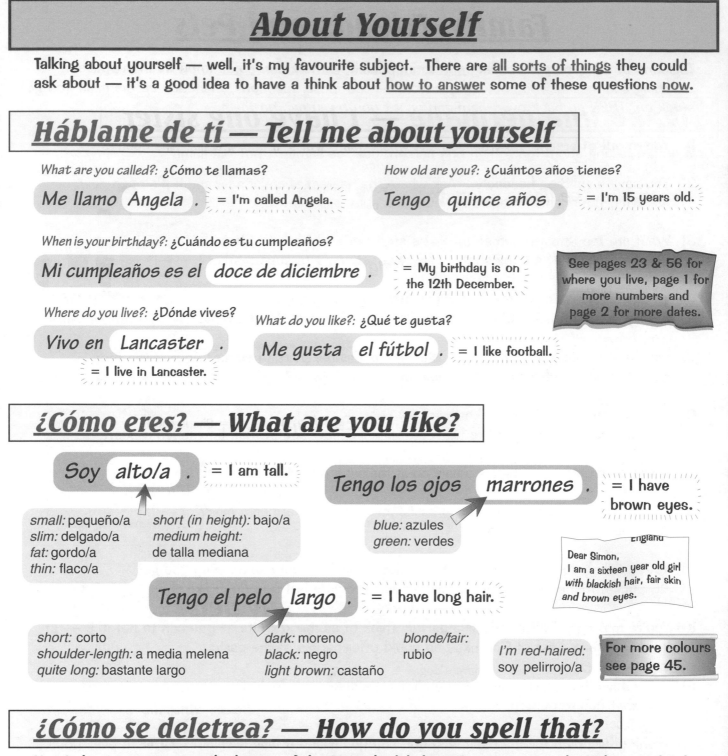

Soy **alto/a** . = I am tall.

small: pequeño/a
slim: delgado/a
fat: gordo/a
thin: flaco/a

short (in height): bajo/a
medium height: de talla mediana

Tengo los ojos **marrones** . = I have brown eyes.

blue: azules
green: verdes

England
Dear Simon,
I am a sixteen year old girl with blackish hair, fair skin and brown eyes.

Tengo el pelo **largo** . = I have long hair.

short: corto
shoulder-length: a media melena
quite long: bastante largo

dark: moreno
black: negro
light brown: castaño

blonde/fair: rubio

I'm red-haired: soy pelirrojo/a

For more colours see page 45.

¿Cómo se deletrea? — How do you spell that?

Here's how to <u>pronounce</u> the letters of the Spanish <u>alphabet</u>. Practise going through it <u>out loud</u> — yes, you'll sound daft, but you'd sound dafter getting it <u>wrong</u> in the Exam.

A — a (like 'cat')	H — achay ('ch' like catch)	Ñ — enyay	U — ooh
B — bay	I — eeh (like 'me')	O — o (like 'pot')	V — oobay
C — they* (like '<u>think</u>')	J — hota ('h' like 'loch')	P — pay	W — oobay doblay
D — day	K — ca (like 'cat')	Q — coo	
E — ay (like 'day')	L — elay	R — eray	X — ekeess
F — efay	M — emay	S — essay	Y — ee greeayga
G — hay ('h' like 'loch')	N — enay	T — tay	Z — thayta*

*In southern Spain and Latin America, they say these as C — <u>say</u>, and Z — <u>sayta</u>.

What I'm like — tall, handsome & a compulsive liar...

<u>Talking about yourself</u> won't be a chore — it's a matter of <u>practice</u>. The alphabet's a <u>pain</u> though.

Family, Friends and Pets

Zzzzz... Families and pets... Like how boring... Still — there are marks to be won I suppose.

Tengo una hermana — I have one sister

If you're talking about more than one person, use "se llaman", not "se llama".

Mi madre **se llama** Janet .

= My mother is called Janet.

Tengo **un hermano** .

= I have one brother.

My father: Mi padre
My brother: Mi hermano
My sister: Mi hermana
My aunt: Mi tía
My uncle: Mi tío
My female cousin: Mi prima
My male cousin: Mi primo
My grandmother: Mi abuela
My grandfather: Mi abuelo
My friend: Mi amigo/a
My boy/girlfriend: Mi novio/a

The average family

Have a bash at describing some of your rellies too:
it's an easy way to pick up extra marks in letters to penpals.

Es **baja** .

= She is short.

Tiene **doce años.**

= He's 12 years old.

Tiene los ojos **azules** .

Tiene el pelo **liso** .

= She has straight hair.

= He has blue eyes.

¿Tienes animales? — Have you any pets?

Tengo **un perro** .

= I have a dog.

a dog: un perro
a cat: un gato
a bird: un pájaro
a rabbit: un conejo
a mouse: un ratón
a horse: un caballo
a guinea pig:
        un conejillo de Indias

Mi perro se llama Enrique.

= My dog is called Henry.

Es **amarillo** .

= He is yellow.

Practise using different descriptive words.

See page 45 for colours and sizes and page 54 for things like fat and thin.

I have 32 brothers, 24 sisters — & 1 tired mother...

Questions about family are a real giveaway — if you know your stuff that is. Learning this stuff will give you a big headstart — practising it will make your chances of doing well even better.

Section 8 — Myself, Family, Friends & Life at Home

56

Where You Live

Describing things — I reckon that's what it's all about. The more info you give, well, the more marks you're gonna get for it. Stands to reason, really...

¿Dónde vives? — Where do you live?

Vivo en la calle de Pitt número cuarenta y cuatro, en Lancaster.

= I live at 44 Pitt Street, in Lancaster.

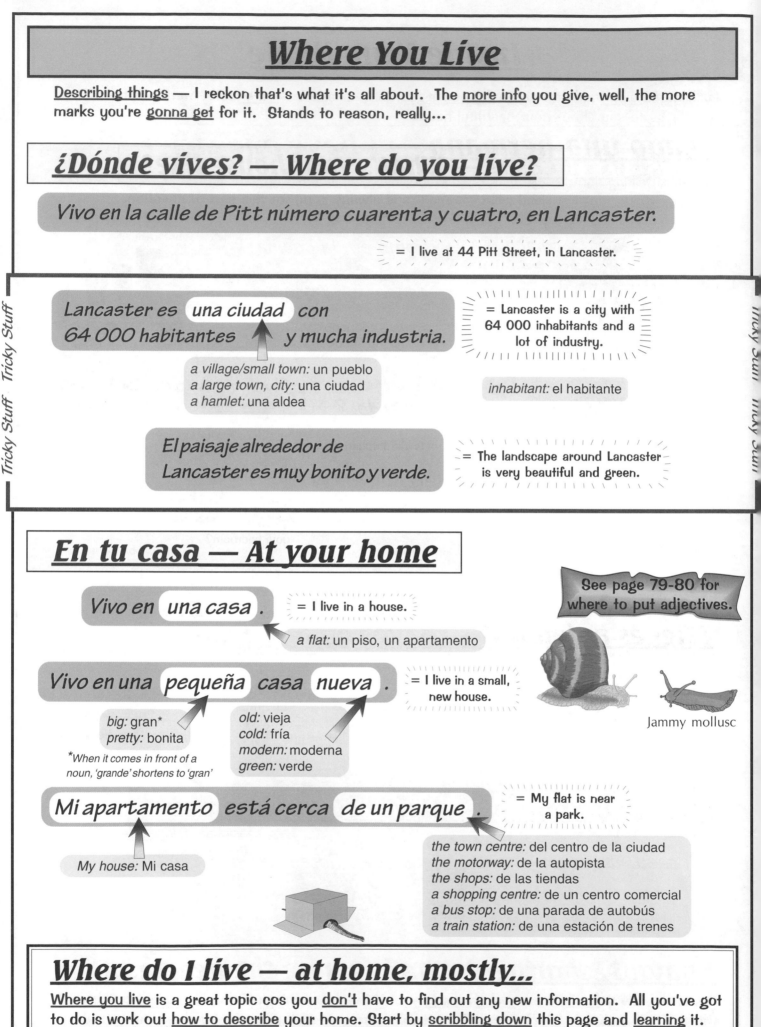

Lancaster es una ciudad con 64 000 habitantes y mucha industria.

= Lancaster is a city with 64 000 inhabitants and a lot of industry.

a village/small town: un pueblo
a large town, city: una ciudad
a hamlet: una aldea

inhabitant: el habitante

El paisaje alrededor de Lancaster es muy bonito y verde.

= The landscape around Lancaster is very beautiful and green.

En tu casa — At your home

Vivo en una casa.

= I live in a house.

a flat: un piso, un apartamento

See page 79-80 for where to put adjectives.

Vivo en una pequeña casa nueva.

= I live in a small, new house.

big: gran*
pretty: bonita

old: vieja
cold: fría
modern: moderna
green: verde

*When it comes in front of a noun, 'grande' shortens to 'gran'

Jammy mollusc

Mi apartamento está cerca de un parque.

= My flat is near a park.

My house: Mi casa

the town centre: del centro de la ciudad
the motorway: de la autopista
the shops: de las tiendas
a shopping centre: de un centro comercial
a bus stop: de una parada de autobús
a train station: de una estación de trenes

Where do I live — at home, mostly...

Where you live is a great topic cos you don't have to find out any new information. All you've got to do is work out how to describe your home. Start by scribbling down this page and learning it.

Section 8 — Myself, Family, Friends & Life at Home

Inside Your Home

Luckily you **won't** need to give a full house tour in your exams — it's just a matter of having a <u>few things</u> to say about your beautiful home.

¿Cómo es tu casa? — What's your house like?

Saying <u>where things are</u> and <u>what they're like</u> is always good for this sort of question.

¿Dónde está **la cocina** ?

= Where is the kitchen?

the living room: el salón
the bathroom: el cuarto de baño
the dining room: el comedor
the bedroom: el dormitorio

¿Cómo es **la cocina** ?

= What's the kitchen like?

small: pequeño/a
tiny: muy pequeño/a

¿ **La cocina** es **grande** ?

= Is the kitchen big?

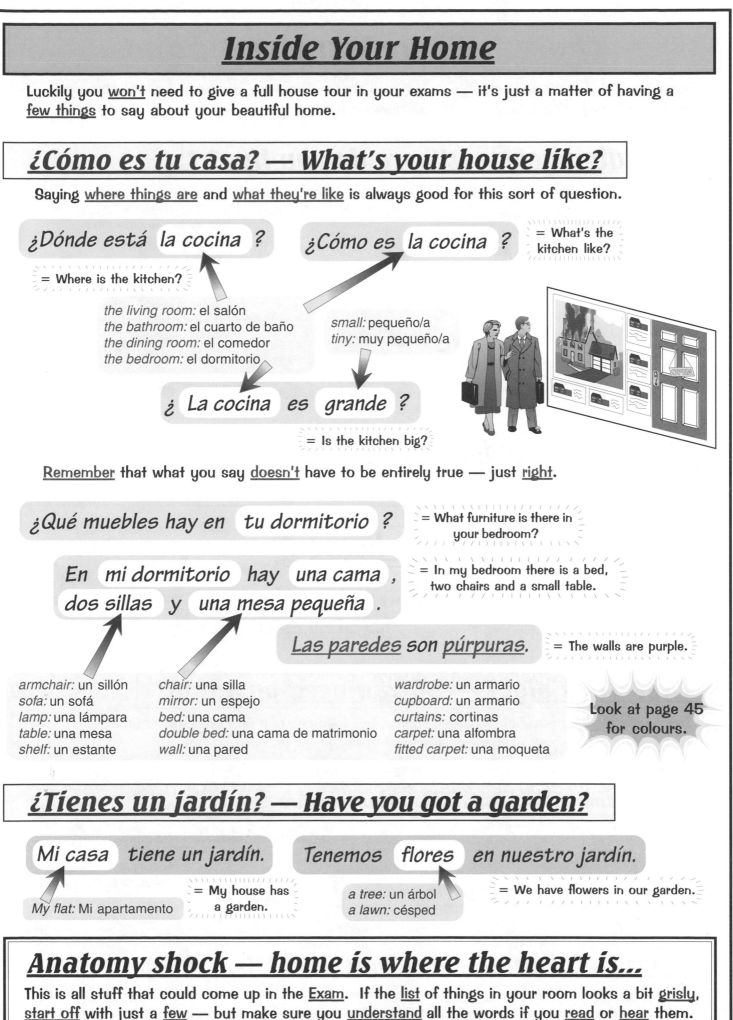

<u>Remember</u> that what you say <u>doesn't</u> have to be entirely true — just <u>right</u>.

¿Qué muebles hay en **tu dormitorio** ?

= What furniture is there in your bedroom?

En **mi dormitorio** hay **una cama** , **dos sillas** y **una mesa pequeña** .

= In my bedroom there is a bed, two chairs and a small table.

<u>Las paredes</u> son <u>púrpuras.</u>

= The walls are purple.

armchair: un sillón
sofa: un sofá
lamp: una lámpara
table: una mesa
shelf: un estante

chair: una silla
mirror: un espejo
bed: una cama
double bed: una cama de matrimonio
wall: una pared

wardrobe: un armario
cupboard: un armario
curtains: cortinas
carpet: una alfombra
fitted carpet: una moqueta

Look at page 45 for colours.

¿Tienes un jardín? — Have you got a garden?

Mi casa tiene un jardín.

My flat: Mi apartamento

= My house has a garden.

Tenemos **flores** en nuestro jardín.

a tree: un árbol
a lawn: césped

= We have flowers in our garden.

Anatomy shock — home is where the heart is...

This is all stuff that could come up in the <u>Exam</u>. If the <u>list</u> of things in your room looks a bit <u>grisly</u>, <u>start off</u> with just a <u>few</u> — but make sure you <u>understand</u> all the words if you <u>read</u> or <u>hear</u> them.

Chores and Household Routines

I <u>can't</u> say this is the <u>most thrilling</u> page ever — in fact, as pages go it's a rancid sock on the bedroom floor of GCSE Spanish. The bad news is it's <u>your job</u> to pick it up.

¿Cuándo se come...? — When do you eat...?

Don't make a meal of it — this vocab'll come in handy for <u>restaurants</u> too.

¿Cuándo se cena ?

= When do you eat dinner?

eat breakfast: se desayuna
eat lunch: se almuerza, se come

breakfast: el desayuno
lunch: el almuerzo, la comida
dinner: la cena

we eat breakfast: desayunamos
we eat lunch: almorzamos, comemos

See page 2 for more times.

Cenamos a las siete.

= We eat dinner at seven o'clock.

¿Tienes que ayudar en casa?
— Do you have to help at home?

Lavo los platos en casa.

= I wash up at home.

I tidy my room: Arreglo mi cuarto
I make my bed: Hago mi cama
I vacuum: Paso la aspiradora

Tengo que lavar/fregar los platos .

= I have to wash up.

vacuum: pasar la aspiradora   *clean:* limpiar
clear the table: quitar la mesa
lay the table: poner la mesa

¿Necesitas algo? — Do you need anything?

These aren't quite household routine phrases, but they can pop up from time to time in Speaking tasks about <u>exchanges</u>, that sort of thing.

¿Me da un poco de pasta de dientes ?

= Can I have some toothpaste?

Have you (informal): ¿Tienes...

a towel: una toalla
soap: jabón

¿Puedo ducharme ?

= May I have a shower?

¿ Tiene pasta de dientes ?

= Have you any toothpaste?

have a bath: bañarme

Oh well — better talking about chores than doing them...

OK, it might not be the most <u>exciting</u> way to spend your youthful years, but it's <u>not really</u> hard. It's about sitting down and <u>learning</u> the words. Then it's all down to <u>practising</u>. It's <u>your choice</u>.

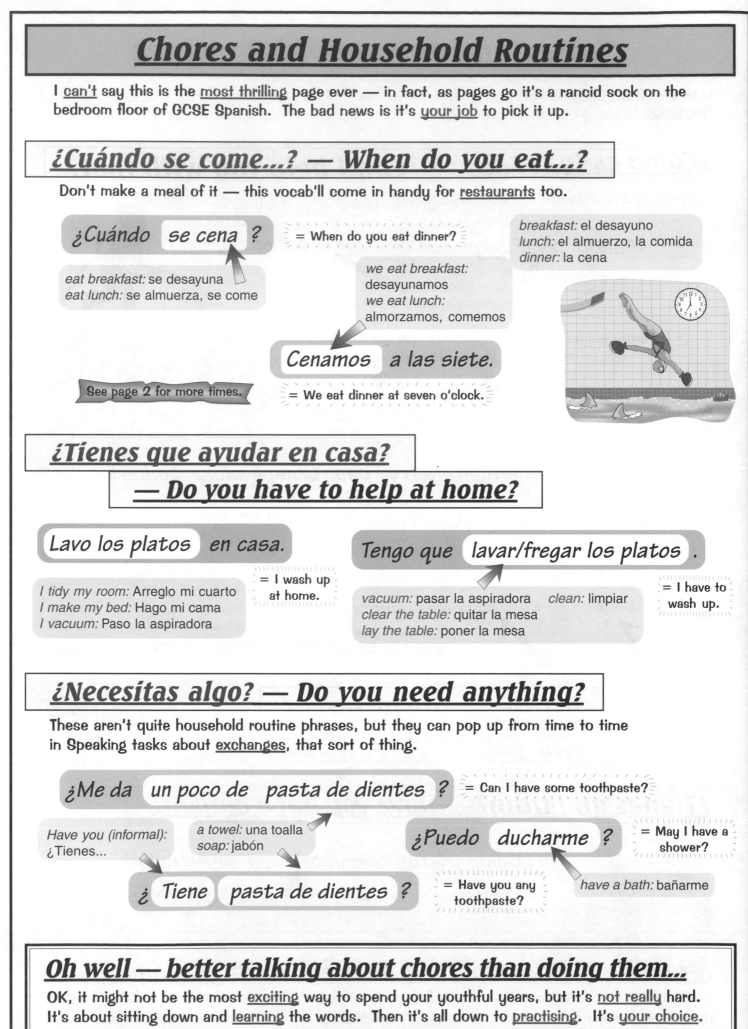

Chores and Household Routines

This stuff isn't just about playing happy home life — it also works a treat for exchange role plays. The trick is using the vocab you know in different settings — which means learning it first.

¿Le puedo ayudar? — Can I help you with that?

Here's how to offer your services when you're staying with someone.

¿Puedo lavar los platos ? = Can I wash up?

vacuum: pasar la aspiradora
clear the table: quitar la mesa

Or for extra politeness marks: '¿Quiere que yo lave los platos?'
(= Would you like me to wash up?)

¿Quién hace cada cosa? — Who does what?

Papá friega los platos .
= Dad does the washing up.

Mi hermana Kerry pasa la aspiradora todos los días .
= My sister Kerry vacuums every day.

washes up: friega los platos
cleans: limpia
vacuums: pasa la aspiradora
lays the table: pone la mesa

every week: todas las semanas

See pages 2–3 for more about time.

Nadie lava los platos en nuestra casa porque tenemos un lavaplatos .
= Nobody washes up in our house because we have a dishwasher.

¿Tienes tu propio dormitorio?
— Do you have your own room?

Tengo mi propio dormitorio. = I have my own room.

Comparto un dormitorio con mi hermano . = I share a room with my brother.

My house is like school — I always have to do homework...

Domestic life is so dull I can never believe they spend so much time asking about it. Still, if the marks are there to be won you might as well learn this vocab. I mean, it'd be daft not to.

Tricky Stuff

Parts of the Body

Anatomy vocab — it takes guts to study it. 'Course it comes in very useful for medical situations...

El cuerpo — The body

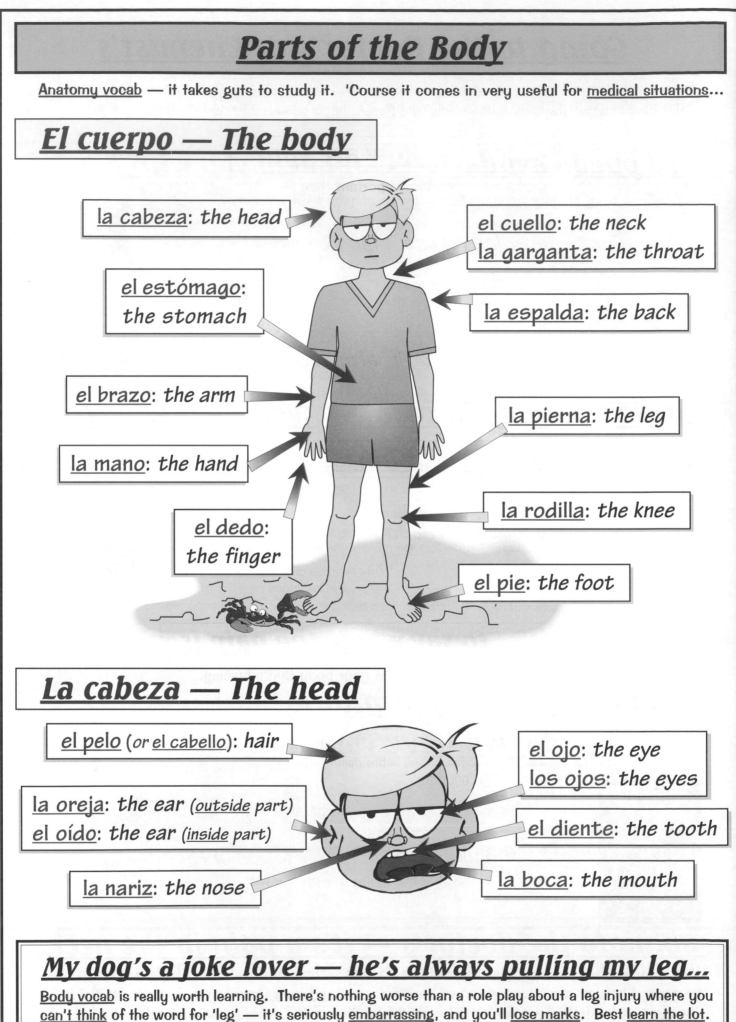

la cabeza: *the head*

el cuello: *the neck*
la garganta: *the throat*

el estómago: *the stomach*

la espalda: *the back*

el brazo: *the arm*

la pierna: *the leg*

la mano: *the hand*

el dedo: *the finger*

la rodilla: *the knee*

el pie: *the foot*

La cabeza — The head

el pelo (*or* el cabello): *hair*

el ojo: *the eye*
los ojos: *the eyes*

la oreja: *the ear* (outside part)
el oído: *the ear* (inside part)

el diente: *the tooth*

la nariz: *the nose*

la boca: *the mouth*

My dog's a joke lover — he's always pulling my leg...

Body vocab is really worth learning. There's nothing worse than a role play about a leg injury where you can't think of the word for 'leg' — it's seriously embarrassing, and you'll lose marks. Best learn the lot.

Going to the Doctor's or Chemist's

Body part vocab is one thing — <u>using it</u> is another. And <u>don't</u> just learn these phrases like a parrot — try using them with <u>different vocab</u>. Believe me, it's the <u>only way</u> to make sure you know 'em.

¿Cómo está usted? — How are you?

Saying <u>how you feel</u>'s gonna be the most important thing — you need to be able to say <u>what's wrong</u>.

Estoy **enfermo/a** . = I am ill.

tired: cansado/a

Me siento **mal** . = I feel ill.

Tengo **calor** . = I am hot.

cold: frío
thirsty: sed
hungry: hambre

Debo ir **al médico** . = I need to go to see the doctor.

to the hospital: al hospital
to the chemist's: a la farmacia

¿Qué le duele? — What hurts?

Here's how you say <u>which bit hurts</u>.

Me **duele** **el dedo** . = My finger hurts.

hurt (plural): duelen

my head: la cabeza
my ears: los oídos

Use 'dolor de...' to say where the pain is

You can use '<u>tengo dolor de</u>' with <u>any</u> part of your body that's hurting.

Tengo **dolor de estómago** . = I have stomach ache.

a headache: dolor de cabeza
a sore throat: dolor de garganta
sunstroke: una insolación

a temperature: fiebre *(fem)*
flu: gripe

This phrase is good too:

Estoy resfriado/a. = I have a cold.

Tengo dolor de **oídos.** = I have earache / my ears hurt.

Practise <u>using</u> this phrase with <u>different pains</u>.

Going to the doctor's — it's a pain in the neck...

You know the score — <u>practise</u> using these phrases as much as you can. If you know 'em well, you <u>won't</u> get 'em wrong. And remember — if you <u>don't know</u> how to say a particular <u>illness</u> in the exam, use '<u>dolor de</u>' with the right part of the body. It'll get you out of trouble nice and neatly.

Polite Conversation

Most of this is basic stuff — it'd be <u>stupid</u> to get it wrong, but every year people <u>do</u>.
See the thing about Spanish is if you can say stuff <u>politely</u>, you're <u>bound</u> to pick up <u>good marks</u>.

¡Buenos días! ¿Qué tal? — Hello! How are you?

Good day / hello: Buenos días
Good evening: Buenas tardes
How are you? (informal): ¿Qué tal?
How are you? (formal): ¿Cómo está?
Good day (to a man): Buenos días señor
Good day (to a woman): Buenos días señora/señorita

Hi: Hola
Goodbye:
Hasta luego / Adiós

To <u>reply</u> to 'Buenos días', just say '<u>Buenos días</u>' back. Do the same with 'Buenas tardes'.

Buenos días

Muy bien, gracias. = (I am) fine thanks.

Not good: no muy bien
Not bad: así así
Great: maravillosamente bien
OK: regular
Terrible: fatal

See page 61 if you're not well and you need to explain why.

Le presento a Nuría — May I introduce Nuría?

My, life's such a social whirl — parties, introductions... oh, have we met before...

Esta es Maria. = This is Maria.

For a man: Este es ...

Pasa. Siéntate. = Come in. Sit down. (Familiar, singular)

Pase. Siéntese. = Come in. Sit down. (Formal, singular)

Pasen. Siéntense. = Come in. Sit down. (Plural)

Encantado/a.
Mucho gusto. = Pleased to meet you.

Muchas gracias. Es muy amable. = Thank you. That is very nice of you.

Use 'lo siento' to say you're sorry

Lo siento. = I'm sorry.

Lo siento mucho. = I'm really sorry.

¿Puedo **sentarme**? = May I sit down?

go to the toilet: ir al baño
have something to drink: beber algo

Polite Ness — a well-mannered Loch monster...

It's a bit <u>boring</u>, I know. But grin, bear it, and most of all <u>learn it</u>, and you'll be fine. It'll be worth it when you hit the exam papers, and realise you can <u>answer all</u> the questions. It's worth the effort.

Tricky Stuff

Revision Summary

The idea isn't that you just do these questions and stop. To make sure you've really learnt this stuff, you need to go back through the section and look up the ones you couldn't do. Then try them all again. Your aim is eventually to be able to glide through them all with the greatest of ease.

1) An easy one to start with — give your name, age and when your birthday is to someone you've just met.

2) Describe three of your friends and say how old they are. Spell out loud their names and the names of the towns where they live.

3) Tell your penfriend what relatives you have — including how many aunts, cousins etc.

4) Your animal-loving friend has six rabbits, a bird, a guinea pig and two cats.
How will she say what these are in her Spanish Speaking Exam?

5) Say your address and describe the place where you live — is it a town or a village, is the landscape nice, and how many people live there?

6) Carina lives in a big house with a garden. It's near a shopping centre, a bus stop and a motorway. How would she say this in Spanish?

7) Give the names of the rooms in your home and say how many bedrooms it has.
Say whether you have a garden and whether it has flowers, grass or trees.

8) Tom has red walls and a brown carpet in his bedroom. He has a bed, two lamps, a wardrobe and a table. He doesn't have a sofa. How will he say all this in Spanish?

9) Describe your bedroom in as much detail as possible.

10) You're telling your host family about your home life. Say that you make your bed and sometimes vacuum and clean at home, you have breakfast at 8 o'clock and lunch at 1 o'clock.

11) You're staying with your host family and have just eaten.
Ask if they would like you to help clearing up.

12) Ask if you can have a bath and if they have a towel for you.

13) Cecilia has a room to herself but Roberto shares one with his brother Xavier.
How would they say this in Spanish?

14) Draw a stick man or woman and label it with as many body parts as you can.

15) How would you say you have each of these ailments in Spanish?
a) stomach ache b) headache c) a cold d) flu

16) Say that you have to go to the chemist's.

17) You're being introduced to a Spanish visitor. Say 'Good morning, how are you?'
When he asks how <u>you</u> are, say 'I'm fine, thanks. Pleased to meet you.'

18) Ask if you may have something to drink — and say thank you.

Telephones

I'd bet my grannie you'll get something on making a phone call in the exam —
if you learn this vocab and practise using it now, I reckon it'll come in pretty handy.

Una llamada telefónica — A phone call

¿Cuál es **tu** número de teléfono?   = What is your telephone number?

If you need to be more formal, use **su** .

Mi número de teléfono es **veintiocho, diecinueve, cincuenta y seis** .

Put your phone number in groups of 2, ie twenty-eight rather than two eight.   = My telephone number is 281956.

Answering the phone: 'Soy Bob' — 'It's Bob'

The trick with phone role plays is saying the things you'd actually say on the phone.

This is how you answer the phone:

¿Dígame?   =Hello?

These are for when you phone someone:

¡Hola! — soy Barbara. = *Hello, it's Barbara.*
¿Puedo hablar con...? = *Can I speak to...?*
¿Está Juana? = *Is Juana there?*
¿Puede llamarme Juana a las siete?
  = *Could Juana call me back at seven?*

¡Dígame!

¡Dígame!

All these phrases are great — but there ain't no substitute for using them yourself.

Quisiera dejar un mensaje — I'd like to leave a message

This is a bit of a twist on the old phone role play — leaving a message.
The important thing is getting all the right info across.

Have a look at this example and scribble down who called, their number and when Claudio should call back:

Hola, soy Paula. Mi número de teléfono es cincuenta y nueve, dieciocho, cuarenta y siete. ¿Puede llamarme Claudio a las siete? Gracias. Hasta luego.

La cabina de teléfono — The telephone box

¿Tiene monedas para el teléfono?   = Have you any coins for the telephone?

Phoning is my vocation — I felt called to it...

Time to cover up the page and write down the key bits of vocab. Then, yep, it's learn and practise.

Post Office

Post offices are great venues for role playing — perhaps it's cos there's lots of vocab potential. You'll be fine with a bit of hard work and practise — as long as you've learnt the words first.

¿Dónde está Correos? — Where is the Post Office?

These phrases all look a bit random, but they're the sort of thing that pop up in role plays. Start by learning the vocab then practising some phrases.

el buzón: *postbox*
los sellos: *stamps*
Correos: *post office*
la carta: *letter*

Señor Pablo Picasso
La Plaza Mayor
Barcelona
Spain

AIR MAIL

¿Dónde está el buzón, por favor? = Where is the postbox, please?

¿Hay un buzón cerca de aquí? = Is there a postbox near here?

¿Tiene sellos? = Have you any stamps?

¿Cuánto cuestan los sellos? = How much do the stamps cost?

Quisiera mandar una carta — I'd like to send a letter

This stuff's a bit more specific — sending letters or parcels abroad or within Spain.

¿Cuánto cuesta mandar una carta a Inglaterra ? = How much does it cost to send a letter to England?

a parcel: un paquete   *a postcard:* una tarjeta postal

¿Cuánto cuesta mandar/enviar una carta en España? = How much does it cost to send a letter within Spain.

¿Tiene sellos para mandar una carta a Inglaterra?

= Do you have stamps for sending a letter to England?

Quisiera mandar una tarjeta postal a Inglaterra.

You can add as many things as you like, using the same phrase.

= I would like to send a postcard to England.

WISH YOU WERE HERE

AIR MAIL

EUROPE

Write each phrase out — and try using it with different vocab.

Find that Michael Caine letter — get carta...

Hard work's the key, I'm afraid. If you want to do well in your GCSE you've got to put the hours in, learning the vocab, covering up each page, and writing it out again. It isn't just enough to read it through — you need to practise using it. And believe me, the examiners can tell if you know it.

Tricky Stuff   Tricky Stuff

Informal Letters

You're <u>bound to</u> have to write a <u>letter</u> in Spanish at some point — it's the law of GCSE. Just remember the secret of writing a good letter in any language is <u>knowing the rules</u>.

Learn this layout for starting and finishing

Here's an incredibly short letter — it shows <u>all</u> the key bits <u>you need</u> for letter-writing.

This means Dear Juan. If you're writing to a woman, you'd put <u>Querida</u> instead of <u>Querido</u>.

Put where you live and the date up here. Check out page 3 for dates.

Millom, 5 de marzo

Querido Juan:

This means: 'Thanks for your letter.'

Gracias por tu carta. Me alegró mucho recibir tus noticias.

This means: 'I was very pleased to hear from you.'

Best wishes.

Saludos

bye for now: Hasta pronto
a hug: un abrazo

Albert

Now <u>you</u> have a go — practise writing <u>your own</u> short letter.

Use plenty of common phrases in your letters

Learning the layout is all very well, but it's only the <u>start</u>. Writing good letters means using lots of nice <u>clear</u> Spanish phrases and vocab. They <u>don't</u> need to be complicated — just <u>right</u>.

¿Qué tal?
= how are you?

¿Qué piensas de...?
= what do you think of...?

¿Cómo va todo?
= how's it all going?

This one's quite good for <u>signing off.</u>

Espero recibir tus noticias pronto.
= I hope to hear from you soon.

Informal letters — the salad dressed down...

Think you've got it sussed? Then <u>cover up</u> the page and <u>practise</u> writing a few short letters — it's the <u>only</u> way to make sure. And always use plenty of <u>nice simple phrases</u> — and <u>get 'em right</u>.

Formal Letters

Sigh... <u>Formal letters</u> are sooo boring. They've got even <u>more rules</u> than informal ones. You've still got to know <u>how to write them</u>, though. It'll come in handy for <u>job applications</u> or <u>booking hotels</u>.

Get the layout and language right

The <u>name and address</u> of who you're writing to goes here.

If you <u>don't know</u> the person's name, write here "Muy señor mío: / Muy señora mía:". Remember to follow the greeting with a colon (:) and not a comma (,).

If you <u>do know</u> the person's name write, say, "Estimado señor García:" or "Estimada señora García:".

Yours faithfully.

Put <u>your</u> name and address up here.

Put the date over here.

This lot means: I would like to reserve three rooms with you for the 4th - 18th June, inclusive. We would like a double room and two single rooms. Please let us know as soon as possible if you have rooms free, and how much they'll cost.

Hotel Miramar
Calle Arenal 16
Málaga
Spain

Aleesha Thompson
16 Rusland Drive
Manchester
M14 7QB
Reino Unido
Manchester, 20 de abril de 2001

Muy señor mío:

Quisiera reservar tres habitaciones en su hotel, desde el cuatro hasta el dieciocho de junio ambos inclusive. Quisiéramos una habitación doble y dos habitaciones individuales. ¿Sería tan amable de informarme cuanto antes si tiene habitaciones libres y de indicarme el precio?

Le saluda atentamente

A Thompson

Aleesha Thompson

Learn these ways to end a letter

Here are a couple of ways to <u>end formal letters</u> — <u>practise</u> using them till they trip off your pen.

Le saluda atentamente. = Yours faithfully/ sincerely

Another useful phrase: *Dándole las gracias por anticipado.* = Many thanks in advance.

Use 'disculparse' to apologise

You may have to write <u>apologising</u> for something — it's worth <u>practising</u> using sentences like this one.

Quisiera disculparme por haber dejado mi bolso en su hotel. = I would like to apologise for having left my bag in your hotel.

Mi bolso..?

How to end a letter — just stop writing...

<u>Practice, practice, practice</u> — that's what GCSE Spanish is all about. You'll pick up <u>lots of marks</u> if you can write in a formal style <u>without</u> sounding like you've just learnt a few stock phrases. It's a matter of practice really — the <u>more letters</u> you write, the <u>more natural</u> the phrases sound,

Revision Summary

Letters and phone calls are places you can really pick up marks if you know your stuff. The beauty is they're so structured. Once you know the vocab and the phrases it's just a matter of getting lots of practice... which is where these questions come in. Have a go at them now, then have another go if there are any you're not sure about. Then use the pages of the section to help you mark them.

1) ¿Cuál es tu número de teléfono? *(No cheating and writing it in numerals — do it in full in Spanish.)*

2) What should you say when you answer the phone in Spanish?

3) Your brother's Mexican friend calls. Write down a message in Spanish for your brother, saying his friend can't go out tonight.

4) Colin phones his friend Pedro and talks to his mother. Pedro isn't in, but his mother says she will tell him Colin rang. Write down the whole phone conversation in Spanish.

5) How do you ask someone if they've got any coins for the phone?

6) Ask at the Post Office if they have stamps for sending a letter to England.

7) You have four postcards and three letters and want to send them to England.
   Ask the Post Office staff how much this will cost.

8) You are in the street in Spain and want to post a letter. How would you ask someone where to find a postbox? (Try to think of two ways of saying it.)

9) Write a letter to your friend Clara. Write your address, say hello and tell her something you've done in the last week.

10) You would like to hear from her soon — how would you say that in your letter?

11) Write down one way you could end the letter.

12) You'd like to reserve 3 single rooms in a hotel in Madrid. Write a letter in Spanish to: Hotel Glorieta, Paseo del Prado 3, Madrid.

13) How would you end a formal letter in Spanish?

14) What does this phrase mean: 'Dándole las gracias por anticipado'? Would you use it in a formal or informal letter?

15) You have left a suitcase in a hotel room. Write a letter to the hotel staff to apologise.

Work Experience & Interviews

These two pages <u>encourage</u> you to think about your <u>future</u> in even more <u>detail</u> — heck it's nearly a public service. If you can't quite manage without a crystal ball then use your <u>imagination</u>.

¿Qué hiciste como experiencia laboral?

= What did you do for work experience?

Work experience is quite simply <u>joyous</u> — I remember my week spent bored to death in a certain high street bank. At least it helped me <u>decide</u> there was no way on this Earth that banking was for me.

Como experiencia laboral , trabajé en la oficina de un abogado .

= For work experience I worked in a lawyer's office.

name or description of company

Trabajé allí durante <u>una semana y media</u>.

= I worked there for a week and a half.

¿Cómo fue el trabajo? Dime qué hiciste.

More <u>opinions</u> wanted — own up, did you or did you not like it..?

= How was the work? Tell me about what you did.

El trabajo fue duro .

= The work was hard.

difficult: difícil
interesting: interesante

comfortable: cómodo/cómoda
at home: en casa
isolated: aislado/aislada

Me sentí muy solo/sola .

= I felt very lonely.

were very friendly: eran muy simpáticos
were interesting: eran interesantes

Mis colegas de trabajo no eran simpáticos .

How many sugars?

SALT

= My work colleagues weren't friendly.

¿Qué quieres hacer en el futuro?

= What do you want to do in the future?

OK, so maybe you've never <u>applied</u> for a job, but it's highly <u>likely</u> that you'll have to one day. And there just might be a job interview <u>role-play</u> in your speaking exam.

En mi trabajo, quiero resolver problemas .

= In my job I would like to solve problems.

meet new people: conocer a personas nuevas
work with numbers: trabajar con números
help people: ayudar a la gente

See <u>page 32</u> for more types of jobs, or look one up in a <u>dictionary</u>.

Me gustaría ser agente de viajes .

= I would like to be a travel agent.

Are you experienced?...

If you <u>haven't</u> done any work experience then you'd better <u>learn</u> how to say that in <u>Spanish</u> in case you're asked. And I'm sure your <u>parents</u> would like you to think about your <u>future job</u> anyway...

Selling Yourself in Interviews

A lot of the stuff in your GCSEs will be addressed to you <u>informally</u>, ie you'll be called 'tú' and not 'usted' by most exam boards. In an <u>interview</u> you'll always be '<u>usted</u>' though. Better get used to it.

Preguntas para una entrevista — Interview Questions

Right, here are <u>examples</u> of answers to the basic questions you could <u>expect</u> to be asked in a job <u>interview</u>. You <u>don't</u> have to learn these sentences — the whole class would sound pretty darned stupid if you all came with the same lines <u>parrot-fashion</u>. Make up some answers for <u>yourself</u>.

¿Cómo se llama usted?   = What is your name?   *¿Cuántos años tiene Ud.?*   = How old are you?

¿Qué trabajo le interesa a Ud?

= Which job are you interested in?

Quisiera trabajar como ayudante en la oficina de turismo en Madrid.   = I'd like to work as an assistant in the tourist information office in Madrid.

¿Por qué quiere Ud este trabajo?

= Why do you want this job?

El turismo me interesa mucho.   = Tourism interests me a lot.

Quisiera mejorar mi español.   = I'd like to improve my Spanish.

qualifications: los títulos   *responsible:* responsable

Tengo la experiencia *necesaria, soy* flexible *y* maduro *.*   = I have the necessary experience, I'm flexible and mature.

¿Qué hizo Ud en el instituto?

= What did you do at school?

Fui al instituto en Fareham.   = I went to school in Fareham.

Mis asignaturas preferidas en el instituto fueron el alemán y el español.   = German and Spanish were my favourite subjects at school.

¿Qué le gusta hacer?

= What do you like to do?

Me encanta la arquitectura.   = I love architecture.

Me gusta viajar al extranjero.   = I like travelling abroad.

"Selling Yourself"..? — isn't that a bit dodgy...

Most of this stuff isn't new, but get used to dealing with it in this <u>context</u>. So when you're asked in your speaking exam to <u>pretend</u> you're <u>applying</u> for a job as a barber in Seville, it won't throw you.

The Environment

Things get <u>serious</u> when the environment comes up, and you're supposed to have an opinion. It's a chance for you to maybe write or say what you <u>think</u> about something real and <u>important</u> not just what colour <u>velour jumpsuit</u> you'd like to buy in the sale.

El medio ambiente — ¿es importante para ti?
Is the environment important to you?

A question like this <u>has</u> to be answered with a <u>yes</u>, or a <u>no</u>, so remember to <u>always</u> listen out first for that in a listening exam... then try to figure out the <u>reason</u>.

<u>No,</u> no tengo ningún interés.
= No, I'm not at all interested in it.

¡Sí! Pienso que el medio ambiente es muy importante.
= Yes, I think the environment is very important.

If you're asked for your own take on a question like this, <u>start</u> with yes or no then explain why. Of course it'll help if you've <u>prepared</u> something earlier (remember Blue Peter...).

Give opinions and arguments

If you're really up on '<u>green</u>' matters then you could get well stuck into this, but if you're not then say so. You'll get as many marks for saying <u>why</u> you're not interested as you would for <u>enthusing</u> about Greenpeace.

¡NO!

Eso no me interesa. Quiero vivir en la ciudad y no en el campo.
= It doesn't concern me. I want to live in the city not in the country.

Las flores y la naturaleza son muy aburridas. Prefiero los juegos de ordenador.
= Flowers and nature are very boring. I prefer computer games.

¡SÍ!

Me preocupa mucho el medio ambiente debido a la contaminación industrial.
= I'm really worried about the environment because of industrial pollution.

Probablemente vamos a perder la biodiversidad de nuestro planeta .
= We are probably going to lose the biodiversity of our planet.

ESSENTIAL ENVIRONMENT VOCAB

exhaust fumes:	el humo de los coches
pollution:	la contaminación
the greenhouse effect:	el efecto invernadero
emissions:	las emisiones
to damage:	dañar
to endanger:	poner en peligro
air pollution:	la contaminación del aire
natural resources:	los recursos naturales
biodiversity:	la biodiversidad
nature:	la naturaleza

Of course there's no <u>denying</u> that you might not be asked your opinion on the environment, which may make you breathe a huge sigh of <u>relief</u> — aaaaaaah...

But, even so you'd be well <u>advised</u> to get friendly with the <u>essential</u> environmental vocab. It could well be <u>sneaked</u> into a <u>reading</u> comprehension or a <u>listening</u> conversation.

My ideal environment has a TV, bed, & pizza...

There are so many <u>different aspects</u> of the environment you could <u>choose</u> to talk about — or not talk about if you really couldn't give a monkey's. As always, <u>be wise</u> and learn the <u>basics</u>, eh...

72

Health & Drugs and Alcohol

¡Qué bueno! — PSHE in Spanish, you lucky, lucky people.
At least you should have an <u>opinion</u> on this without having to try too hard.

Diet — Un régimen

No, I'm not talking about any ridiculous <u>lettuce-only</u>, weightloss diet.
This is about your normal everyday diet and how <u>healthy</u> it is, or isn't.

¿Comes **bien** ?

regularly: regularmente

> For more food
> see page 48.

= Do you eat well?

Sí, como muchas ensaladas y fruta.

= Yes, I eat lots of salads and fruit.

No, como patatas fritas casi todos los días, y bebo solamente limonada.

= No, I eat chips almost every day and I only drink lemonade.

El ejercicio — Exercise

It doesn't matter if you don't do any, just be able to say so.

¿Qué haces para mantenerte en buena salud?

= What do you do to stay healthy?

Hago mucho deporte.

= I play a lot of sport.

Como bien, me mantengo delgado y tengo mucha energía.

= I eat very healthily, stay slim and have a lot of energy.

Juego al fútbol y al tenis regularmente.

= I regularly play football and tennis.

Smoking, Drugs, Alcohol & Rock'n'Roll

OK, so I lied about the rock'n'roll bit...

¿Qué piensas de **las drogas** ?

alcohol: del alcohol

= What do you think of drugs?

NO FUMO

= I don't smoke

Los cigarrillos me dan asco. Lo odio cuando la gente fuma. Los cigarrillos tienen un olor horrible. No saldría nunca con un fumador / una fumadora.

= Cigarettes disgust me. I hate it when people smoke.
Cigarettes have a terrible smell. I'd never go out with a smoker.

ME GUSTA FUMAR

= I like smoking.

Sé que no es muy sano, pero me parece muy elegante fumar.

= I know it's unhealthy, but I think it's very stylish to smoke.

Salud — I like lettuce and tomatoes myself...

There is loads you might want to say about these <u>exciting</u> things, but learning the stuff on this page is a <u>good</u> start. <u>Think</u> about what else you might want to say, write it down, and <u>practise</u> it.

The Wider World — Section 10

Famous People

Now this choice of topic seems a tad weird to me, but apparently you are supposed to be <u>fascinated</u> by celebs. So much so that you wanna <u>talk</u> about them in Spanish with your penfriends and <u>exchange partners</u> — or summat like that.

¿Admiras a las personas famosas?

Talking about celebrities and famous people you admire mostly involves all the same old

Do you admire celebrities?

<u>straightforward</u> stuff that you need to talk about yourself and your family. You're gonna have to start with their <u>name</u>, then <u>what</u> they do, and follow that up with <u>why</u> you like them.

WHO → *Pienso que Britney Spears es fantástica.* = I think Britney Spears is fantastic.

WHAT → *Es una cantante famosa de los Estados Unidos.* = She is a famous singer from the USA.

WHY → *Britney es muy bonita y lleva siempre ropa de moda.* = Britney looks so pretty and always wears fashionable clothes.

Canta como un ángel. = She sings like an angel.

¡Es mi heroína! = She is my heroine!

La influencia de la gente famosa

¿Piensas que se puede considerar a la gente famosa como un ejemplo positivo para los jóvenes?

The Influence of Celebrities

Celebrities are often <u>role models</u> for young people. You may be expected to have an <u>opinion</u> on this and the role the media plays in the whole cult of celebrity.

= Do you think famous people can be seen as a positive example for young people?

¡SÍ!

¡Por supuesto! Tienen mucho éxito.

= Of course. They are very successful.

Se les puede admirar.

= You can admire them.

POSITIVE EXAMPLE?

¡NO!

¡De ninguna manera! No son personas normales.

= No way. They aren't normal people.

Algunas chicas piensan que deben estar tan flacas como las 'Supermodelos'. Muchas veces ésto es la causa de problemas dietéticos.

= Some girls think they have to be as thin as the 'Supermodels'. This is often the cause of dietary problems.

PRETTY DARNED USEFUL VOCAB

famous: famoso / famosa	*admire:* admirar
singer: un/una cantante	*hero / heroine:* un héroe / una heroína
anorexia: la anorexia	*the media:* los medios (de comunicación)
bulimia: la bulimia	*influence:* una influencia
role model: un modelo	*responsibility:* la responsabilidad
example: un ejemplo	*responsible:* responsable
actor / actress: un actor / una actríz	*cause:* causar

Social Issues

Urg, social issues — the words alone are <u>almost</u> guaranteed to make you remember you needed to tidy your room, or go to the doctor's etc... Talking about them can seem <u>daunting</u> enough in your own language, let alone another one, but keep a <u>cool head</u> and don't start anything you can't <u>finish</u>.

El desempleo — Unemployment

There's not really very much that needs saying here. Unemployment sucks whichever way you look at it. End of story.

Hay muchos desempleados en la ciudad .
= There are lots of unemployed people in the town.

few: pocos
some: algunos

area: la región
village: el pueblo

El desempleo en Gran Bretaña no es un problema hoy en día.
= Unemployment in Britain isn't a problem nowadays.

Nadie tiene problemas en encontrar trabajo.
= Nobody has a problem finding work.

La igualdad de derechos — Equal Rights

This is your chance for a good <u>rant</u>, in Spanish of course.

For more <u>countries</u> see <u>page 13</u>.

Pienso que la igualdad de derechos es muy importante .

unimportant: no es muy importante

= I think equal rights are very important.

Es verdad que a veces hay mucha hostilidad hacia las personas de otros países .

discrimination: discriminación

women: las mujeres

= It's true there's sometimes a lot of hostility towards people from other countries.

Me parece racista .
= It seems racist to me.

sexist: sexista
unfair: injusto

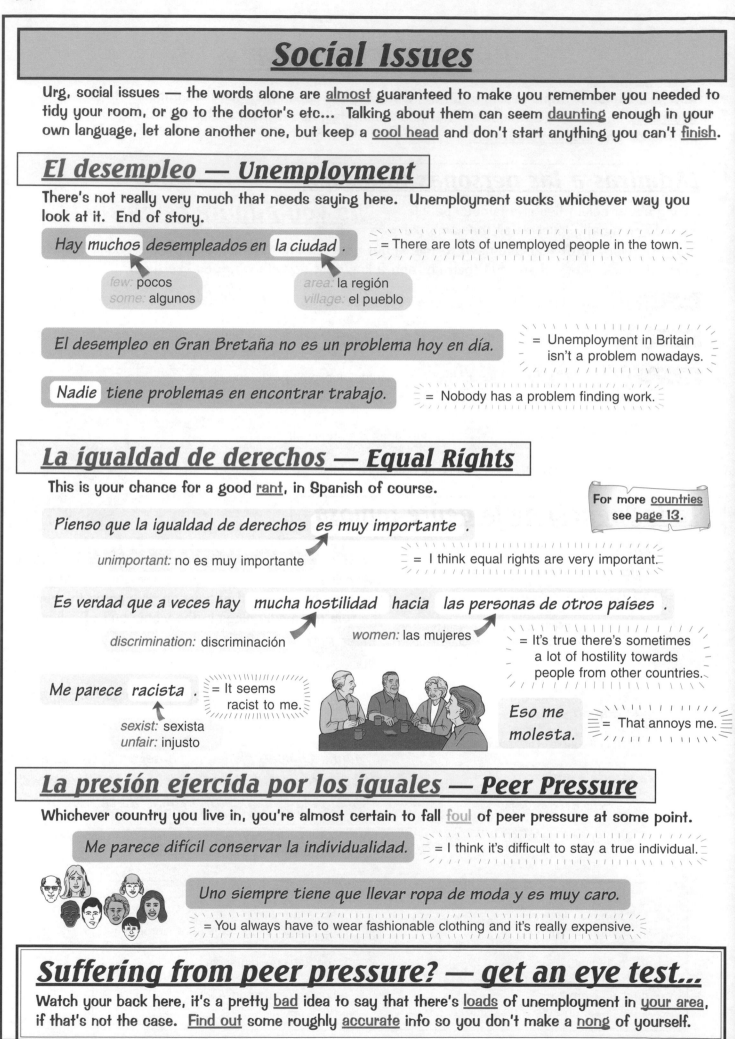

Eso me molesta.
= That annoys me.

La presión ejercida por los iguales — Peer Pressure

Whichever country you live in, you're almost certain to fall <u>foul</u> of peer pressure at some point.

Me parece difícil conservar la individualidad.
= I think it's difficult to stay a true individual.

Uno siempre tiene que llevar ropa de moda y es muy caro.
= You always have to wear fashionable clothing and it's really expensive.

Suffering from peer pressure? — get an eye test...

Watch your back here, it's a pretty <u>bad</u> idea to say that there's <u>loads</u> of unemployment in <u>your area</u>, if that's not the case. <u>Find out</u> some roughly <u>accurate</u> info so you don't make a <u>nong</u> of yourself.

Revision Summary

By now you surely know that everything in this book is here because it's megatastically important. This section on the wider world is all about taking your Spanish language skills and using them in other situations. You need to use your initiative and imagination maybe a touch more, and get to feel happy using what you already know to answer unexpected queries.

1) Write a full Spanish sentence explaining what you did for your work experience. If you didn't do work experience anywhere then write that down.

2) Write a Spanish sentence saying whether you liked your work experience and why, or saying whether you would have liked to do work experience and where.

3) You have two Spanish penfriends Pilar and José. Pilar wants to have a job where she works with animals and José wants to travel. How would each of them say that?

4) Write down how you'd respond to the question '¿Cómo se llama usted?'.

5) How would you write a reply in Spanish to a job advert for an assistant in a bookshop. Explain why you want the job and why you think you're suitable.

6) Write down the Spanish for: a) friendly; b) responsible; c) flexible.

7) Pilar wants to know what your interests are. Tell her at least two things.

8) José is really worried about industrial pollution, explain what you think about the problem.

9) There's no stopping José: he's just told you he'd like to live in a remote wooden hut and be at one with nature. Tell him whether you fancy this idea and why.

10) What is the Spanish for: a) air pollution; b) emissions; c) biodiversity?

11) Write down a list of all the things you'd normally eat in a day — in Spanish, of course.

12) ¿Comes bien y regularmente?

13) ¿Por qué? / ¿Por qué no?

14) Do you play a lot of sport? Why? Why not? Answer in Spanish, of course.

15) ¿Admiras a las personas famosas? ¿A quiénes? ¿Y por qué?

16) ¿Qué piensas de la situación de las mujeres en Inglaterra hoy en día?

17) Eric thinks it's hard to stay individual nowadays. How would he say it Spanish?

NOUNS	## Words for People and Objects

Stop — before you panic, this stuff is a lot less scary than it looks.
It's all <u>pretty simple</u> stuff about words for <u>people</u> and <u>objects</u> — nouns. This is <u>really important</u>.

No kidding!

Every Spanish noun is masculine or feminine

Whether a word is <u>masculine</u>, <u>feminine</u> or <u>plural</u> affects a lot of things. All 'the' and 'a' words change, and as if that weren't enough, the adjectives (like big, red, shiny) change to fit the word.

> **EXAMPLES:** *a small dog:* <u>un</u> perro pequeño (masculine)
>
> *a small house:* <u>una</u> casa pequeña (feminine)

For more on this, see pages 79 and 80.

It's no good just knowing the Spanish words for things, you have to know whether each one's <u>masculine</u> or <u>feminine</u> too.

> *THE GOLDEN RULE*
>
> Each time you <u>learn</u> a <u>word</u>, remember the <u>el</u> or <u>la</u> to go with it — don't think 'dog = perro', think 'dog = <u>el</u> perro'.

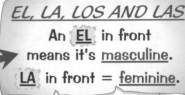

EL, LA, LOS AND LAS
An **EL** in front
means it's <u>masculine</u>.
LA in front = <u>feminine</u>.

These rules help you guess what a word is

Tricky Stuff

You can't tell whether a noun ending in 'e' or 'ista' is <u>masculine</u> or <u>feminine</u>, eg.

the car: <u>el</u> co<u>che</u>
the people: <u>la</u> gen<u>te</u>
the tourist (man): <u>el</u> tur<u>ista</u>
the tourist (woman): <u>la</u> tur<u>ista</u>

Rules of Thumb for Masculine and Feminine Nouns	
MASCULINE NOUNS: most nouns that end: -o -l -n -r -s -ma -pa -ta -aje also: male people, languages, days, months, seas, rivers, oceans, and mountains.	FEMININE NOUNS: most nouns that end: -a ción -sión -tad -tud -dad -umbre also: female people, letters of the alphabet.

Making Nouns Plural

1) Nouns in Spanish are usually made plural by adding an '<u>s</u>' when they end in a vowel and '<u>es</u>' when they end in a consonant.

    eg: una naranja → dos naranjas
    one orange → two oranges

2) Family surnames and nouns which finish in an unstressed syllable ending in 's' stay the same in the plural.
    eg. *the Jiménezs (family)*
      ⇨ Los Jiménez
    eg. *Tuesday — Tuesdays*
      ⇨ el martes — los martes

3) You may need to add or remove an accent when nouns become plural to keep the pronunciation.
    eg. *one young man — two young men*
      ⇨ un <u>joven</u> — dos <u>jóvenes</u>
    eg. *one Englishman — two Englishmen*
      ⇨ un <u>inglés</u> — dos in<u>gleses</u>

4) Nouns ending in 'z' change the 'z' to a 'c' before adding 'es'.
    eg. *one pencil — two pencils*
      ⇨ un lápi<u>z</u> — dos lápi<u>ces</u>

TOP TIP FOR PLURALS
Each time you <u>learn</u> a <u>word</u>, learn how to make it into a plural too.

5) When you make a masculine noun plural, instead of '<u>el</u>' you have to use '<u>los</u>' to say '<u>the</u>'. For feminine nouns '<u>la</u>' becomes '<u>las</u>' when it's plural — see <u>page 78</u>.

Masculine words — butch, hunky, stud...

The bottom line is — <u>every time</u> you learn a word in Spanish, you <u>have</u> to learn whether it's <u>el</u> or <u>la</u>, and you have to learn what its <u>plural</u> is. So start as you mean to go on — get into <u>genders</u>.

Joining Words — Longer Sentences

CONJUNCTIONS

Everyone knows <u>long</u> sentences are <u>clever</u> — and Examiners <u>like</u> clever people. So learn these joining words to <u>help</u> you make longer sentences, and get <u>more marks</u> for being smart.

Y = And

Me gusta jugar al fútbol. **AND** *Me gusta jugar al rugby.* **=** *Me gusta jugar al fútbol y al rugby.*

= I like playing football.

= I like playing rugby.

= I like playing football <u>and</u> rugby.

BUT: if '<u>y</u>' comes in front of a word beginning with '<u>i</u>' or '<u>hi</u>' it changes to '<u>e</u>'.

Hablo español e inglés. = I speak Spanish <u>and</u> English.

O = Or

Juega al fútbol todos los días. **OR** *Juega al rugby todos los días.* **=** *Juega al fútbol o al rugby todos los días.*

= He plays football every day.

= He plays rugby every day.

= He plays football <u>or</u> rugby every day.

BUT: when '<u>o</u>' comes in front of a word beginning with '<u>o</u>' or '<u>ho</u>' it changes to '<u>u</u>'.

Cuesta siete u ocho libras. = It costs seven <u>or</u> eight pounds.

Pero = But

Like, duh — this is different from '<u>perro</u>', which means 'dog'.

Me gusta jugar al fútbol. **BUT** *No me gusta jugar al rugby.* **=** *Me gusta jugar al fútbol pero no me gusta jugar al rugby.*

= I like playing football.

= I don't like playing rugby.

= I like playing football <u>but</u> I don't like playing rugby.

When '<u>but</u>' means 'on the contrary' it becomes '<u>sino</u>': *Mi amigo no es americano sino australiano.*

= My friend isn't American, but (on the contrary) he's Australian.

Porque = Because

This is a really important one you need to use to explain yourself. There's loads more about it on <u>page 7</u>.

Me gusta el tenis porque es divertido. = I like tennis <u>because</u> it's fun.

Other wee joining words to understand

You don't have to use all of these, but you should understand them if you see or hear them.

well, then: pues, entonces
if: si   *with:* con
as, like: como
so, therefore: por lo tanto, así (que), de manera (que)
while, during: mientras (que)

EXAMPLES:

Puedes salir si quieres.
= You can go out <u>if</u> you want.

Es como su hermano.
= He's <u>like</u> his brother.

Tengo hambre, así que voy a comer.
= I'm hungry, <u>so</u> I'm going to eat.

Juega al hockey mientras que llueve.
= She plays hockey <u>while</u> it's raining.

Si — not something to swim in...

You use '<u>and</u>', '<u>or</u>' and '<u>but</u>' all the time when you're speaking English — if you <u>don't</u> use them when you speak <u>Spanish</u>, you'll sound a bit <u>weird</u>. But don't confuse '<u>si</u>' (if) and '<u>sí</u>' (yes). It's good if you can <u>recognise</u> all the <u>extra</u> words in the last bit too, and it's even better if you can <u>use</u> them.

Tricky Stuff

ARTICLES	*'The' and 'A'*

'The' and 'a' are essential words. They're tricky in Spanish, because there are different ones for <u>masculine</u>, <u>feminine</u> or <u>plural</u> words (see page 76).

'A' — *un, una*

Grammar Fans: these are called '<u>Indefinite Articles</u>'.

Masculine: UN	Feminine: UNA
Tengo <u>un</u> hermano.	*Tengo <u>una</u> hermana.*
= I have <u>a</u> brother.	= I have <u>a</u> sister.

In Spanish 'a' is often left out:

a) after the verb 'ser' when talking about someone's occupation or nationality: eg. *I'm a student* ⇨ *Soy estudiante*

b) after a negative word: eg. *I haven't got a cat.* ⇨ *No tengo gato.*

c) in front of 'otro/a': eg. *Do you want another coffee?* ⇨ *¿Quieres otro café?*

When you make 'un' or 'una' plural, they mean 'some' or 'a few'.

Pasé <u>unos</u> días en la playa. = I spent <u>a few</u> days on the beach.

Tengo <u>unas</u> fotos muy buenas.

= I have <u>some</u> very good photos.

'The' — *el, la, los, las*

1) Spanish 'the' changes for <u>masculine</u>, <u>feminine</u> or <u>plural</u>.

masculine singular	feminine singular	masculine plural	feminine plural
el	la	los	las

<u>EXAMPLES</u>:   *El chico.*   *La chica.*   *Los hombres.*   *Las mujeres.*

= <u>The</u> boy.   = <u>The</u> girl.   = <u>The</u> men.   = <u>The</u> women.

Grammar Fans: these are called '<u>Definite Articles</u>'.

2) But remember 'el' is used before feminine nouns which start with a stressed 'a':   eg. *The water is cold.* ⇨ <u>El</u> *agua está fria.*

3) 'El' also changes with '<u>a</u>' (to) and '<u>de</u>' (of).

4) You <u>can't</u> say 'a el', 'de el'.

	el
+ a	al
+ de	del

That's an affirmative

Absolutely! No doubt at all.

100% positive. Couldn't be surer.

voy a + <u>*el café*</u> = *Voy al café.* = I go to the café.

5) Sometimes you need a definite article in Spanish when you <u>wouldn't</u> use one in English.

a) with nouns used in a general sense: eg. *I don't like coffee.* ⇨ No me gusta <u>el</u> café.

b) in front of days of the week and times: eg. *Every Monday at five o'clock.* ⇨ Todos <u>los</u> lunes a <u>las</u> cinco.

c) in front of weights and measurements: eg. *200 pesetas a kilo.* ⇨ Doscientas pesetas <u>el</u> kilo.

d) when you talk about a <u>person</u> and give their title: eg. *How is Mr Jiménez?* ⇨ ¿Cómo está <u>el</u> señor Jiménez?

6) There's also a neuter article 'lo' for things that aren't masculine or feminine. You'll mostly come across it in <u>phrases</u>:   Lo mejor/peor = *the best/worst thing*   Lo que = *what/that which*

No sé <u>lo</u> que quiere = *I don't know what he wants.*

You <u>don't</u> normally need to say 'any' in Spanish

Here's something worth knowing — you <u>don't need</u> a special word for any...

¿Tienes manzanas?

= Have you got <u>any</u> apples?

Juan no quiere tortilla.

= Juan doesn't want <u>any</u> omelette.

Secretly masculine — hidden a gender....

Blimey, am I glad I speak English — just one word for 'the', and no genders... This stuff's none too tricky but it is important — <u>cover up</u> the page, and write out <u>both tables</u> till you can do it in your sleep.

Words to Describe Things

Gain <u>more marks</u> and show what an interesting person you are by using some <u>juicy describing</u> words. Make sure you <u>understand</u> what you're saying as well.

Adjectives must 'agree' with the thing they're describing

1) In <u>English</u>, you can use the <u>same</u> describing word (adjective) for whatever you like — like big bus, big buses, big boy, big girl...

2) In <u>Spanish</u>, the describing word has to <u>change</u> to <u>match</u> whether what it's describing is <u>masculine/ feminine</u>, <u>singular/plural</u>. Look at these examples where 'pequeño' has to change:

MASCULINE SINGULAR	MASCULINE PLURAL	FEMININE SINGULAR	FEMININE PLURAL
el chico <u>pequeño</u>	los chicos <u>pequeños</u>	la chica <u>pequeña</u>	las chicas <u>pequeñas</u>
(the <u>small</u> boy)	(the <u>small</u> boys)	(the <u>small</u> girl)	(the <u>small</u> girls)

The Rules Are: ① Add an '-a' to the describing word if the word being described is **feminine** (see page 76).

② Add an '-s' or an '-es' to the describing word if the word being described is **plural** (see page 76).

(Of course, that means if it's feminine plural, then you have to add '-as'.)

IMPORTANT NOTE: When you look an adjective up in the <u>dictionary</u> it's listed in the <u>masculine singular</u> form. Don't ask me why — it must have been a load of single blokes who wrote the dictionary.

"You stink!"   "I agree"

3) Some colours <u>never change</u> at all, because they are actually the names of *things*, and are not real adjectives. The commonest ones are:

> See page 45 for more Colours.

beige crema	naranja púrpura rosa	turquesa violeta

eg. *Three orange hats.*
⇨ *Tres sombreros <u>naranja</u>.*

Here are 22 <u>describing words</u> — they're the ones you really <u>have</u> to know.

Top 22 Describing Words

good: bueno/a	*sad:* triste	*interesting:* interesante	*big/great:* grande	*old:* viejo/a
bad: malo/a	*easy:* fácil	*boring:* aburrido/a	*tall:* alto/a	*young:* joven
pretty/nice: bonito/a	*difficult:* difícil	*strange:* raro/a	*small:* pequeño/a	*new:* nuevo/a
happy: feliz	*nice(character):* simpático/a	*long:* largo/a	*short (height):* bajo/a	*fast:* rápido/a
		handsome/pretty: guapo/a		*slow:* lento/a

Most describing words go after the word they describe

It's the opposite of English — in Spanish <u>most</u> describing words (adjectives) <u>go after</u> the word they're describing (the noun).

noun (dress)

el vestido rojo   (the red dress)

adjective (red)

EXAMPLE: *Tengo un coche <u>rápido</u>.*

= I have a <u>fast</u> car.

Some adjectives lose the final 'o' before masculine nouns

Some adjectives lose the final 'o' when they go in front of a masculine noun:

good: bueno/a	*some:* alguno/a
first: primero/a	*none:* ninguno/a
third: tercero/a	*bad:* malo/a

EXAMPLE: *Un <u>buen</u> día.*   = A <u>good</u> day.

Be aware that 'alguno' and 'ninguno' both drop an 'o' and add an accent: *No hay <u>ningún</u> taxi libre.*   = There isn't <u>any</u> taxi free.

Unlike siblings — adjectives always agree...

Aaaargh — more tables to learn, but then that's the nature of Spanish grammar. For these endings to be of any <u>use</u> to you, you need to learn the <u>genders</u> of the nouns in the first place. You have to know <u>what</u> your adjective needs to <u>agree</u> with. To get it right — <u>get learning</u>.

ADJECTIVES
Words to Describe Things

Two totally odd adjectives

grande = *big, great*
ciento = *100*

1) 'Grande' is the only adjective that drops 'de' in front of both masculine and feminine words.

    eg. *A great lady.*   eg. *A great day.*
    ⇨ Una <u>gran</u> señora.   ⇨ Un <u>gran</u> día.

2) 'Ciento' drops '-to' when it comes in front of anything that isn't another number (but not before 'mil' or 'millón').

eg. *one hundred pesetas*
⇨ <u>cien</u> pesetas

There are some odd ones out that always go in front

cada = *each, every*   poco/a = *little (not much)*
mucho/a = *a lot of*   pocos/as = *few*
otro/a = *another*   tanto/a = *so much*

eg. *Every day Felipe eats another omelette.*
⇨ <u>Cada</u> día Felipe come <u>otra</u> tortilla.

Some change what they mean depending on position

Some adjectives <u>change their meaning</u> according to whether they are <u>before</u> or <u>after</u> the noun. Here are some important ones — learn them <u>carefully</u>.

You can also add '<u>ito</u>' to lots of adjectives to make things seem smaller or cuter, or '<u>ísimo/a</u>' to make the meaning stronger.

adjective	meaning if <u>before</u>	meaning if <u>after</u>
grande	great un <u>gran</u> hombre (a <u>great</u> man)	big un hombre <u>grande</u> (a <u>big</u> man)
mismo	same el <u>mismo</u> día (the <u>same</u> day)	self yo <u>mismo</u> (me <u>myself</u>)
nuevo	new (different) tengo un <u>nuevo</u> coche (I have a <u>new</u> [to me] car)	(brand) new tengo un coche <u>nuevo</u> (I have a <u>brand new</u> car)
viejo	old (longstanding) un <u>viejo</u> amigo (an <u>old</u> friend)	old (elderly) un amigo <u>viejo</u> (an <u>elderly</u> friend)

eg. *My little sister is beautiful.*
⇨ Mi herman<u>ita</u> es guap<u>ita</u>.

eg. *The book is absolutely awful.*
⇨ El libro es mal<u>ísimo</u>.

My, your, our — who things belong to

You have to be able to <u>use</u> and <u>understand</u> these words to say that something <u>belongs</u> to someone:

You have to choose masculine, feminine or plural to <u>match</u> the thing it's describing (<u>NOT</u> the person who owns it).

<u>Mi</u> hermano es alto,
<u>mis</u> padres son bajos.

= <u>My</u> brother is tall, <u>my</u> parents are short.

	masculine singular	feminine singular	masculine plural	feminine plural
my	mi	mi	mis	mis
singular familiar your	tu	tu	tus	tus
his/her/its/singular polite your	su	su	sus	sus
our	nuestro	nuestra	nuestros	nuestras
plural familiar your	vuestro	vuestra	vuestros	vuestras
their/plural polite your	su	su	sus	sus

Mine, yours, ours — other belonging words

These adjectives always come after the noun ('nuestro' and 'vuestro' etc. are the same as above).

¿Esa casa es <u>tuya</u>?

= Is that house <u>yours</u>?

	masculine singular	feminine singular	masculine plural	feminine plural
mine	mío	mía	míos	mías
yours	tuyo	tuya	tuyos	tuyas
his/hers/yours/theirs	suyo	suya	suyos	suyas

Boring, boring, boring — three key describing words

You need a <u>whole lot</u> of Spanish describing words to make what you say <u>fascinating</u>. Remember to learn which ones go <u>before</u> the noun — and don't forget the ones which go <u>before or after</u> the noun and <u>change</u> their meaning. Be sure you learn <u>how</u> to <u>use</u> them properly — by <u>practising</u>.

Making Sentences More Interesting
ADVERBS

The 2 pages before this are about describing <u>objects</u>, eg the bus is <u>red</u>.
This page is about describing things you <u>do</u>, eg I speak Spanish <u>perfectly</u>,
and about adding <u>more info</u>, eg the bus is <u>very</u> red or I speak Spanish <u>almost</u> perfectly.

Make your sentences better by saying how you do things

1) In <u>English</u>, you don't say 'We talk slow', you have to
   <u>add</u> a '<u>ly</u>' on the end to say 'We talk slow<u>ly</u>'.

> Grammar Fans:
> These are '<u>adverbs</u>'.

2) In <u>Spanish</u>, you have to <u>add</u> a '<u>mente</u>' on the end, but first you have to
   make sure the describing word is in the <u>feminine</u> form (see page <u>79</u>).

EXAMPLE: Habla **lentamente** .   = He speaks <u>slowly</u>.

quickly: rápidamente
rarely: raramente

> The Spanish word for 'slow' is 'lento', but the feminine form
> is 'lent**a**'. Add 'mente' and you get 'lentamente' = slowly.

3) <u>Unlike</u> normal describing words (see page <u>79</u>)
   you <u>don't</u> ever have to <u>change</u> these words —
   even if what it's about is <u>feminine</u> or <u>plural</u>.

EXAMPLES:

Feminine → *Ana habla* **lentamente** . → Always the same.

Plural → *Hablamos* **lentamente** . → the same.

Learn these odd ones out off by heart

Just like in English there are <u>odd ones out</u> —
for example, you <u>don't</u> say I sing '<u>goodly</u>'...

Spanish Odd Ones Out	
ENGLISH	**SPANISH**
good → well	bueno/a → bien
bad → badly	malo/a → mal

MORE EXAMPLES OF ADDING DESCRIBING WORDS:

Canto.
I sing.

Canto <u>bien</u>.
I sing <u>well</u>.

Canto <u>mal</u>.
I sing <u>badly</u>.

Use one of these four words to give even more detail

Stick one of these <u>four</u> words in <u>front</u> of
the <u>describing word</u> in a sentence to add
extra detail and impress the Examiners.

very: muy
quite: bastante
almost: casi
too: demasiado

You can use them for sentences
saying <u>how something is done</u>...

Ella habla **casi** *perfectamente el español.*

She speaks Spanish <u>almost</u> perfectly.

...and for sentences about
<u>what something is like</u>.

Bob está **muy** *feliz.*   = Bob is <u>very</u> happy.

Lentamente — how Spanish should be spoken...

Alrightee — this is <u>a bit like</u> English — you have a set ending (-mente) to learn and stick on, and it's
not too tricky either. Make sure you <u>really know</u> the standard <u>rule</u> and all the <u>exceptions</u>.

COMPARATIVES AND SUPERLATIVES

Comparing Things

Often you don't just want to say that something is <u>tasty</u>, or <u>juicy</u> or whatever, you want to say that it's the <u>tastiest</u>, or <u>juicier than</u> someone else's...

How to say more brave, most brave

In Spanish you can't say 'stranger' or 'strangest', it's gotta be 'more strange' or 'the most strange':

Dave es valiente.

= Dave is brave.

Dave es más valiente.

= Dave is more brave/braver.

Dave es el más valiente.

= Dave is the most brave/bravest.

old: viejo ⇨	*older:* más viejo ⇨	*oldest:* el más viejo
tall: alto ⇨	*taller:* más alto ⇨	*tallest:* el más alto

Add '<u>más</u>'.

Add '<u>el más</u>'.

You can do this with almost any <u>describing word</u>. Check out page 79 for more describing words.

BUT, just like in English, there are <u>odd ones out</u>:

good: bueno ⇨	*better:* mejor ⇨	*best:* el mejor
bad: malo ⇨	*worse:* peor ⇨	*worst:* el peor
big: grande ⇨	*bigger:* mayor ⇨	*biggest:* el mayor
/old	/older	/oldest
young: pequeño ⇨	*younger:* menor ⇨	*youngest:* el menor
/small	/smaller	/smallest

El gorro azul es el mejor .

= The blue cap is the best.

Tricky Stuff

It's 'la más...' for feminine, 'las más...' for plural

Instead of '<u>el</u> más' you have to use '<u>la</u> más' or '<u>las</u> más' to match the word you're describing (see page 76).

Liz es <u>la</u> más alt<u>a</u>.

= Liz is the tallest.

Ed y Jo son <u>los</u> más alt<u>os</u>.

= Ed and Jo are the tallest.

You also have to change the <u>describing word</u> — usually add an '<u>a</u>' for <u>feminine</u>, and/or an '<u>s</u>' or '<u>es</u>' for <u>plural</u> (see page 79). NB — you <u>only</u> do this for adjectives, <u>NOT</u> for adverbs (see below).

More or most strangely is pretty much the same...

When you're saying that someone <u>does</u> something <u>more</u> or <u>most</u> ...ly, you follow the <u>same pattern</u> as above, but instead of <u>adjectives</u> (describing words — see pages 79 and 80), you use <u>adverbs</u> (see page 81).

eg: **Dave habla** valientemente .

= Dave talks bravely.

Dave habla más valientemente .

= Dave talks more bravely.

Dave es él que habla más valientemente .

= Dave talks the most bravely / Dave is the one who talks the most bravely.

There are two <u>odd ones out</u> you need to know:

well: bien ⇨	*better:* mejor
badly: mal ⇨	*worse:* peor

Learn these three great ways of comparing things

You just stick the words in purple <u>on either side of</u> the describing word, like this:

Ed es <u>más</u> **joven** <u>que</u> **Tom.**

= Ed is younger <u>than</u> Tom.

Ed es <u>menos</u> **joven** <u>que</u> **Tom.**

= Ed is <u>less</u> young <u>than</u> Tom.

Ed es <u>tan</u> **joven** <u>como</u> **Tom.**

= Ed is <u>as</u> young <u>as</u> Tom.

Comparing things — yep, size does matter...

Make sure you learn how to say <u>bigger</u> or <u>biggest</u>, and how to say bigger <u>than</u>, <u>as</u> big <u>as</u> and <u>less</u> big <u>than</u>. And don't just learn the rule, <u>learn all</u> those <u>exceptions</u> to it as well. Best just to use your imagination and <u>make up</u> some comparing sentences to make sure you really <u>know it all</u>.

Sneaky Wee Words

You've got to <u>learn</u> these if you want tip-top marks. They're really useful words anyway.

TO — a

Where we use 'to', they usually use '<u>a</u>':

Va <u>a</u> Madrid. = He's going <u>to</u> Madrid.

Voy <u>a</u> casa. = I'm going (<u>to</u>) home.

For 'the train <u>to</u> London' see 'the train <u>for</u> London' below.

For things like <u>to go</u>, <u>to do</u>, just use the <u>infinitive</u> (see page 88), you <u>don't</u> need an extra word for '<u>to</u>'. Eg ir = to go, hacer = to do/make.

ON — sobre, en

For 'on top' of, it's '<u>sobre</u>' or '<u>en</u>': *<u>Sobre</u> la mesa.* = <u>On</u> the table.

When it's <u>not</u> 'on top', it's usually '<u>en</u>':

Lo vi <u>en</u> la tele. = I saw it <u>on</u> TV.

For days of the week, it's <u>left out</u>:

Me voy el lunes. = I'm leaving on Monday.

IN — en, dentro de

'En' is just 'in', 'inside' is usually '<u>dentro</u>'.

Está <u>en/dentro de</u> la caja. = It's <u>in/inside</u> the box.

If it's in a town, it's '<u>en</u>':

Vivo <u>en</u> Málaga. = I live <u>in</u> Malaga.

Don't forget to add '<u>en</u>' when going into a place:

Teresa entra <u>en</u> la tienda. = Teresa enters (<u>into</u>) the shop.

FROM — de, desde or a partir de

Where we use 'from', they usually use '<u>de</u>':

Soy <u>de</u> Cardiff. = I come <u>from</u> Cardiff.

'<u>Desde</u>' is used where there is a starting and finishing point:

<u>Desde</u> Londres hasta Madrid. = <u>From</u> London to Madrid.

For dates, it's '<u>a partir de</u>':

<u>A partir del</u> 4 de junio. = <u>From</u> the 4th of June.

OF — de

Where we use 'of', they usually use '<u>de</u>':

Una botella <u>de</u> leche. = A bottle <u>of</u> milk.

'Made of' is '<u>de</u>':

Es un cinturón <u>de</u> cuero. = It's a leather belt.

WATCH OUT: sometimes it's hard to spot the <u>de</u> in a sentence, because de+el=<u>del</u>.

Salgo <u>del</u> supermercado. = I go out <u>of</u> the supermarket.

AT — en, a

Very few English phrases with 'at' in them use '<u>a</u>' in the Spanish — most use '<u>en</u>':

<u>A</u> las seis. = <u>At</u> six o'clock.

Ella está <u>en</u> la escuela. = She is <u>at</u> school.

<u>En</u> casa. = <u>At</u> home.

Don't forget — a + el = <u>al</u> Sometimes it can be tricky to spot.

Learn these words for saying where something is

You need these little words a lot, for saying where things are in your <u>town</u> or your <u>house</u>.

El banco está | enfrente del | hotel y del café. = The bank is <u>opposite</u> the hotel and the cafe.

next to/beside: al lado de	*under:* bajo/debajo de	*against:* contra	*here:* aquí
behind: detrás de	*below:* abajo	*in/into:* en	*there:* allí, ahí, allá
in front of: delante de	*on/upon:* en, sobre	*at the end of:* al final de	*inside:* dentro de
between: entre	*above:* encima de	*at the back of:* al fondo de	*outside:* fuera de

Don't forget to use <u>está/están</u> for describing where things are/go.

Of, at, from, on, to — in, out, shake it all about...

Prepositions have loads of <u>different</u> meanings in English — it's important to remember they do in Spanish <u>too</u>, just <u>not</u> the same ones. You have to learn the words from a <u>Spanish perspective</u>.

'Por' & 'Para'

'Por' and 'para' are two <u>nightmare words</u> for English-speakers cos they both mean 'for' — but in different ways. This bit's gonna be tricky I'm afraid, but it's really important — it's <u>worth</u> learning.

Por and Para both mean FOR

This pair of words cause endless confusion. Thing is, they <u>don't</u> mean exactly the same thing. The only way to <u>get 'em right</u> time after time is by <u>learning these rules</u> and <u>practising</u>.

Use Para for...

1) Sentences with 'for' looking forwards:

Este dinero es <u>para</u> ti.   *Una habitación <u>para</u> dos personas.*   *El tren <u>para</u> Buenos Aires.*

This money is for you.   A room for two people.   The train for Buenos Aires.

2) When you want to say 'to'/'in order to':

Se fue de vacaciones <u>para</u> descansar.   *Pon más sal <u>para</u> darle más sabor.*

He went on holiday in order to rest.   Put in more salt to give it more flavour.

3) When you want to say 'by' in time phrases: *Para mañana*   *Para entonces*

= <u>by</u>/<u>for</u> tomorrow   = <u>by</u>/<u>for</u> then

4) 'For' in sentences 'for X days...'

Quiero el coche <u>para</u> tres días.   I want the car for three days.

5) 'In...view':

<u>Para</u> mí, ella es la chica más atractiva de todos.

In my view she's the most attractive girl of all.

6) 'On the point of' (confusingly in Latin America they use 'por')

Está <u>para</u> llover.   It's about to rain.

Use Por for...

1) Time sentences with 'for':   *Vivió en Málaga <u>por</u> un año.*   *<u>por</u> la mañana*

He lived in Malaga for a year.   in the morning

2) Direction/place sentences:

El tren va <u>por</u> el túnel.   3) Number phrases: *veinte <u>por</u> ciento*

The train goes through the tunnel.   *dos veces <u>por</u> día* = twice a day   = twenty per cent

4) Exchange: *Pagó mil pesetas <u>por</u> el libro.*   He paid 1000 pesetas for the book.

5) On behalf of: *Lo hace <u>por</u> ti.*   He does it for you.

NB with 'gracias' it's <u>always</u> 'por':   *Gracias <u>por</u> todos los peces.*   Thanks for all the fish.

Por & para — wish I knew what they're for...

Phew... Think this is bad? In Portuguese they've got <u>another</u> word — pora... This is one of the <u>hardest things</u> in all of Spanish, I'm afraid — but if you can get it right, it'll seriously <u>impress the examiners</u> and <u>boost your marks</u>. So get <u>practising</u>. And remember 'gracias' <u>always</u> needs 'por'.

I, You, Him, Them...

Pronouns are words that replace nouns — like 'you' or 'them'.

> Dave has a new job at the poodle parlour. He likes shaving poodles.

> 'He' is a pronoun. It means you don't have to say 'Dave' again.

Yo, tú, él, ella — I, you, he, she

'I', 'you', 'he', etc are not usually needed in Spanish — unless you want to emphasise or make it clear exactly who you're talking about. You definitely need to know them though — or you'll end up getting seriously confused.

The subject pronouns

I:	yo		
you (informal singular)	tú	nosotros/as	:we
he/it:	él	vosotros/as	:you (informal plural)
she/it:	ella	ellos	:they (masc. or mixed masc. & fem.)
you (formal singular):	usted	ellas	:they (all fem.)
one:	se	ustedes	:you (formal plural)

THE FOUR 'YOU's

Remember — there are 4 ways of talking to 'you'. 'Tú' is for one person who's your friend, a member of your family or about your age. For a group of people you know, use 'vosotros/as'. You use 'usted' to be polite to one person (for older people who aren't your family or friends), or 'ustedes' if there's more than one of them.

Me, te, lo, la — me, you, him, her

These are for the person/thing in a sentence that's having the action done to it (the direct object).

> Dave lava el perro. = Dave washes the dog.
>
> Dave lo lava. = Dave washes it.

The direct object pronouns

me:	me	nos	:us
you (inf. sing.):	te	os	:you (inf. plu. or formal)
him/it/you (form. sing. masc.):	lo	los	:them/you (formal pl.m)
her/it/you (form. sing. fem.):	la	las	:them/you (formal pl.f)

There are special words for to me, to her, to them

For things that need 'to', 'for' or 'by' — like writing to someone — use the indirect object pronouns.

> El perro da el cepillo a Dave. = The dog gives the brush to Dave.
>
> El perro le da el cepillo. = The dog gives the brush to him.

The indirect object pronouns

to me:	me	nos	:to us
to you (inf. sing.):	te	os	:to you (inf. plu. or formal)
to him/her/it/ you (form. sing):	le	les	:to them/you (form. pl)

These pronouns usually come before the verb, but when you tell someone to do something they are tacked on to the end of the verb.

¡Escríbele! = Write to him/her! ¡Dígame! = Tell me!

You'll definitely need these pronouns for saying you like something. You have to say 'it is pleasing to me' etc..

Watch out — it doesn't matter if the person is singular or plural. You need 'gusta' if the thing you like is singular, or 'gustan' if it's plural.

Me gusta la música. = I like music.

No nos gusta el pulpo. = We don't like octopus.

¿Te gustan los árboles? = Do you like trees?

No les gustan las flores. = They don't like flowers.

Tricky Stuff

More on Pronouns

Sometimes you'll need the pronouns on the first bit of this page — they can be a bit confusing, so learn them.

Special words for me, you, him, her...

There are some pronouns which change when they come after a preposition:

The prepositional pronouns

me:	mí	nosotros/as	:*us*
you (informal sing.):	ti	vosotros/as	:*you* (inf. plu. or formal)
him/it:	él	ellos	:*them* (m. or mixed m. & f.)
her/it:	ella	ellas	:*them* (all fem.)
you (formal sing.):	usted	ustedes	:*you* (formal plu.)

El regalo no es para ti, es para ella.

= The present isn't for you, it's for her

¿Hablas de mí?

= Are you talking about me?

'With me' and 'with you'(fam. sing.) have their own special words:

Va conmigo. = He's going with me.
Voy contigo. = I'm going with you.

The Personal — 'a'

It sounds confusing but it isn't:

Extra preposition alert — you need to put an extra 'a' in before the word for any human being after every single verb except 'tener'.

Tengo dos hermanos. = I have two brothers.

Veo a mi hermano. BUT *Veo el árbol.*
= I see my brother.   = I see the tree.

Estoy buscando a Juan. BUT *Estoy buscando un taxi.*
= I'm looking for Juan.   = I'm looking for a taxi.

Que — that, which, who

'Que' is a special kind of pronoun (a relative pronoun). It can mean 'which', 'who', 'what' or 'that' — and it can't be left out of sentences.

Dice que va a llover. He says that it's going to rain.

It's not like English — you can't leave out the 'that'.

Fui a Menorca, que es una isla preciosa.
= I went to Menorca, which is a lovely island.

La persona que vive aquí.
= The person who lives here.

Getting the Order Right

1) These pronouns usually go before the verb — though they can go before OR after an infinitive or a present conditional:

Le voy a hablar. / Voy a hablarle. = *I'm going to speak to him.*
Lo estamos mirando. / estamos mirándolo. = *We are watching it.*

...and they must go after a command to do something:

Déme su pasaporte, por favor. = *Give me your passport please.*

2) Whenever there are two object pronouns in the same sentence, the indirect ones always go first:

Me los da. = *He gives them to me.*
Te la enviaré. = *I'll send it to you.*

3) But, if the indirect pronoun is 'le' or 'les', then it changes to 'se' when it comes in front of lo, la, los or las (even though the final meaning may not be very clear!)

Se las da. = *He gives them to him/her/them/you (sing)/ you (plu)*
Se lo regalé. = *I gave it to him/her/them/you (sing)/ you (plu)*

It could be any one of these — you need to look at the sentences around to work out who it's on about.

This & That, Something & Someone

DEMONSTRATIVES & INDEFINITE PRONOUNS

This page is about <u>pointing things out</u>, and generally making it clear <u>which</u> thing you're on about.

How to say this, that or the other

Use 'este', etc... for saying things like '<u>this man</u>', '<u>these apples</u>' —
ie when you're using 'this' as a <u>describing</u> word.

	Masculine singular	Feminine singular		Masculine plural	Feminine plural
THIS	este	esta	THESE	estos	estas
THAT	ese	esa	THOSE	esos	esas
THAT	aquel	aquella	THOSE (further away)	aquellos	aquellas

This bird?

EXAMPLES: este pájaro   aquella casa   estos bolis   esas manzanas
              this bird   that house   these pens   those apples

Use the neuter when you're <u>not</u> talking about a <u>particular thing</u>:

Neuter	
THIS	esto
THAT	eso

¿Qué es <u>ésto</u>?   = What's this?   *¡<u>Éso</u> es!*   = That's it!

It's different when the 'this' or 'these' is a noun

When you say things like '<u>this</u> is mine', you're using 'this' as a <u>noun</u>.
That means you need to <u>stick an accent</u> on the 'this' word: eg <u>éstos</u>, <u>ése</u> etc...

Tengo dos perros; <u>éste</u> es simpático, pero <u>ése</u> es malo.

I've got two dogs; <u>this one here</u> is nice, but <u>that one there</u> is nasty.

Algo — Something   Alguien — Someone

There's nothing particularly special about these, you just need to be able to <u>understand</u> and <u>use</u> them:

¿Quiere <u>algo</u>?

= Do you want <u>something</u>?

Hay <u>algo</u> en mi bolso.

= There's <u>something</u> in my bag.

<u>Alguien</u> ha llevado el dinero.

= <u>Someone</u> has taken the money.

Buscan a <u>alguien</u> muy gordo.

= They're looking for <u>someone</u> very fat.

So, what are you studying — Oh, this and that...

None of this stuff is too tricky — as long as you're absolutely one-hundred percent <u>sure</u> you've got it clear. Remember — 'este', 'eso' and the others <u>always</u> go with another word, like '<u>este hombre</u>'. If they're <u>on their own</u>, they must have <u>accents</u> ('éste', 'éso' etc)— so <u>don't</u> forget 'em.

The Lowdown on Verbs

Oh boy — you just <u>can't</u> get away from this stuff, I'm afraid.
But think about this — if you <u>learn it now</u>, it'll make the <u>whole</u> of Spanish GCSE easier... Bargain!

Verbs are action words — they tell you what's going on

Ethel plays football every Saturday.

These are <u>verbs</u>.

And so is this.

Alex wished his grandma preferred knitting.

There's a lot you need to know about verbs, but it all boils down to these two things...

1) The verb is different for different times

You say things differently if they happened last week, or aren't going to happen till tomorrow.

HAS ALREADY HAPPENED
I went to Tibet last year.
I have been to Tibet.
I had been to Tibet.

PAST

HAPPENING NOW
I go to Tibet.
I am going to Tibet.

PRESENT

These are all different <u>tenses</u>, in case you're interested.

HASN'T HAPPENED YET
I go to Tibet on Monday.
I will go to Tibet.
I will be going to Tibet.

FUTURE

2) The verb is different for different people

You'd say 'he <u>plays</u>', but <u>never</u> 'I plays' — it'd be daft. The verb <u>changes</u> to fit the person.

HAPPENING TO ME
I am miserable.

HAPPENING TO YOU
You are miserable.

HAPPENING TO HER
She is miserable.

OK, you get the picture — verbs are dead important. You use them all the time, after all.

The infinitive means 'to...'

In Spanish infinitives always end in 'r'.

When you look up a verb <u>in the dictionary</u>, this is what you get:

(to) give: dar
(to) go: ir

Most of the time, you won't want the verb in its <u>raw state</u> — you'll have to <u>change</u> it so it's right for the <u>person</u> and <u>time</u> you're talking about.

BUT: if you want to use two verbs together, the <u>second one</u> usually needs to be <u>infinitive</u>.

Quiero <u>comer</u>. = I want to eat.

Preferimos <u>bailar</u>. = We prefer to dance.

Action words round the edge — a verbacious border...

I'm not kidding — this is <u>mega-important</u> stuff. Over the next few pages I'll give you <u>loads of stuff</u> on verbs because there's loads you <u>need to know</u>. Some of it's easy, some of it's tricky — but if you <u>don't understand</u> the things on <u>this page</u> before you start, you'll have <u>no chance</u>.

Verbs in the Present Tense

Sadly, this is nothing to do with Christmas gifts — it's the easiest of the <u>verb forms</u> in Spanish.
That <u>doesn't mean</u> you can skip it though — you've <u>still</u> got to get it <u>right</u>.

The present tense is what's happening now

You'll use it more than anything else, so it's <u>really important</u>.

It's all about sticking 'endings' onto something (the 'stem').
For the present tense, the 'stems' that you stick the endings onto are dead easy:

Formula for Present Tense Stems
stem = infinitive – last two letters

Example of Present Tense Stems			
Infinitive	hablar	vivir	comer
Stem	habl	viv	com

Endings for -er verbs

To form the present tense of <u>regular</u> '-er' verbs,
add the following endings to the verb's stem — eg:

See page 85 for when to use which form of 'you'.

comer = to eat

I eat =	com **o**	com **emos**	= we eat
you (inf. sing.) eat =	com **es**	com **éis**	= you (inf. pl. & form.) eat
he/she/it/one eats =	com **e**	com **en**	= they eat
you (formal singular) eat =	com **e**	com **en**	= you (formal plural) eat

The first bit ('<u>com</u>') doesn't change.

NOTE A: <u>he</u>, <u>she</u>, <u>it</u> and <u>you</u> (formal. sing.) always have the <u>same</u> ending.

Endings for -ir verbs

To form the present tense of <u>regular</u> '-ir' verbs,
add the following endings to the verb's stem — eg:

vivir = to live

I live =	viv **o**	viv **imos**	= we live
you (inf. sing.) live =	viv **es**	viv **ís**	= you (inf. pl. & form.) live
he/she/it/one lives =	viv **e**	viv **en**	= they live
you (formal singular) live =	viv **e**	viv **en**	= you (formal plural) live

The first bit ('<u>viv</u>') doesn't change.

NOTE B: <u>they</u> and <u>you</u> (formal plural) always have the <u>same</u> ending.

Endings for -ar verbs

To form the present tense of <u>regular</u> '-ar' verbs,
add the following endings to the verb's stem — eg:

hablar = to speak

I speak =	habl **o**	habl **amos**	= we speak
you (informal singular) speak =	habl **as**	habl **áis**	= you (informal plural) speak
he/she/it speaks =	habl **a**	habl **an**	= they speak
you (formal singular) speak =	habl **a**	habl **an**	= you (formal plural) speak

So if you want to say something like 'He <u>talks</u> a lot', it's dead easy:

hablar = to speak

1) Start by <u>knocking off</u> the '<u>ar</u>':
hablar

2) Then <u>add on</u> the <u>new ending</u>:
habl a

3) And — <u>ta da</u>...
Habla mucho.
= He <u>talks</u> a lot.

Present tense — aargh, I feel a 'tents' joke coming...

All you have to do is learn the endings for '<u>-ar</u>', '<u>-er</u>' & '<u>-ir</u>' verbs. They aren't too bad, really,
because a lot of them are <u>the same</u> — especially the '-er' ones. <u>Learn</u> them and <u>practise them</u>.

Verbs in the Present Tense

OK, on the last page you got the nice regular verbs. Now you get the horrible <u>irregular</u> ones. Enjoy.

Some Spanish Verbs are almost Irregular

How's that? Well, some verbs change their spelling (but only in the present tense). These are called <u>stem</u> or <u>radical</u> changing verbs, and they change the '<u>e</u>' to an '<u>ie</u>' and the '<u>o</u>' or '<u>u</u>' to a '<u>ue</u>'.

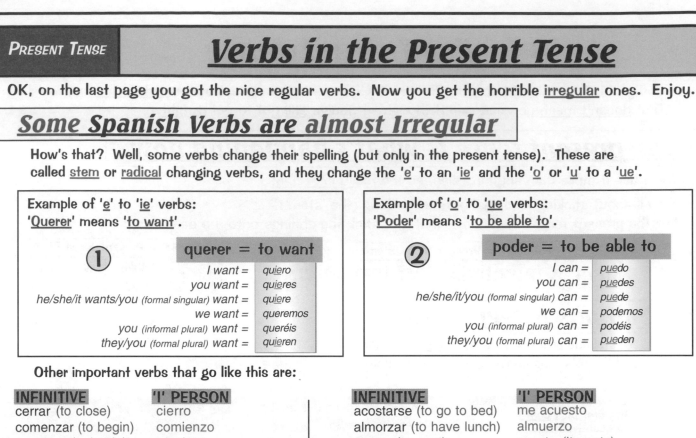

Example of '<u>e</u>' to '<u>ie</u>' verbs:
'<u>Querer</u>' means '<u>to want</u>'.

① querer = to want

I want =	quiero
you want =	quieres
he/she/it wants/you (formal singular) want =	quiere
we want =	queremos
you (informal plural) want =	queréis
they/you (formal plural) want =	quieren

Example of '<u>o</u>' to '<u>ue</u>' verbs:
'<u>Poder</u>' means '<u>to be able to</u>'.

② poder = to be able to

I can =	puedo
you can =	puedes
he/she/it/you (formal singular) can =	puede
we can =	podemos
you (informal plural) can =	podéis
they/you (formal plural) can =	pueden

Other important verbs that go like this are:

INFINITIVE	'I' PERSON
cerrar (to close)	cierro
comenzar (to begin)	comienzo
empezar (to begin)	empiezo
pensar (to think)	pienso
preferir (to prefer)	prefiero
sentarse (to sit down)	me siento
sentir (to feel)	siento
tener (to have)	tengo (tú tienes)
venir (to come)	vengo (tú vienes)

INFINITIVE	'I' PERSON
acostarse (to go to bed)	me acuesto
almorzar (to have lunch)	almuerzo
costar (to cost)	cuesta (it costs)
doler (to hurt)	duele (it hurts)
dormir (to sleep)	duermo
jugar (to play)	juego
llover (to rain)	llueve (it rains)
morir (to die)	muero
volver (to return)	vuelvo

Some of the most Useful Verbs are totally Irregular

Here are the most useful irregular verbs:

'<u>Ser</u>' and '<u>estar</u>' both mean '<u>to be</u>' — they're probably the two <u>most important</u> Spanish verbs in the whole world... ever.

① ir = to go

I go =	voy
you go =	vas
he/she/it goes/you (formal singular) go=	va
we go =	vamos
you (informal plural) go =	vais
they/you (formal plural) go =	van

② ser = to be

I am =	soy
you are =	eres
he/she/it is/you (formal singular) are =	es
we are =	somos
you (informal plural) are =	sois
they/you (formal plural) are =	son

③ estar = to be

I am =	estoy
you are =	estás
he/she/it is/you (formal singular) are =	está
we are =	estamos
you (informal plural) are =	estáis
they/you (formal plural) are =	están

'<u>Ser</u>' and '<u>estar</u>' both mean '<u>to be</u>' but are used differently.
It takes plenty of <u>practice</u> to use the right one all the time.

Use '<u>ser</u>' for pretty <u>permanent</u> things, such as nationality, height, occupation:

> *Julio <u>es</u> español, <u>es</u> alto y moreno.*

= Julio is Spanish, he is tall and dark.

Use '<u>estar</u>' for either fairly <u>temporary</u> things:

> *<u>Estamos</u> tristes hoy.* = We are sad today.

<u>OR</u> for saying <u>where</u> things are:

> *Madrid <u>está</u> en España.* = Madrid is in Spain.

Talking About the Future

You'll need to talk about things that are <u>going to happen</u> at some point in the <u>future</u>.
There are <u>two ways</u> you can do it — and the first one's a <u>piece of cake</u>...

1) You can use 'I'm going to' to talk about the future

This is pretty easy, so there are no excuses for not learning it.

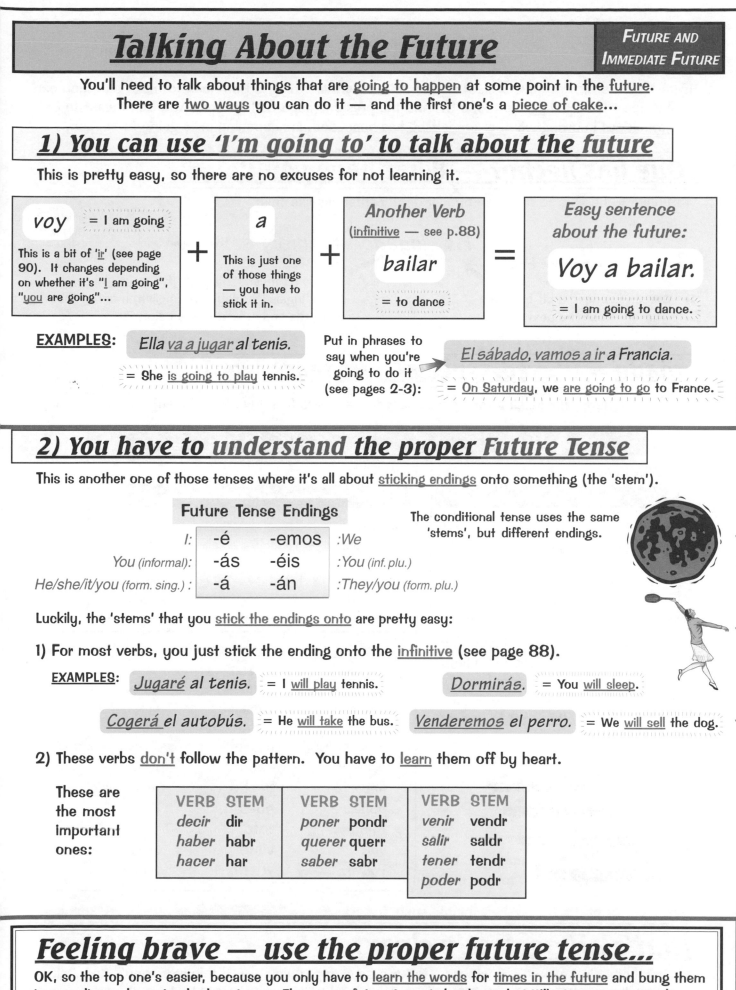

voy = I am going

This is a bit of '<u>ir</u>' (see page 90). It changes depending on whether it's "<u>I</u> am going", "<u>you</u> are going"...

+

a

This is just one of those things — you have to stick it in.

+

Another Verb
(<u>infinitive</u> — see p.88)

bailar

= to dance

=

Easy sentence about the future:

Voy a bailar.

= I am going to dance.

EXAMPLES:

Ella <u>va a jugar</u> al tenis.

= She <u>is going to play</u> tennis.

Put in phrases to say when you're going to do it (see pages 2-3):

<u>El sábado</u>, <u>vamos a ir</u> a Francia.

= <u>On Saturday</u>, we <u>are going to go</u> to France.

2) You have to understand the proper Future Tense

This is another one of those tenses where it's all about <u>sticking endings</u> onto something (the 'stem').

Future Tense Endings

I:	-é	-emos	:We
You (informal):	-ás	-éis	:You (inf. plu.)
He/she/it/you (form. sing.):	-á	-án	:They/you (form. plu.)

The conditional tense uses the same 'stems', but different endings.

Luckily, the 'stems' that you <u>stick the endings onto</u> are pretty easy:

1) For most verbs, you just stick the ending onto the <u>infinitive</u> (see page 88).

EXAMPLES: *<u>Jugaré</u> al tenis.* = I <u>will play</u> tennis. *<u>Dormirás</u>.* = You <u>will sleep</u>.

<u>Cogerá</u> el autobús. = He <u>will take</u> the bus. *<u>Venderemos</u> el perro.* = We <u>will sell</u> the dog.

2) These verbs <u>don't</u> follow the pattern. You have to <u>learn</u> them off by heart.

These are the most important ones:

VERB	STEM	VERB	STEM	VERB	STEM
decir	dir	poner	pondr	venir	vendr
haber	habr	querer	querr	salir	saldr
hacer	har	saber	sabr	tener	tendr
				poder	podr

Feeling brave — use the proper future tense...

OK, so the top one's easier, because you only have to <u>learn the words</u> for <u>times in the future</u> and bung them in an ordinary, bog-standard sentence. The <u>proper future tense</u> is harder — but it'll win you <u>more marks</u>. But definitely make sure you can <u>understand</u> it, in case it crops up in your Reading or Listening papers.

Talking About the Past

Uh oh, it's the first of several past tenses now. The main thing is you need to make sure you can tell it apart from the <u>future</u> (page 91) and the <u>present</u> (page 89) tenses. You don't want to be stuck not knowing whether something has happened, is happening or is going to happen.

¿Qué has hecho? — What have you done?

You have to be able to make and <u>understand</u> sentences like this:

> **Grammar Fans:**
> This is the
> <u>Perfect Tense</u>.

He **jugado** al tenis.   = I have played tennis.

There are <u>two</u> important bits.

1) You always need a bit to mean '<u>I have</u>' — see the next page.

2) This bit means '<u>played</u>'. It's a <u>special version</u> of 'jugar' (to play). In English, most of these words end in '-ed'. See below.

jugado = played: special past tense words

> **Grammar Fans:**
> These are the
> <u>Past Participles</u>.

Learn the <u>patterns</u> for making the special past tense words like 'jugado' (played).

-ar verbs	-er/-ir verbs
FORMULA:	**FORMULA:**
Remove '-<u>ar</u>', then add '-<u>ado</u>'	Remove '-<u>er</u>' or '-<u>ir</u>' then add '-<u>ido</u>'
EXAMPLES:	**EXAMPLES:**
jugar → jug<u>ado</u> *to play played*	vender → vend<u>ido</u> salir → sal<u>ido</u> *to sell sold to leave left*
esperar → esper<u>ado</u> *to wait waited*	beber → beb<u>ido</u> elegir → eleg<u>ido</u> *to drink drunk to choose chosen*

Some verbs <u>don't</u> follow the patterns. It's dead annoying, because a lot of the <u>most useful</u> verbs are <u>irregular</u> — you just have to <u>learn</u> them off <u>by heart</u>:

Verb	Past tense version*	Translation
abrir:	**abierto**	*opened*
cubrir:	**cubierto**	*covered*
decir:	**dicho**	*said*
descubrir:	**descubierto**	*knew/discovered*
escribir:	**escrito**	*written*
hacer:	**hecho**	*done/made*
poner:	**puesto**	*put*
romper:	**roto**	*broken*
ver:	**visto**	*seen*
volver:	**vuelto**	*returned*

* ie the past participle.

That's all perfectly clear...

OK, this page ain't easy — no sirreee. But it's dead important — in the Exams, you'll definitely need to <u>talk or write</u> about something that's <u>happened in the past</u>. Scribble down the table of <u>past participles</u> at the bottom of the page and <u>learn</u> it — they'll come in handy for <u>other verb forms</u> too.

Past & Conditional Tenses

The last page was about the <u>participles</u> — the special words for 'played', 'done' etc.
You have to bring it together with the '<u>have</u>' part to make the <u>whole perfect tense verb</u>.

I have played: for 'have' use 'haber'

For the '<u>have</u>' bit of these past tense phrases, you use the present tense of '<u>haber</u>'.

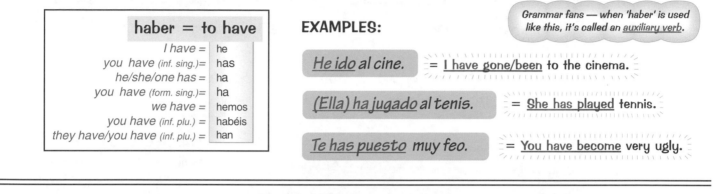

haber = to have	
I have =	he
you have (inf. sing.)=	has
he/she/one has =	ha
you have (form. sing.)=	ha
we have =	hemos
you have (inf. plu.) =	habéis
they have/you have (inf. plu.) =	han

Grammar fans — when 'haber' is used like this, it's called an <u>auxiliary verb</u>.

EXAMPLES:

He ido al cine. = <u>I have gone/been</u> to the cinema.

(Ella) ha jugado al tenis. = <u>She has played</u> tennis.

Te has puesto muy feo. = <u>You have become</u> very ugly.

The Conditional Tense: What would you do?

The <u>conditional</u> tense (for saying '<u>would</u>') uses the stems from the future tense (see page 91) and adds the imperfect endings like '-ía' (see page 95).

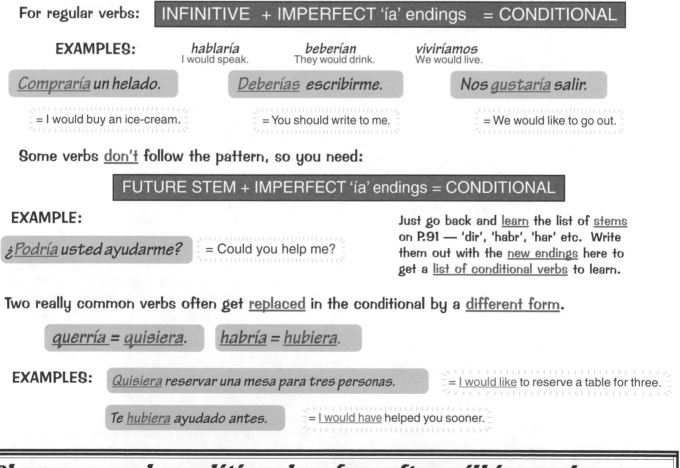

For regular verbs: INFINITIVE + IMPERFECT 'ía' endings = CONDITIONAL

EXAMPLES: *hablaría*
I would speak.   *beberían*
They would drink.   *viviríamos*
We would live.

Compraría un helado.   *Deberías escribirme.*   *Nos gustaría salir.*

= I would buy an ice-cream.   = You should write to me.   = We would like to go out.

Some verbs <u>don't</u> follow the pattern, so you need:

FUTURE STEM + IMPERFECT 'ía' endings = CONDITIONAL

EXAMPLE:

¿Podría usted ayudarme? = Could you help me?

Just go back and <u>learn</u> the list of <u>stems</u> on P.91 — 'dir', 'habr', 'har' etc. Write them out with the <u>new endings</u> here to get a <u>list of conditional verbs</u> to learn.

Two really common verbs often get <u>replaced</u> in the conditional by a <u>different form</u>.

querría = <u>quisiera</u>.   *habría = <u>hubiera</u>.*

EXAMPLES: *Quisiera reservar una mesa para tres personas.*   = <u>I would like</u> to reserve a table for three.

Te <u>hubiera</u> ayudado antes.   = <u>I would have</u> helped you sooner.

Shampoo and conditional — for softer, silkier verbs...

Don't get confused between the <u>conditional</u> and the future or the imperfect.
Watch out for '<u>quisiera</u>'.

PRETERITE	# Another Past Tense: 'Did'

This is the most useful tense for talking about what happened in the past, but, guess what, it's the one with the most irregular bits! Make sure you learn this page <u>carefully</u> — you'll <u>need it</u>.

¿Qué hiciste después? — What did you do next?

This is like saying '<u>I did</u>', rather than 'I have done' — just take the <u>stem</u> of the infinitive, and add the following <u>endings</u> onto it:

> Grammar Fans:
> This is the <u>PRETERITE</u>.

Preterite Endings for '-ar' verbs

I:	-é	-amos	:We
You (inf. sing.):	-aste	-asteis	:You (inf. plu.)
He/she/it/ you (form. sing.):	-ó	-aron	:They/you

Preterite Endings for '-er'/'-ir' verbs

I:	-í	-imos	:We
You (inf. sing.):	-iste	-isteis	:You (inf. plu.)
He/she/it/ you (form. sing.):	-ió	-ieron	:They/you

EXAMPLES:

<u>Pasó</u> toda la vida en Badajoz. = <u>He spent</u> all his life in Badajoz.

<u>Nací</u> en Portsmouth. = <u>I was born</u> in Portsmouth.

<u>Bailamos</u> hasta medianoche. = <u>We danced</u> until midnight.

<u>WATCH OUT</u>: The accents are really important. They can <u>change the meaning</u> of words:

eg: '<u>hablo</u>' - I speak, to '<u>habló</u>' - he spoke!

There are four vital irregular verbs in the preterite

Typical — the words you'll need <u>most often</u> are the irregular ones. Make sure you get 'em <u>learnt</u> pronto:

Ser — to be/Ir — to go (they have the same preterite)

I was/went:	fui	fuimos	:We were/went
You were/went:	fuiste	fuisteis	:You were/went
He/she/it was/went You were/went:	fue	fueron	:They/you were/went

Estar — to be

I was:	estuve	estuvimos	:We were
You were:	estuviste	estuvisteis	:You were
You were/ He/she/it was:	estuvo	estuvieron	:You/They were

Hacer — to do or make

I did/made:	hice	hicimos	:We did/made
You did/made:	hiciste	hicisteis	:You did/made
You/He/she/it did/made:	hizo	hicieron	:You/ They did/made

> <u>All</u> these verbs are really <u>worth learning</u> off by heart — <u>scribble</u> them down, <u>cover</u> them up and see how many you can write out <u>from memory</u>. Then do it <u>again</u>.

Here are some other common <u>irregular</u> ones:

Infinitives	yo	él/ella/usted
dar	di	dio
decir	dije	dijo
poder	pude	pudo
poner	puse	puso
querer	quise	quiso
tener	tuve	tuvo
traer	traje	trajo
venir	vine	vino

EXAMPLES:

No <u>dijeron</u> nada. = <u>They didn't say</u> anything.

<u>Dijiste</u> que <u>no te gustó</u>. = <u>You said</u> <u>you didn't like it</u>.

¿Dónde <u>pusiste</u> el queso? = Where <u>did you put</u> the cheese?

'Was Doing', or 'Used to Do'
IMPERFECT TENSE

...And another page of <u>verbs</u>. ...And another <u>tense</u> for talking about the <u>past</u> — you lucky thing!

What you were doing or used to do

This is another dead useful one.
There are <u>3 easy steps</u> to making this tense:

> Grammar Fans:
> This is the IMPERFECT TENSE.

1) Get the <u>infinitive</u> of the verb you want to use (see page 88).

2) Knock the '-ar', '-er' or '-ir' off the end.

3) Add on the <u>correct ending</u> from the first or second list:

> I used to
> have a life

Imperfect Tense Endings for '-ar' verbs

I:	-aba	-ábamos	*:We*
You (inf. sing.):	-abas	-abais	*:You (inf. plu.)*
He/she/it/ you (form. sing.):	-aba	-aban	*:They/you (form. plu.)*

Imperfect Tense Endings '-er'/'-ir' verbs

I:	-ía	-íamos	*:We*
You (inf. sing.):	-ías	-íais	*:You (inf. plu.)*
He/she/it/ you (form. sing.):	-ía	-ían	*:They/you (form. plu.)*

EXAMPLES:

I was doing/used to do: hacer → hacía
He was speaking/used to speak: hablar → hablaba
We were/used to be: estar → estábamos

SOME UNBELIEVABLY GOOD NEWS:

there are only 3 verbs that don't follow the pattern — <u>ser</u>, <u>ir</u>, and <u>ver</u>.

VER is almost regular, just add normal '-er' endings onto 've-'.

Ir = to go

I used to go = iba
you (inf. sing.)used to go = ibas
he/she/it used to go = iba
you (form. sing.) used to go = iba
we used to go = íbamos
you (inf. plu.) used to go = ibais
they/you (form. plu.) used to go = iban

Ser = to be

I used to be = era
you (inf. sing.)used to be = eras
he/she/it used to be = era
you (form. sing.) used to be = era
we used to be = éramos
you (inf. plu.) used to be = erais
they/you (form. plu.) used to be = eran

Había... — There was...   Era... — It was...

'Había' is the <u>imperfect</u> version of 'hay'. And instead of using 'es'(it is), you can use 'era' (it was).

Hay un mono en el árbol. = <u>There is</u> a monkey in the tree.

Había un mono en el árbol. = <u>There was</u> a monkey in the tree.

Es demasiado caro. = <u>It is</u> too expensive.

Era demasiado caro. = <u>It was</u> too expensive.

When to use the imperfect

1) What you <u>used to do</u> by habit/repeatedly in the past: *Iba al cine cada jueves.* = <u>I used to go</u> to the cinema every Thursday.

2) <u>Descriptions</u> about something in the <u>past</u>, including what <u>was going on</u> when something else happened: *Saqué una foto mientras dormía.* = I took a photo, while <u>she was sleeping</u>.

Hacía mucho calor. = <u>It was</u> very hot.

Use the <u>Preterite Tense</u> for the <u>key event</u>, and the <u>Imperfect Tense</u> for the <u>on-going situation</u>.

REFLEXIVE VERBS

Myself, Yourself, etc

Sometimes you'll have to talk about things you do to <u>yourself</u> — like 'washing yourself' or 'getting yourself up' in the morning. It sounds weird in English, but in Spanish they do it <u>all the time</u>.

Talking about yourself — me, te, se...

'<u>Se</u>' means '<u>oneself</u>'. Here are all the different ways to say 'self':

You can tell <u>which</u> verbs need 'self' by checking in the <u>dictionary</u>. If you look up '<u>to wash</u>', it'll say '<u>lavarse</u>'.

myself:	me
yourself (inf.):	te
himself:	se
herself:	se
oneself:	se
yourself (form. sing):	se

ourselves:	nos
yourselves (inf. plu.) :	os
themselves, each other:	se
yourselves (form. plu.) :	se

Grammar fans call these <u>reflexive verbs</u>.

Me lavo — I wash myself

These verbs are really useful for talking about <u>daily routine</u> stuff... getting up, getting washed, getting dressed. All you've got to do is <u>learn</u> the pattern:

lavarse = to wash oneself

I wash myself =	me lavo	nos lavamos	= we wash ourselves
you wash yourself (informal) =	te lavas	os laváis	= you wash yourselves (inf. plu.)
he washes himself /	se lava	se lavan	= they wash themselves /
she washes herself /			you wash yourselves (form. plu.)
one washes oneself /			
you wash yourself (form. sing.)			

There are lots of these verbs, but here are the ones you <u>should know</u> for the Exam:

8 IMPORTANT REFLEXIVE VERBS	EXAMPLES
to go to bed: acostarse	Me acuesto a las once. = _I go to bed at 11 o'clock._
to get up: levantarse	Me levanto a las ocho. = _I get up at 8 o'clock_
to feel: sentirse	¿Te sientes mal? = _Do you feel ill?_
to be called (literally = to call oneself): llamarse	Me llamo Bob. = _I'm called Bob._ (literally = I call myself Bob)
to wake up: despertarse	Me despierto muy temprano. = _I wake up very early._
to be spelt: escribirse	¿Cómo se escribe? = _How is that spelt?_
to go away: irse	Se va por la mañana. = _He's leaving in the morning._
to wear: vestirse	Siempre se viste de negro. = _She always wears black._

Perfect tense reflexive verbs are pretty easy

When you want to use reflexive verbs in the <u>perfect tense</u>, you just put the '<u>me</u>', '<u>se</u>' or whatever, in front of <u>all the bits</u> of the <u>verb</u> as usual:

EXAMPLE:

ponerse = to put on

<u>Me he puesto</u> el sombrero.   = I've put the hat on.

Stick the '<u>me</u>' at the start.

Then put the <u>whole</u> of the <u>perfect tense verb</u> (see page 92).

¿Se habla español?

Here's another use of '<u>se</u>' — to be <u>impersonal</u>.

Instead of saying someone does something, it says that things have something <u>done to them</u>. It can also mean '<u>one</u>' — eg 'Can one come in?'

Las puertas <u>se abren</u> a las nueve. = The doors are opened at nine.

¿<u>Se puede</u> entrar? = Can one come in?

How to say 'No', 'Not' & 'Nobody'

This stuff's easy enough. Well, most of it is...

Use 'no' to say not

In English you change a sentence to mean the opposite by adding 'not'.
For example, 'I am Bob' ➡ 'I am not Bob'.
In Spanish, you have to put 'no' in front of the action word (verb).

EXAMPLE:

Soy Bob. ➡ No soy Bob.

= I am Bob.

This is the verb. The 'no' goes in front, easy.

= I am not Bob.

Tricky Stuff

You do the same with all the tenses. For example, the perfect tense goes: -

EXAMPLES:

No lo he visto. = I have not seen that.

Ella no ha llegado. = She has not arrived.

Tricky Stuff

No, I don't!

'No' in Spanish means both 'no' and 'not', so answering a question, you may need to say 'no' twice:

No, no quiero pulpo, gracias.

= No, I don't want any octopus thanks.

No, prefiero no ver una película.

= No, I prefer not to see a film.

Tricky Stuff

no ... nunca — never   no ... nada — nothing

There are more negatives you need to understand, and for top marks you should use them too.

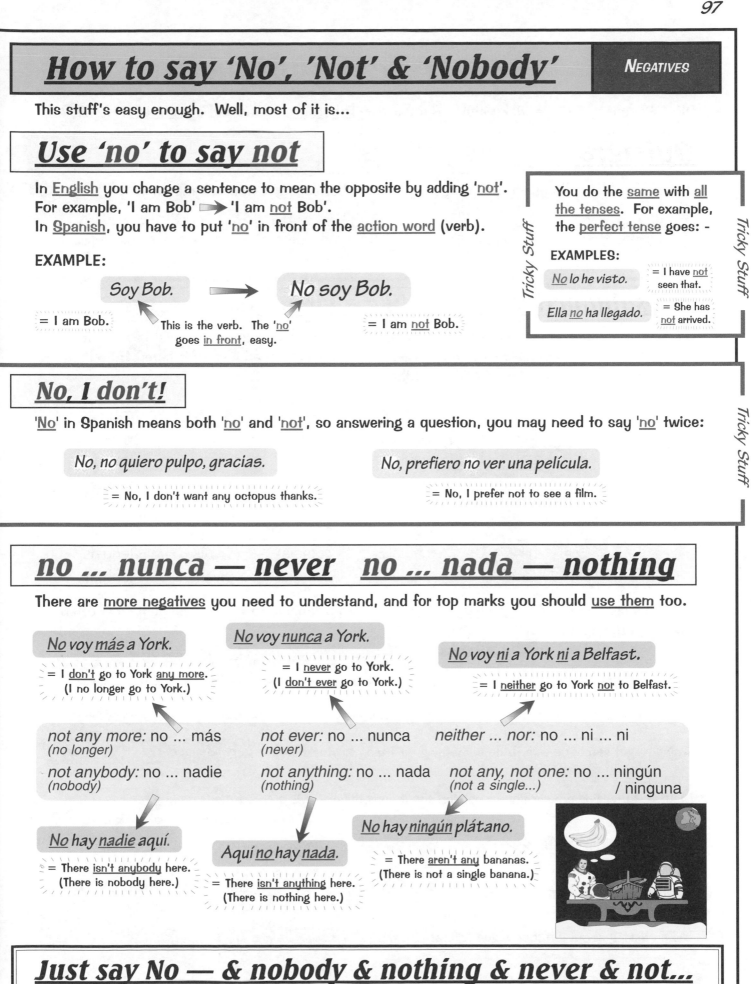

No voy más a York.

= I don't go to York any more. (I no longer go to York.)

No voy nunca a York.

= I never go to York. (I don't ever go to York.)

No voy ni a York ni a Belfast.

= I neither go to York nor to Belfast.

not any more: no ... más (no longer)

not anybody: no ... nadie (nobody)

not ever: no ... nunca (never)

not anything: no ... nada (nothing)

neither ... nor: no ... ni ... ni

not any, not one: no ... ningún / ninguna (not a single...)

No hay nadie aquí.

= There isn't anybody here. (There is nobody here.)

Aquí no hay nada.

= There isn't anything here. (There is nothing here.)

No hay ningún plátano.

= There aren't any bananas. (There is not a single banana.)

Just say No — & nobody & nothing & never & not...

Good news — it's nowhere near as bad as it looks. It seems confusing because you need 'no' with everything — but it actually makes life a lot easier when you're trying to spot negative sentences. Have a go at writing sentences using all the negative phrases here — it's the best way to learn 'em.

Present Subjunctive

OK, I'll admit it. This <u>is</u> tricky stuff. But it's very <u>important</u> if you want a <u>top grade</u>.

Quisiera — I would like

Remember this? It's handy for being <u>polite</u>, instead of saying 'I want' all the time.

| *Quisiera leche.* | = <u>I would like</u> some milk. | | *Quisiera ir al hospital.* | = <u>I would like</u> to go to the hospital. |

The subjunctive *is more like a mood than a tense*

This <u>isn't</u> another tense, but a different mood, and Spanish speakers are really keen on it. In fact, there is so much to learn, I can only try and give you an <u>idea</u> of it here. If you can manage to <u>use it</u> a bit, it could add the * to your 'A'.

	HABLAR (hablo — I speak)	**COMER** (como — I eat)	**VIVIR** (vivo — I live)	**TENER** (tengo — I have)
I	habl<u>e</u>	com<u>a</u>	viv<u>a</u>	teng<u>a</u>
you (inf sing)	hables	comas	vivas	tengas
he/she/it/you (form sing)	hable	coma	viva	tenga
we	hablemos	comamos	vivamos	tengamos
you (inf plu)	habléis	comáis	viváis	tengáis
they/you (form plu)	hablen	coman	vivan	tengan

When a sentence has <u>two linked subjects</u>, the verb belonging to the <u>second subject</u> is often put into the subjunctive.

EXAMPLE   *Elena quiere que Jorge <u>lave</u> los platos.*

= Elena wants Jorge to wash the dishes. (ie: Elena wants that Jorge should wash the dishes.)

The rules and reasons are <u>too tricky</u> to go into — just <u>learn</u> these <u>common examples</u>:

(1) Trying to get someone else to do something, or trying to stop them: *Espero que me <u>escribas</u> pronto.*
= I hope (that) you will write to me soon.

(2) After expressing an emotion or opinion about something : *Me alegro de que <u>podáis</u> venir mañana.*
= I'm pleased that you can come tomorrow.

(3) After any doubts: *Dudamos que el tren <u>llegue</u> a tiempo.* = We doubt that the train will arrive on time.

(4) When there is a need or requirement: *Necesito a un amigo que <u>sepa</u> cocinar.* = I need a friend who knows how to cook.

(5) When talking about a rather vague future: *Cuando <u>sea</u> mayor, quiero ser bombero.* = When I'm grown up, I want to be a fireman.

(6) After the phrases '<u>para que</u>' (so that), '<u>antes de que</u>' (before), '<u>como si</u>' (as if) and '<u>aunque</u>' (even if):
Vamos a la playa para que <u>veas</u> el mar. = We're going to the beach so that you can see the sea.

Tricky Stuff   Tricky Stuff   Tricky Stuff   Tricky Stuff

Ordering People Around

Of course you need to understand this, and for top marks you need to be able to <u>do it yourself</u> too.

You need this stuff for bossing people about

Luckily, the single informal bit is <u>dead easy</u>. It's just like the 'tú' part of the Present Tense but <u>without</u> the 's' at the end.

hablas = you speak   *bebes* = you drink.   *escribes* = you write.   ¡Escucha ésto!

¡*habla!* = speak!   ¡*bebe!* = drink!   ¡*escribe!* = write!   = Listen to this!

Grammar fans: this is called the <u>Imperative</u>.

There are a few <u>common irregular</u> ones:

decir	hacer	ir	oír	poner	salir	tener	venir
di	haz	ve	oye	pon	sal	ten	ven

It seems really <u>odd</u>, but if you want to tell <u>several people</u> what to do, you take the infinitive and <u>change</u> the final '<u>r</u>' to a '<u>d</u>', even with the irregular ones:

hablar ➡ ¡hablad!   salir ➡ ¡salid!   hacer ➡ ¡haced!   escribir ➡ ¡escribid!   beber ➡ ¡bebed!

¡Terminad vuestros deberes!   = Finish your homework!

Politely Telling People what to Do

This can be more <u>difficult</u>. You have to take the <u>'I' person of the verb</u> in the <u>Present Tense</u>, and change the last '<u>o</u>' to an '<u>a</u>' or an '<u>e</u>', whichever is the opposite ending to the one you would expect. Confused? The examples should help:

hablo ➡ ¡hable!   como ➡ ¡coma!   escribo ➡ ¡escriba!

EXAMPLES:

Siga todo recto. = Continue straight on.   Coja la primera a la derecha. = Take the first on the right.
(seguir ➡ sigo)   (coger ➡ cojo)

At least, the <u>polite plural</u> is easy - just add an '<u>n</u>' as usual:

¡hablen!   ¡coman!   ¡escriban!

And the only real exceptions are:

dar	haber	ir	saber	ser
dé	haya	vaya	sepa	sea

Orders with Pronouns

If you tell someone to do something, any <u>pronouns</u> (me, it, them etc) are <u>stuck on the end</u>, in the <u>normal word order</u>:

Me lo trae. = You bring it to me.

Te levantas. = You get up.   ¡Levántate! = Get up!

¡Tráigamelo! = Bring it to me!

Add 'no' for saying what not to do

Also, change the normal endings to their opposites in all cases:

¡No escuches! = Don't listen!

Orders where you say no are in the <u>Subjunctive</u>.

And move any pronouns from the end to the beginning:

¡Tócalo! = Touch it!   ¡No lo toques! = Don't touch it!

SABER, CONOCER AND PODER	# 'Know' and 'Can'

Here are <u>three really useful verbs</u> that people are always getting <u>wrong</u> — make sure <u>you don't</u>.

'To know information' is 'Saber'

1) <u>Saber</u> means '<u>to know</u>', in the sense of having <u>learnt</u> something (like how to play the piano), or knowing <u>information</u> (eg knowing what time the bus leaves).

Have a look at these examples:

Ella <u>sabe</u> la respuesta a la pregunta.	*She knows the answer to the question.*
No <u>sé</u> si tenemos plátanos.	*I don't know if we have any bananas.*
¿<u>Sabe</u> usted cuándo llega el tren?	*Do you know when the train arrives?*

2) <u>Saber</u> followed by an *infinitive* means '*to know how to do something*', in the sense of a skill, eg:

Sabe esquiar.   *No sabe leer.*   *Sé conducir.*
He knows how to ski.   *She cannot read.*   *I can drive.*

IMPORTANT: '<u>saber</u>' is a regular verb, except for the '<u>I</u>' <u>person</u>, which is '<u>sé</u>'.

'To be familiar with' is 'Conocer'

Conocer means <u>to know</u> a person or place — to 'be familiar with'.
If someone asks you if you know their mate Gertrude, this is the one to use.

Conozco la luna.

<u>Conozco</u> Madrid.	= *I know Madrid.*
No <u>conoce</u> esta ciudad.	= *He doesn't know this town.*
¿<u>Conoces</u> a mi amigo?	= *Do you know my friend?*

IMPORTANT: like '<u>saber</u>', '<u>conocer</u>' is also a <u>normal verb</u> with an <u>odd</u> '<u>I</u>' <u>person</u> = '<u>conozco</u>'.

'Poder' means 'to be able to'

Poder (<u>to be able to/can</u>) has three very important meanings:

1) Being <u>able</u> to do something (<u>not</u> knowing <u>how</u> to do it, but just being able to — like 'Yes, I can come tomorrow').

Si quieres, <u>puedo</u> llevar el equipaje.   = I can carry the luggage if you like.

2) <u>Permission</u> to do something.   *Se <u>pueden</u> sacar fotos aquí.*   = You can take photos here.

3) <u>Possibility</u> — something <u>could</u> be the case.   *Eso <u>puede</u> pasar.*   = That can happen.

I love fine food and wine — I'm a conocer...

Three mega-handy verbs that you need to sort out. Don't forget the difference between <u>saber</u> and <u>conocer</u>, and make sure that you know the three meanings of <u>poder</u>. Wonderful stuff...

Section 11 — Grammar

'Had Done', '-ing' & 'Just Done'

3 more bits to <u>learn</u> — you may come across them in the <u>Listening</u> or <u>Reading</u> papers.

Había hecho — 'I had done'

Grammar fans: this is the <u>Pluperfect Tense</u>.

1) You need to be able to <u>understand</u> this stuff if it comes up in the <u>Reading</u> or <u>Listening Exams</u>.

2) It's <u>similar</u> to the Perfect Tense (see page 93) — that's for saying what you <u>have</u> done, <u>but</u> this is for saying what you <u>had</u> done.

3) It's still made of a bit of <u>haber</u> + <u>a past participle</u>, but the bit of haber is in the <u>imperfect tense</u>.

For stuff on the imperfect tense, see page 95.

IMPERFECT TENSE OF HABER + PAST PARTICIPLE

EXAMPLES:

<u>Había escrito</u> una carta.   = I <u>had written</u> a letter.

Betty <u>había llegado</u>.   = Betty <u>had arrived</u>.

Doing, saying, thinking are present participles

<u>Most</u> of the time you'd translate things like 'I am doing' and 'I was doing' with <u>normal tenses</u> — those two would be 'hago' (present tense), and 'hacía' (imperfect tense).

But sometimes you want <u>to stress</u> that something <u>is ongoing</u> at the moment, or <u>was ongoing</u> in the past.

eg: *Estoy <u>almorzando</u>.*   = I'm having my lunch.

Estaba <u>durmiendo</u> cuando sonó el teléfono.   = He was sleeping when the phone rang.

There are <u>two bits</u> to this:

a) the correct part of '<u>estar</u>' (to be) in the <u>present</u> or the <u>imperfect tense</u>, and

b) the <u>special word</u> to describe the '<u>ing</u>' <u>bit</u> — called the <u>present participle</u>.

'-ar' verbs eg. hablar	'-er' verbs eg. comer	'-ir' verbs eg. vivir
stem (eg. habl) + ando	stem (eg. com) + iendo	stem (eg. viv) + iendo
hablando	comiendo	viviendo

There are only a few irregular ones:
1) caer ➡ estoy ca<u>y</u>endo (I'm falling).
2) leer ➡ estamos le<u>y</u>endo (we're reading).
Also:
servir ➡ <u>sirviendo</u>   pedir ➡ <u>pidiendo</u>
dormir ➡ <u>durmiendo</u>   morir ➡ <u>muriendo</u>

Acabo de... — 'I have just...'

To say what's <u>just</u> happened, use the present tense of '<u>acabar</u>' + '<u>de</u>' + the verb you want in the <u>infinitive</u>.

ACABAR: to finish	
acabo	acabamos
acabas	acabáis
acaba	acaban

EXAMPLES: *<u>Acabo de</u> ducharme.*   = I have just taken a shower.

<u>Acaba de</u> salir.   = She has just left.

The end of the grammar — you deserve a medal...

Phew.

Revision Summary

The stuff in this section really helps you to put words together to say what you want to. The way to make sure you've learnt it is to check you can do all these questions. Try them all, and look up any you can't do. Then try them all again. Keep doing that until you can answer all of them. THEN you'll really know this stuff.

1) What are the Spanish words for   a) 'and',   b) 'or',   c) 'but',   d) 'because'?

2) Use the Spanish word for 'and' to turn these two phrases into one sentence that says 'I have a bird <u>and</u> a carrot': 'Tengo un pájaro.' = I have a bird. 'Tengo una zanahoria.' = I have a carrot.

3) What are the words for 'the' and 'a' that go with each of these words?
   a) 'pie' (masculine)   b) 'flor' (feminine)

4) How would you say these in Spanish? a) I'm going to London. b) I live in Swansea.

5) What are the Spanish words for   a) <u>my</u> horse,   b) <u>our</u> house,   c) <u>his</u> clothes,   d) <u>her</u> house?

6) This sentence means 'I speak Spanish' — 'Hablo español'.
   How would you change the sentence to mean 'I speak Spanish well'?
   How would you change the sentence to mean 'I speak Spanish very well'?

7) How do you say 'Bob is taller than me' in Spanish? How do you say 'Bob is the tallest'?

8) This sentence means 'I speak slowly' — 'Hablo lentamente'.
   How would you say 'I speak the slowest'?

9) What are the Spanish words for
   'I', 'you' (informal, singular), 'he', 'she', 'we', 'you' (formal, plural) and 'they'?

10) What do these Spanish words mean? a) 'me' b) 'te' c) 'le' d) 'les'

11) How would you say these in Spanish: a) This dog is green. b) These cats are blue.

12) What do these sentences mean?   a) Me gustan las manzanas, pero no me gusta ésta.
                                      b) ¿Tiene pantalones rojos? Esos son naranja.

13) How do you say these in Spanish?
    a) I have b) she has c) they have d) I am e) he is f) we are

14) What do each of these phrases mean? a) 'Como un pastel'   b) 'He comido un pastel'
    c) 'Comí un pastel'   d) 'Comía un pastel'   e) 'Voy a comer un pastel f) 'Comeré un pastel'
    g) 'Comería un pastel'.

15) How would you say these in Spanish?
    a) 'I like to eat a cake.'   b) 'I will eat a cake next year.'   c) 'I had eaten a cake.'

16) Fill in the missing Spanish words (past participles). I've done the first one for you.
    a) to make/do = hacer;   made/done = hecho
    b) to buy = comprar;   bought = ?   c) to ask = pedir;   asked = ?
    d) to finish = terminar;   finished = ?   e) to sell = vender;   sold = ?

17) How do you say these in Spanish?   a) I have gone. b) I have come.

18) This sentence means 'I'm called Jim' — 'Me llamo Jim'. How would you say
    a) She's called Sarah,   b) You're called (informal singular) Marigold,
    c) We're called Hopkins,   d) You're called (formal) Fitzgerald.

19) How do you say these in Spanish?   a) I don't go out. b) I never go out.

20) How do you say these in Spanish? a) Get out! b) Let's go out! c) Come here!

21) For each word, write out a sentence in Spanish that includes it: a) nada b) ni...ni.

22) What does this sentence mean? 'Acabo de llegar.'

23) Write out these sentences in Spanish:
    a) I have just left. b) She has just said 'hello'. c) We have just started.

A

la a f a (letter)
a pron at, to
abajo ad down, downstairs, below
el abanico m fan
abatido/a a depressed
la abeja f bee
abierto/a a open
el/la abogado/a a mf lawyer
abonar v to pay
abonarse vr to subscribe to
el abono m subscription, payment
abrazar v to hug
el abrazo m hug
el abrebotellas m bottle opener
el abrelatas m tin opener
abrigar v to shelter, keep warm
el abrigo m overcoat
abril m April
abrir v to open
abrochar v to fasten
la abuela f grandmother
el abuelo m grandfather
aburrido/a a bored, boring
aburrirse vr to be/get bored
acabar v to finish acabar de to have just…(done something)
acampar v to camp
el acantilado m cliff
el aceite m oil
la aceituna f olive
acelerar v to speed up
aceptar v to accept
la acera f pavement
acerca de prep about
acercarse (a) vr to get near (to)
el acero m steel
acertar v to guess, to be right
acogedor(a) a welcoming
acoger v to receive
la acogida f reception, welcome
acompañar v to accompany
aconsejar v to advise
acordarse (de) v to remember
acostarse vr to go to bed
la actitud f attitude
la actividad f activity
la actuación f performance
las actualidades fpl news
actualmente nowadays
actuar v to act
el acuerdo m agreement
adelantar v to overtake, move forward
adelante ad forward
además ad in addition
adentro ad inside
el adiós m & excl goodbye
adivinar v to guess
adjunto/a ad attached
¿adónde? ad where?
adrede ad on purpose
la aduana f the customs
el/la aduanero/a mf customs officer
advertir v to warn
el aerodeslizador m hovercraft
el aeropuerto m airport
afeitarse vr to shave
la afición f hobby
el/la aficionado/a mf enthusiast, fan
afuera ad outside
las afueras fpl outskirts
agarrar v to grip
la agencia de viajes f travel agency
agitar v to wave, to shake
agosto m August
agotar v to wear out, extinguish
agradable a pleasant
agradecer v to thank
agradecido/a a grateful
el agrado m pleasure
el agua f water
aguantar v to put up with, stand
aguardar v to wait, to wait for

agudo/a a sharp, pointed
la aguja f needle
el agujero m hole
ahí ad there
ahogarse vr to drown/choke
ahora ad now
ahorrar v to save
aislado/a a isolated
el ajedroz m chess
el ajo m garlic
al aparato speaking (on phone)
alargar v to stretch
el albañil m bricklayer
el albaricoque m apricot
el albergue m hostel, shelter
el alcalde m mayor
alcanzar v to reach
la aldea f hamlet
alegrarse vr to be happy
alegrarse de to be pleased about
alegre a happy
la alegría f happiness, joy
alejarse vr to go/move away
el alfiler m pin
la alfombra f carpet
algo pron something, anything
el algodón m cotton
alguien pron somebody, anyone
algún sitio ad somewhere
algunas veces ad sometimes
alguno/a a some
el aliento m breath
la alimentación f food, nutrition
el alimento m food
aliviar v to relieve
allá ad there
allí ad there
el almacén m store, warehouse
la almendra f almond
la almohada f pillow
almorzar v to have lunch
el almuerzo m lunch
alojarse v to stay, to lodge
el alpinismo m mountain climbing
el/la alpinista mf mountain climber
alquilado/a a rented
alquilar v to rent, to hire
el alquiler m rent
alrededor (de) ad around, about
alto/a a high, tall
la altura f height
el/la alumno/a mf pupil
el ama de casa f housewife
amable a kind
el amanecer m dawn
amar v to love
amargo/a a bitter
amarillo/a a yellow
ambiente m atmosphere
ambos a/pron both
amenazar v to threaten
el/la amigo/a mf friend
la amistad f friendship
amistoso/a a friendly
el/la amo/a mf owner, boss
el amor m love
amplio/a a large, spacious
amueblado/a a furnished
añadir v to add
ancho/a a wide
anciano/a a old
el/la anciano/a mf old man/woman
andar v to walk
el andén m platform
el anfiteatro m amphitheatre
el anillo m ring
animado/a a lively, animated
animar v to liven up, cheer up
el año m year
anoche ad last night
el anochecer m nightfall
anteayer a day before yesterday
antes (de) a before

antiguo/a a old, antique
antipático/a a unpleasant, horrible
anunciar v to announce
el anuncio m advert, announcement
apagar v to turn out, to put out, switch off
el aparador m sideboard
el aparato m appliance, telephone
el aparcamiento m car park
aparcar v to park
aparecer v to appear
aparte adj separate, ad separately
el apellido m surname
apenado/a a sorry, sad
apenas ad hardly, scarcely
la apertura f opening
apetecer v to feel like, to crave
apetitoso/a a appetizing
aplastar v to crush, to squash
aplicado/a a conscientious
el apodo m nickname
apoyar v to lean, to support
apreciar v to like, to value
aprender (a) v to learn (to)
el aprendizaje m apprenticeship
apresurarse v to hurry
aprobar v to pass (exam), to approve
apropiado/a a suitable
aprovecharse (de) v to take advantage
apto/a a suitable, capable
los apuntes notes
aquel/aquella a that
aquél/aquélla pron that, that one
aquí ad here
aquí tiene here it is
el/la árbitro/a mf referee, umpire
el árbol m tree
el arbusto m bush
archivar v to file
arder v to burn
la arena f sand
el arma f weapon
el armario m cupboard, wardrobe
arrancar v to pull out/start vehicle
arreglar v to arrange/settle/repair
arreglarse v to get ready
arrepentirse v to be sorry, regret
arriba ad above, upstairs, up
arriesgar v to risk
arrojar v to throw, to throw out
el arroyo m stream
el arroz m rice
arruinar v to ruin
el arte dramático m drama, theatre
el artículo m article
asado/a a roast
asar v to roast
el ascensor m lift
el asco m disgust
asegurar v to insure, secure
los aseos mpl toilets
asesinar v to murder
el asesinato m murder
así ad so, like this/that
el asiento m seat
la asignatura f subject (school)
asistir v to attend
asomarse v to look/lean out of
asombrar v to astonish
asombroso/a a amazing
el aspecto m aspect, appearance
la aspiradora f vacuum cleaner
asqueroso/a a disgusting
el asunto m matter, subject
asustarse v to be frightened
atacar v to attack
el ataque cardíaco m heart attack
atar v to tie, to tie up
el atasco m obstruction, traffic jam

atento/a a attentive
el aterrizaje m landing (plane)
aterrizar v to land
el ático m attic
el/la atleta mf athlete
el atletismo m athletics
atónito/a a amazed
el atraco m holdup, robbery
atraer v to attract
atrás ad behind
atrasar v to be late, to be slow
atravesar v to go across
atreverse v to dare
atrevido/a a daring, cheeky
atropellar v to run over
el atún m tuna fish
el aula f classroom, lecture room
aumentar v to increase
el aumento m increase
aún ad still, yet
aunque conj although
el autobús m bus
el autocar m coach
la autopista f motorway
el/la autor/a mf author
la autoridad f authority
el autostop m hitch-hiking
el AVE m (alta velocidad española) high speed train
la avenida f avenue
la aventura f adventure
averiarse vr to break down
averiguar v to find out
el avión m aeroplane
avisar m to inform, warn
el aviso m notice, warning
la avispa f wasp
ay excl ouch!, oh dear!
ayer ad yesterday
la ayuda f help
ayudar v to help
el ayuntamiento m town hall
la azafata f air hostess
azar m chance, fate
el azúcar m sugar
azul a blue

B

el bacalao m cod
el bachillerato m secondary course/examination
bachillerato elemental lower certificate (GCSE) bachillerato superior higher certificate (A Level)
la bahía f bay
bailar v to dance
el baile m dance
bajar v to take/go down
bajar de get off (a vehicle)
bajo/a a low, short
bajo prep low, below
el balcón m balcony
el balón m ball
el baloncesto m basketball
el/la bañador/a mf swimmer
los bañadores mpl bathing trunks
bañar(se) vr to bathe
el/la bancario/a mf bank employee
la bandeja f tray
la bandera f flag
la bañera f bathtub
el baño m bath, bathroom
barato/a a cheap
la barba f beard
la barbacoa f barbecue
la barbaridad f atrocity
¡Qué barbaridad! how awful!
la barbilla f chin
la barca (de pesca) f (fishing) boat
el barco m boat, ship
la barra (de pan) f loaf (of bread)
la barra de labios f lipstick
barrer v to sweep
la barrera f barrier
el barrio m district, neighbourhood

bastante a/ad enough, quite a lot
¡Basta! Enough!
la basura f rubbish
el/la basurero/a mf dustman/woman
la bata f dressing gown
la batalla f battle
la batería f battery, drums
batido/a a beaten
el batido m milk shake
el bebé m baby
beber v to drink
la bebida f drink
belga a Belgian
Bélgica f Belgium
bello/a a beautiful
besar v to kiss
el beso m kiss
la biblioteca f library
la bicicleta f bicycle la bici bike
bien ad well/good
bien hecho well done
bienvenido/a a welcome
el biftec m steak
el bigote m moustache
el billete m ticket billete sencillo/de ida single ticket billete de ida y vuelta/regreso return ticket
el billete m bank note
el billetero m wallet
el bistec m steak
blanco/a a white
el bloque m block
la boca f mouth
el bocadillo m sandwich
la boda f wedding
la bodega f wine cellar/shop
la bofetada f slap
la bola f ball, scoop (of ice cream)
la bolera f bowling alley
el boletín f bulletin
el bolígrafo/el boli m ballpoint pen
el bolo m skittle los bolos skittles
la bolsa f bag
el bolsillo m pocket
el bolso m bag, handbag bolso de mano handbag
la bomba f bomb, pump lo pasé bomba I had a wonderful time
el bombero m fireman
la bombilla f light bulb
el bombón m chocolate, sweet
bonito/a a pretty, nice
el bonobús m bus pass
el boquerón m fresh anchovy
el borde m edge
(el bordo m) a bordo on board
borracho/a a drunk
el borrador m (board) rubber
borrar v to rub out, delete
la borrasca f storm
el bosque m wood
la bota f boot
el bote m jar, pot
bote de remo rowing boat
la botella f bottle
el botón m button
el brazo m arm
brevemente ad briefly
el bricolaje m do-it-yourself
brillar v to shine
la broma f joke
broncearse v to get a suntan, sunbathe
la bruma f mist
brusco/a a sharp, sudden, rude
bucear v to dive, go under water
bueno/a a good
la bufanda f scarf
el búho m owl
el buque m ship, boat
burlarse vr to joke
burlarse de to make fun of
el burro m donkey
buscar v to look for, fetch
la butaca f armchair, seat (in cinema, theatre)

el buzón m *post box*

C

el caballero m *gentleman, knight*
el caballo m *horse*
el cabello m *hair*
caber v *to fit*
la cabeza f *head*
la cabina f *booth*
el cable m *wire, cable*
el cabo m *cape, end*
la cabra f *goat*
la cacerola f *saucepan*
cada a *each, every*
la cadena f *chain*
caer v *to fall* caer enfermo *fall ill* caerse vr *to fall, fall over*
el café m *coffee, café*
la cafetera f *coffee pot/machine*
la caja f *box, till* caja de ahorros *savings bank*
el/la cajero/a mf *cashier*
el cajero automático m *cash dispenser*
el cajón m *drawer*
los calamares mpl *squid*
el calcetín m *sock*
el caldo m *soup, broth*
calentar v *to heat*
caliente a *hot*
la calificación f *grade, mark, rating*
calificado/a a *qualified*
callado/a a *quiet, reserved*
callar(se) v(r) *to say nothing*
la calle f *street*
la callejuela f *side street*
el calor m *heat*
caluroso/a a *warm, hot*
calvo/a a *bald*
el calzado m *footwear*
calzar v *to wear (shoes etc.)*
los calzoncillos mpl *underpants*
la cama f *bed*
la cámara f *camera*
el/la camarero/a mf *waiter/ waitress*
el camarote m *cabin*
cambiar v *to change*
el cambio m *change, bureau de change*
caminar v *to walk*
la caminata f *long walk, hike*
el camino m *road, track, route*
el camión m *lorry*
la camioneta f *van*
la camisa f *shirt*
la camiseta f *T-shirt*
la campana f *bell*
la campaña f *campaign*
el/la campeón/a mf *champion*
el campeonato m *championship*
campesino/a a *rural*
el camping m *campsite*
el/la campista mf *camper*
el campo m *field, country*
la caña f *small glass of beer, stalk*
caña de pesca (r) *fishing rod*
el canal m *canal, channel*
la cancha f *court* cancha (de tenis etc.) *(tennis etc.) court, ground*
la canción f *song*
el cangrejo m *crab*
el canguro m *kangaroo* hacer de canguro *to baby-sit*
cansado/a a *tired*
cansador/a a *tiring*
el cansancio m *tiredness*
cansarse v *to get tired*
el/la cantante mf *singer*
cantar v *to sing*
la cantidad f *quantity*
la capa f *cloak, layer*
capacitar(se) vr *to prepare yourself, qualify*
capaz a *capable*
la cara f *face*
el caracol m *snail*
caramba excl *good gracious*

el caramelo m *sweet, caramel*
la cárcel f *prison*
cargar v *to load*
carillo/a a *a bit expensive*
cariñoso/a a *affectionate*
el carnaval m *carnival*
la carne f *meat* carne de cerdo *pork* carne de vaca *beef*
el carnet m *card* carnet de conducir *driving licence*
la carnicería f *butcher's*
el/la carnicero/a mf *butcher*
caro/a a *expensive*
la carpeta f *folder, file*
el carpintero m *carpenter*
la carrera f *run, race, course, career*
la carretera f *road* la carretera nacional *"A" road*
el carro m *cart*
la carta f *letter, menu, card*
las cartas fpl *playing cards*
cartearse (con) vr *to correspond*
el cartel m *poster*
la cartelera f *billboard*
la cartera f *wallet, schoolbag*
el cartón m *cardboard*
la casa f *house*
casado/a a *married*
el casamiento m *marriage, wedding*
casarse vr *to get married*
el casco m *helmet*
casi ad *almost*
la casilla f *pigeonhole, hut*
el caso m *case*
castaño/a a *chestnut brown*
las castañuelas fpl *castanets*
castellano/a a *Spanish, Castilian*
el castellano m *Spanish (language)*
castigar v *to punish*
el castigo m *punishment*
el castillo m *castle*
el catarro m *cold, catarrh*
cavar v *to dig*
la caza f *hunting*
cazar v *to hunt*
la cebolla f *onion*
(el ceda m) ceda el paso *give way*
celebrar v *to celebrate*
célebre a *famous*
celoso/a a *jealous*
la cena f *dinner, evening meal*
cenar v *to have dinner*
el cenicero m *ashtray*
la central telefónica f *telephone exchange*
el centro m *centre*
cepillar v *to brush*
el cepillo m *brush* cepillo de dientes *toothbrush*
cerca (de) ad *near (to)*
cercano/a a *close, nearby*
el cerdo m *pig*
el cereal m *cereal, grain*
la cereza f *cherry*
la cerilla f *(wax)match*
el cero m *zero*
cerrado/a a *closed* cerrado con llave *locked*
la cerradura f *lock*
cerrar v *to shut*
el certificado m *certificate*
la cerveza f *beer*
la cervezería f *bar, brewery*
cesar (de) v *to stop*
el césped m *lawn*
la cesta f *basket*
el cesto m *basket*
el chaleco m *waistcoat, vest*
el champiñon m *mushroom*
el champú m *shampoo*
la chaqueta f *jacket*
la charcutería f *pork butcher's, cooked pork products*
charlar v *to chat*
el cheque m *cheque* cheque de viaje *traveller's cheque*

la chica f *girl*
el chicle m *chewing gum*
el chico m *boy*
chillar v *to shriek, scream*
la chimenea f *chimney, fireplace*
el chisme m *thingummy*
el chiste m *joke*
chocar v *to collide, crash, shock*
el chófer m *driver*
el choque m *crash*
el chorizo m *spicy hard pork sausage*
el chubasco m *heavy shower*
la chuleta f *chop, cutlet*
el churro m *flour fritter*
el ciclismo m *cycling*
el/la ciclista mf *cyclist*
ciego/a a *blind*
el cielo m *sky, heaven*
cien a *100*
la ciencia f *science*
cierto conj *true, certain, sure*
la cifra f *figure, number*
el cigarrillo m *cigarette*
el cigarro m *cigarette, cigar*
la cima f *summit, peak*
el cine m *cinema*
la cintura f *waist*
el cinturón m *belt*
el circo m *circus*
la circulación f *traffic, circulation*
el círculo m *circle*
la ciruela f *plum*
el/la cirujano/a mf *surgeon*
la cita f *appointment, date*
citarse vr *to arrange to meet*
la ciudad f *city, large town*
el/la ciudadano/a mf *citizen*
claro/a a *clear, obvious, light (coloured)* ¡Claro! *Of course!*
la clase f *class, lesson*
clásico/a a *classical*
clasificar v *to classify*
el clavo m *nail*
el/la cliente mf *customer,client*
el clima m *climate*
climatizado/a a *air-conditioned*
la clínica f *clinic*
el club m *club*
cobarde a *cowardly*
el/la cobarde mf *coward*
el/la cobayo/a f *guinea pig*
el/la cobrador/a mf *train/ bus conductor*
cobrar v *to charge, collect (cash)*
el cobro revertido m *reverse charge*
el coche m *car*
cocido/a a *boiled, cooked*
el cocido m *stew*
la cocina f *kitchen, cookery, cooker*
cocinar v *to cook*
el/la cocinero/a mf *cook*
codiciado/a a *sought after*
el código m *code*
el codo m *elbow*
coger v *to take, pick, hold, catch*
el cojín m *cushion*
cojo/a a *lame*
la col f *cabbage*
la cola f *queue, tale, glue*
el colchón m *mattress*
coleccciónar m *to collect,*
el/la colega mf *colleague*
el colegio m *school, college*
colgar v *to hang, hang up, put down (phone)*
la coliflor f *cauliflower*
la colina f *hill*
el collar m *necklace*
colocar v *to place, arrange*
el color m *colour*
el columpio m *swing*
la comedia f *comedy, play*
el comedor m *dining room*
comenzar v *to begin*
comer v *to eat*

los comestibles mpl *food, groceries*
cometer v *to commit*
la comida f *food, meal, lunch*
el comienzo m *start*
la comisaría f *police station*
el comité m *committee*
como ad *how, like, as, about* ¿cómo? *How, pardon?*
la cómoda f *chest of drawers*
la comodidad f *comfort*
cómodo/a a *comfortable*
el/la compañero/a mf *companion*
la compañía f *company*
compartir v *to share, divide*
complicado/a a *complicated*
componer v *to compose, make up*
el comportamiento m *behaviour*
comportarse vr *to behave*
la compra f *purchase*
comprar v *to buy*
las compras fpl *shopping*
comprender v *to understand*
el comprimido m *pill, tablet*
comprobar v *to check, confirm*
el compromiso m *commitment*
la computadora f *computer*
con prep *with*
el concierto m *concert*
concurrido/a a *busy, crowded*
el concurso m *competition*
conducir v *to drive, lead*
el/la conductor/a mf *driver, motorist*
el conejo m *rabbit*
el conejillo de Indias m *guinea pig*
la confianza f *confidence*
confiar v *to trust*
la confitería f *sweet shop, confectionary*
confortable a *comfortable*
el congelador m *freezer*
congelar v *to freeze*
conjunto/a adj *joint, combined*
el conjunto m *group, outfit, team*
conmigo, contigo pron *with me, with you*
conocer v *to know, meet*
el conocimiento m *knowledge*
la consecuencia f *consequence*
conseguir v *to achieve, manage, get*
el consejo m *advice*
el conserje m *caretaker, janitor*
la consigna f *left-luggage office*
el constipado m *cold* estar constipado/a *to have a cold*
el/la constructor/a mf *builder*
construir v *to build*
el consulado m *consulate*
la contaminación f *pollution*
contar v *to count, tell*
contenido/a a *controlled, restrained*
el contenido m *contents*
el contestador automático m *telephone answering machine*
contestar v *to reply, answer*
continuar v *to continue*
contra prep *against*
el/la contrabandista mf *smuggler*
el contrabando m *smuggled goods,*
contrario/a a *opposing, opposite*
convencer *to convince*
la copa f *cup, trophy, wine glass* copa mundial *World Cup*
el corazón m *heart*
la corbata f *tie*
el corcho m *cork*
el/la cordero/a mf *lamb*
el cordón m *cord, string, wire*
el coro m *choir, chorus*
corregir v *to correct*
el correo m *post, mail* correo electrónico *email* correo aéreo *airmail*

Correos *post office*
correr v *to run*
el/la corresponsal mf *penfriend*
la corrida (de toros) f *bullfight*
el cortacésped m *lawnmower*
el cortalápiz m *pencil sharpener*
cortar v *to cut*
el corte de pelo m *haircut*
cortés a *polite*
la cortina f *curtain*
corto/a a *short*
la cosa f *thing*
coser v *to sew*
la costa f *coast*
costar v *to cost*
el coste m *cost*
costoso/a a *costly, expensive*
la costumbre f *custom*
la costura f *sewing*
cotidiano/a a *daily, everyday*
crear v *to create*
crecer v *to grow*
creer v *to think, believe*
crema a *cream, cream-coloured*
la crema f *cream* crema bronceadora *suntan lotion*
la cremallera f *zip*
la criada f *maid*
criar v *to bring up (children), raise*
el crimen m *crime*
el/la crío/a mf *child*
el cristal m *glass, window pane*
criticar v *to criticize*
el cruce m *junction (road)*
el crucigrama m *crossword*
la cruz f *cross* Cruz Roja *Red Cross*
cruzar v *to cross*
el cuaderno m *exercise book*
cuadrado/a a *square*
el cuadro m *square, picture, painting*
cual(es) pron (pl) *which, what*
la cualidad f *quality*
cualquier/a a *any*
cuando ad *when* ¿Cuándo? *When?*
cuanto/a a *how much*
cuarto/a a *fourth*
el cuarto m *room, quarter* cuarto de baño *bathroom* cuarto de hora *quarter of an hour*
cubierto/a a *covered, overcast*
el cubierto m *cover, place setting*
el cubo m *bucket, cube* cubo de basura *dustbin*
cubrir v *to cover*
la cucaracha f *cockroach*
la cuchara f *spoon*
la cucharada f *spoonful*
la cucharilla f *teaspoon*
el cuchillo m *knife*
el cuello m *neck*
la cuenta f *bill, sum, account*
el cuento m *short story*
la cuerda f *rope, string, cord*
el cuero m *leather*
el cuerpo m *body*
la cuesta f *slope, hill*
la cueva f *cave, wine cellar*
¡Cuidado! *Careful!*
cuidadoso/a a *careful*
cuidar v *to look after, take care of*
la culebra f *snake*
el culebrón m *soap opera*
la culpa f *blame*
culpable a *guilty*
cultivar v *to cultivate, grow*
la cumbre f *summit, top*
el cumpleaños m *birthday*
cumplido/a a *complete, full*
cumplir v *to carry out, complete*
el/la cuñado/a mf *bro/sister-in-law*

nouns — **m**: masculine   **f**: feminine   **pl**: plural   **v**: verb   **vr**: reflexive verb   **a**: adjective

el cura m *priest*
la cura f *cure*
 curar v *to cure*
la curiosidad f *curiosity*
el curso m *course*
el cursor m *slide (technical)*
la curva f *bend, curve*
 cuyo/a a *whose, of whom*

D

 dañar v *to harm, damage, spoil*
el daño m *harm, damage*
 dañoso/a a *damaging*
 dar v *to give*
 darse cuenta *to realize*
los datos mpl *facts, data*
 de prep *of, from*
 deber v *to owe, must, should*
el deber m *duty*
los deberes mpl *homework, duties.*
 débil a *weak*
una decena f *ten*
 decepcionado/a a *disappointed*
 decidir v *to decide*
 décimo/a a *tenth*
 decir v *to say*
el dedo m *finger*
 dedo del pie *toe*
 dejar v *to leave, allow* dejar de (hacer) *stop (doing)*
 dejar caer *drop*
el delantal m *apron*
 delante (de) *in front (of)*
 deletrear v *to spell*
 delgado/a a *thin, slim*
el delito m *crime, offence*
 demás a *other, others*
 demasiado ad *too, too much*
la demora f *delay*
 dentro (de) ad *inside*
 denunciar v *to report, denounce*
el/la dependiente/a mf *shop assistant*
el deporte m *sport*
el depósito m *tank (petrol), warehouse, deposit*
 deprisa ad *quickly*
la derecha f (der – abrev.) *right*
 derecho/a a *straight*
el derecho m *right, law, duty*
los derechos mpl *rights*
 desafortunado/a a *unfortunate*
 desagradable a *unpleasant*
 desaparecer v *to disappear*
la desaparición f *disappearance*
el desastre m *disaster*
 desastroso/a a *disastrous*
 desayunar v *to have breakfast*
el desayuno m *breakfast*
 descansar v *to rest*
el descanso m *rest, break*
 descolgar v *to pick up (phone), to unhook*
 desconfiar v *to distrust*
 desconocido/a a *unknown*
el/la desconocido/a mf *stranger*
 descortés/a a *impolite*
el descubrimiento m *discovery*
 descubrir v *to discover, uncover*
el descuento m *discount*
 descuidado/a a *careless, untidy*
 desde prep *from*
 desear v *to want*
 desempleado/a a *unemployed*
el desempleo m *unemployment*
 deshacer las maletas v *to unpack*
 desierto/a a *bleak, deserted*
el desierto m *desert*
 desmayarse v *to faint*
 desnudarse v *to get undressed*
el desodorante m *deodorant*
el despacho m *office, study*
 despacio ad *slowly*

 desparecido/a a *disappeared*
 despedirse vr *to say goodbye*
 despegar v *to take off (plane), unstick*
 despejado/a a *clear*
 despejar v *to clear*
el despertador m *alarm clock*
 despertarse vr *to wake up*
 desplazar v *to move, transfer*
 después (de) ad *after, later on*
 destruir v *to destroy*
el desván m *attic*
la desventaja f *disadvantage*
 desviar v *to divert*
el desvío m *diversion*
el detalle m *detail, small gift*
 detenerse vr *to stop*
 detestar v *to detest, hate*
 detrás (de) ad *behind*
 devolver v *to give back, return*
el día m *day*
la diapositiva f *slide (photographic)*
 diario/a a *daily*
el diario m *daily newspaper*
 dibujar v *to draw*
el dibujo m *drawing, art*
los dibujos animados m *cartoons*
el diciembre m *December*
el diente m *tooth*
 difícil a *difficult*
 ¡diga! v *speak* ¡dígame! *speak to me (when answering the phone)*
 dinámico/a a *dynamic*
el dinero m *money*
 dinero de bolsillo *pocket money*
 Dios m *God*
la dirección f *direction, address*
 dirección obligatoria *one-way*
 directo/a a *straight, direct*
el/la director/a mf *director, head*
 dirigir(se) v *to speak to, head for, go towards*
el disco m *record, disc* disco compacto/CD *compact disc*
 disculpar v *to forgive*
 disculparse vr *to apologize*
el discurso m *speech*
 discutir v *to argue*
el/la diseñador/a mf *designer*
 diseñar v *to design*
el diseño m *design, sketch*
 disfrutar v *to enjoy*
el disgusto m *quarrel, upset*
 disminuir v *to diminish*
 disponible a *available*
 dispuesto/a a *arranged, ready*
la disputa f *argument*
 distinguir v *to distinguish*
 distinto/a a (de) *different (from)*
la/s distracción / distracciones f/ fpl *entertainment*
 distribuir v *to distribute*
 divertido/a a *fun, funny, amusing*
 divertirse vr *to enjoy yourself*
 dividir v *to divide*
 divorciado/a a *divorced*
el DNI m (documento nacional de identidad) *ID (identity) card*
 doblar v *to turn, to fold*
 doble a *double*
la docena f *dozen*
el documental m *documentary*
 doler v *to hurt*
el dolor m *pain, ache*
el domicilio m *home, residence*
el domingo m *Sunday*
 donde ad *where*
 ¿dónde? *Where?*
 dormido/a a *asleep*
 dormir v *to sleep*
 dormirse vr *to go to sleep*
el dormitorio m *bedroom*
la droga f *drug*
el/la drogadicto/a mf *drug addict*
la droguería f *chemist's without a pharmacy, drugstore*

la ducha f *shower*
 ducharse vr *to have a shower*
 dudar v *to doubt*
el/la dueño/a mf *owner, landlord*
 dulce a/ad *sweet, soft, gentle*
 durante prep *during*
 durar v *to last*
 duro/a a *hard*

E

 echar v *to throw, throw away, put, pour, show*
 echar al buzón *to post* echar de menos *to miss*
 echar sangre *to bleed*
 echar una mirada/un vistazo *to glance*
la ecología f *ecology*
 económico/a a *economic, cheap*
la edad f *age*
el edificio m *building*
 EEUU abrev (mpl) *USA*
el efecto m *effect*
 eficaz a *effective, efficient*
 egoísta a *selfish*
el ejemplo m *example*
el ejercicio m *exercise*
el ejército m *army*
 el def. art. m *the*
el/la mío/a pron *mine*
la elección f *election*
la electricidad f *electricity*
 eléctrico/a a *electric, electrical*
 electrónico/a a *electronic*
el/la elefante/a mf *elephant*
 elegir v *to choose*
 elevado/a a *high, noble, important*
 embarazada a *pregnant*
 emborracharse vr *to get drunk*
el embotellamiento m *traffic jam*
 emigrar v *to emigrate*
 emocionante a *moving, exciting*
 emparejar v *to pair, match*
el empate m *draw (match)*
 empezar v *to begin*
el/la empleado/a mf *employee*
 emplear v *to employ*
el empleo m *employment, work, job*
la empresa f *company, enterprise*
el/la empresario/a mf *businessman*
 empujar v *to push*
 en prep *in, on*
 enamorado/a (de) a *in love (with)*
 enamorarse (de) vr *to fall in love (with)*
 encantado/a a *delighted*
 encantar v *to bewitch* me encanta *I love*
el/la encargado/a mf *manager*
 encender v *to light, turn on, ignite*
 encerrar v *to shut (up), enclose*
 enchufar v *to plug in*
el enchufe m *plug, socket*
 encima (de) ad *on, above, over*
 encoger(se) vr *to shrug*
 encontrar v *to find*
 encontrarse *to find, meet, be*
el encuentro m *meeting*
la encuesta f *survey*
el/la enemigo/a mf *enemy*
la energía f *energy*
 enero m *January*
 enfadarse vr *to get angry*
la enfermedad f *illness*
el/la enfermero/a a *nurse*
 enfermo/a a *ill*
 enfrente ad *opposite, in front*
 engañar v *to deceive, trick*
 enganchar v *to hook (up)*
 ¡Enhorabuena! *Congratulations!*
 enojar v *to anger*
 enojarse vr *to get angry*

la ensalada f *salad*
el ensayo m *essay, test, trial*
la enseñanza f *education, teaching*
 enseñar v *to teach, show*
 ensuciar v *to dirty, get dirty*
 entender v *understand*
 entonces ad *then, after*
el entorno m *environs, surroundings*
la entrada f *entry, entrance, ticket*
 entrar v *to enter*
 entre prep *between, among*
la entrega f *delivery, handover*
 entregar v *to deliver, hand over*
el entremés m *interlude*
los entremeses mpl *hors d'oeuvres*
 entrenarse vr *to train*
 entretanto ad *meanwhile*
la entrevista f *interview*
 enviar v *to send*
 envolver v *to wrap (up)*
la época f *age, period*
 equipado/a a *equipped*
el equipaje m *luggage*
el equipo m *team, equipment*
la equis f *"X"*
la equitación f *horse riding*
 equivocarse vr *to make a mistake*
la escala f *scale, stopover (on trip)*
 escalar v *to climb*
la escalera f *stairs, ladder*
 escapar(se) v *to escape, leak*
el escaparate m *shop window*
la escarcha f *frost*
la escena f *scene*
 escoger v *to choose*
 esconder v *to hide*
 escribir v *to write*
 escribir a máquina *to type*
el/la escritor/a mf *writer*
el escritorio m *desk, bureau*
 escuchar v *to listen (to), hear*
la escuela f *school*
el/la escultor/a mf *sculptor*
la escultura f *sculpture*
la ese f *"S"*
 ese/a a *that* ése/a pron *that one*
el esfuerzo m *effort*
la esgrima f *fencing, swordfighting*
 eso pron *that*
el espacio m *space* espacio en blanco *blank space*
la espalda f *back*
 espantar v *to scare*
 espantoso/a a *frightening, scary*
el esparadrapo m *sticking plaster*
el espárrago m *asparagus*
la especialidad f *speciality*
la especie f *type, species*
el espectáculo m *show, performance*
el espejo m *mirror*
la esperanza f *hope*
 esperar v *to hope, expect, wait for*
 espeso/a a *thick, heavy*
las espinacas fpl *spinach*
el espíritu m *spirit, mind*
el/la esposo/a mf *husband, wife*
el esquí m *skiing*
 esquiar v *to ski*
la esquina f *corner*
la estación f *station* estación del año *season of the year*
el estacionamiento m *car park*
 estacionar v *to park*
el estadio m *stadium*
el estado m *state* (civil) *marital*
 estadounidense a *US citizen*
 estallar v *to explode, burst*
la estancia f *stay, ranch*
el estanco m *tobacco/cigaretteshop*
 estar v *to be*

la estatua f *statue*
 este/a a *this*
 éste/a pron *this one*
el este m *the East*
el estéreo m *stereo*
el estilo m *style*
 esto pron *this*
el estómago m *stomach*
 estrecho/a a *narrow*
la estrella f *star*
 estremecer v *to shake, shudder*
 estrenar v *to wear/use something for the first time*
el estrés m *stress*
 estricto/a a *strict*
 estropear v *to spoil/damage/break*
el estuche m *case (for glasses etc)*
el/la estudiante mf *student*
 estudiar v *to study*
el estudio m *study*
los estudios mpl *studies*
 estupendo/a a *wonderful*
 estúpido/a a *stupid*
la etapa f *stage, phase*
la ética f *ethics*
 evitar v *to avoid*
 exagerar v *to exaggerate*
el examen m *examination*
 exigente a *demanding*
 exigir v *to demand*
el éxito m *success*
 experimentado/a a *experienced*
la explicación f *explanation*
 explicar v *to explain*
 exponer v *to display, exhibit*
la exposición f *exhibition*
el expreso m *express train*
el extracto m *extract*
 extranjero/a a *foreign*
el/la extranjero/a mf *foreigner*
 extraño/a a *strange*

F

la fábrica f *factory*
 fabricar v *to manufacture*
 fácil a *easy*
la faena f *task, chore*
la falda f *skirt*
la falta f *lack*
 faltar v *to lack, be missing, need*
la fama f *fame*
la familia f *family*
los familiares mpl *relations, relatives*
 famoso/a a *famous*
el/la farmacéutico/a mf *chemist*
la farmacia f *chemist's*
el faro m *headlamp, lighthouse*
 fastidiar v *to annoy*
 febrero m *February*
la fecha f *date*
la felicidad f *happiness*
 felicidades/felicitaciones *congratulations*
 felicitar v *to congratulate*
 feliz a *happy*
 feo/a a *ugly*
la feria f *fair, festival, market*
el ferrocarril m *railway*
la festividad f *festivity, holiday*
la fianza f *deposit, bond*
 fiarse vr *to trust*
la ficha f *file, counter, token*
la fiebre f *fever, temperature*
la fiesta f *party, holiday, festival*
 fijar v *to fix, focus*
la fila f *line, row*
el filete m *fillet*
el fin m *end*
 fin de semana *weekend*
la finca f *farm*
la firma f *company, signature*
 firmar v *to sign*
la física f *physics*
 físico/a a *physical*
el/la físico/a mf *physicist*

---

nouns — **m**: *masculine*   **f**: *feminine*   **pl**: *plural*   **v**: *verb*   **vr**: *reflexive verb*   **a**: *adjective* | Spanish–English Dictionary |

flaco/a a *thin, skinny*
el flan m *crème caramel*
la flauta f *flute, recorder*
la flecha f *arrow*
flojo/a a *loose, weak*
la flor f *flower*
(silvestre) *wild flower*
el/la florero/a mf *florist*
el florero m *vase*
flotar v *to float*
el folleto m *brochure*
el fondo m *end, bottom, back*
el/la fontanero/a mf *plumber*
el/la forastero/a m *stranger, outsider*
la forma f *shape, way, method, form*
la formación f *training*
el formulario m *form*
forzar v *to force*
el fósforo m *match*
fracasar v *to make a mess of, fail*
la frambuesa f *raspberry*
franco/a a *frank, honest*
la frase f *phrase*
el fregadero m *sink*
fregar v *to wash*
freír f *to fry*
frenar v *to brake*
la frente f *forehead*
el frente m *front*
la fresa f *strawberry*
fresco/a a *fresh, cool*
el frigorífico m *refrigerator*
el frigo *fridge*
frío/a a *cold*
la fruta f *fruit*
la frutería f *fruit shop, greengrocer's*
el fuego m *fire*
fuegos artificiales *fireworks*
la fuente f *fountain, dish, source*
fuera (de) ad *outside (of)*
fuerte a *strong*
la fuerza f *strength, force*
el/la fumador/a mf *smoker*
fumadores mpl *smoking compartment*
fumar v *to smoke*
el/la funcionario/a mf *civil servant*
fundir v *to melt*
el futuro m *future*

G

las gafas fpl *(eye)glasses* gafas de sol *sunglasses*
la galería (de arte) f *(art) gallery*
la galleta f *biscuit*
la gallina f *hen*
el gallo m *cockerel*
la gamba f *prawn*
el gamberro m *hooligan*
(la gana f) con ganas *with enthusiasm*
el/la ganador/a mf *winner*
ganar v *to earn, win*
ganarse la vida *to earn a living*
la ganga f *bargain*
el ganso m *goose*
el garaje m *garage*
el/la garajista f *garage owner/attendant*
la garganta f *throat*
la gaseosa f *fizzy drink, soda*
la gasolina f *petrol* gasolina sin plomo *lead free petrol*
la gasolinera f *petrol station*
gastado/a a *worn, used*
gastar v *to spend (money), wear away*
el gasto m *expense, expenditure*
el/la gato/a mf *cat*
el gazpacho m *cold spicy soup*
el/la gemelo/a mf *twin*
generoso/a a *generous*
la gente f *people*
el/la gerente mf *manager*
el gimnasio m *gymnasium, gym*
la gimnasia f *gymnastics, P.E.*

la gimnástica f *gymnastics*
girar v *to turn, go round, spin*
la glorieta f *(large)roundabout*
el gobierno m *government*
el gol m *goal*
goloso/a a *sweet-toothed, greedy*
golpear v *to hit*
la goma f *glue, rubber*
goma (de borrar) f *eraser, rubber*
gordo/a a *fat*
la gota f *drop*
gozar v *to enjoy*
las gracias fpl *thanks*
Gracias *Thankyou*
gracioso/a a *funny*
el grado m *degree, stage, grade*
el gramo m *gramme*
grande a *big, great*
los grandes almacenes *dept stores*
el granizo m *hail*
la granja f *farm*
el/la granjero/a mf *farmer*
la grasa f *fat, grease*
gratis a/ad *free, for nothing*
grato/a a *pleasing*
gratuito/a a *free*
el grifo m *tap*
la gripe f *flu, influenza*
gris a *grey*
gritar v *to shout*
el grito m *shout*
grosero/a a *rude, vulgar*
grueso/a a *thick, stout, fat*
el grupo m *group*
el guante m *glove*
guapo/a a *beautiful, handsome*
guardar v *to guard, put away*
el guardarropa m *wardrobe, cloakroom*
la guardería f *nursery, play school*
el/la guardia mf *policeman/woman, guard* guardia civil *civil guard*
guay excl *great!, wonderful!*
la guerra f *war*
el/la guía mf *guide*
la guía (turística) f *guidebook*
guiar v *to guide*
el guisante m *pea*
la guitarra f *guitar*
gustar v *to like*
el gusto m *taste, pleasure*

H

la haba f *broad bean*
haber aux v *to have*
hábil a *skilful*
la habitación f *room, bedroom*
el habla f *speech, language*
hablar v *to talk, speak*
hacer v *to do, make*
hacerse vr *to become*
hacerse daño *to hurt yourself*
hacia prep *towards, about*
hallar v *to find*
hallarse vr *to be, find yourself*
el hambre f *hunger*
la hamburguesa f *hamburger*
la harina f *flour*
harto/a a *fed up, tired (of), full up*
hasta prep *until, up to*
hay v *there is, there are*
el haz m *bundle*
he ad he aquí *here is, here are*
el hecho m *deed, fact*
el helado m *ice-cream*
helar v *to freeze*
la herida f *wound, injury*
herir v *to wound, hurt, injure*
herirse vr *to injure yourself*
el/la hermano/a mf *brother/sister*
el/la hermanastra/o mf *stepbrother/sister*
hermoso/a a *beautiful*
la herramienta f *tool*

hervir v *to boil*
el hidrodeslizador m *hovercraft*
el hielo m *ice*
la hierba f *grass*
el hierro m *iron*
el hígado m *liver*
el higo m *fig*
el/la hijo/a mf *son/daughter*
hijo/a único/a *only child* mf
el hilo m *thread, yarn*
el/la hincha mf *fan*
hinchar v *to inflate*
el hipermercado m *hypermarket*
la historia f *story, history*
el hogar m *home, hearth*
la hoja f *leaf* hoja de solicitud *application form*
hola excl *hello!*
el hombre m *man*
el hombro m *shoulder*
honesto/a a *honest*
honrado/a a *honourable, honest*
la hora f *hour*
hora de comer *lunch time*
hora punta *rush hour*
el horario m *timetable*
el horno m *oven*
horroroso/a a *dreadful, horrible*
la hortaliza f *vegetable*
hortalizas *garden produce*
hoy ad *today*
la huelga f *strike*
el huerto m *kitchen garden*
el hueso m *bone, stone (in fruit)*
el huésped m *guest*
el huevo m *egg*
la huida f *flight, escape*
huir v *to escape, flee*
húmedo a *damp*
el humo m *smoke*

I

la ida f *departure*
la identidad f *identity*
el idioma m *language*
la iglesia f *church*
ignorar v *to not know, ignore*
igual (a) a *equal (to)*
la imagen f *image*
impedir v *to prevent*
el impermeable m *raincoat*
imprescindible a *vital, essential*
impresionante a *impressive*
la impresora f *printer*
imprimir v *to print*
el impuesto m *tax, duty*
el incendio m *fire*
inclinar v *to lean, incline*
incluido/a a *included*
incluir v *to include*
incluso ad *even*
increíble a *incredible*
indicar v *to indicate, show*
el individuo m *individual*
la industria f *industry*
informar v *to inform*
informarse vr *to find out, get info*
la informática f *computing, IT*
el informe m *report*
el/la ingeniero/a mf *engineer*
Inglaterra f *England*
el inglés m *English (language)*
el/la inglés/esa mf *Englishman/woman*
el/la ingeniero/a mf *engineer*
el ingreso m *admission, entry,*
los ingresos *income*
injusto/a a *unjust, unfair*
inmediatamente ad *immediately*
inmenso/a a *immense*
inmóvil a *immobile, unmoving*
inquieto/a a *worried, unsettled*
la insignia f *badge, emblem*
la insolación f *sunstroke*
insoportable a *unbearable*
las instalaciones fpl *facilities*

instalar v *to install*
el instituto m *secondary school, college*
intentar v *to try*
intercambiar v *to exchange, swap*
el intercambio m *exchange*
interesar v *to interest*
interesarse vr *to be interested in*
el/la interno/a mf *boarder*
intervenir v *intervene, take part in*
introducir v *to insert, enter*
la inundación f *flood*
inútil a *useless*
el invierno m *winter*
la inyección f *injection*
ir v *to go* ir a + infinitive *to be going to (Future Tense)*
las Islas Baleares fpl *Balearic Isles*
las Islas Canarias fpl *Canary Islands*
irritar v *to irritate*
la isla f *island*
irse vr *to go away, leave*
el IVA m (impuesto sobre el valor añadido) *VAT*
la izquierda f *left*

J

el jabón m *soap*
jamás ad *never*
el jamón m *ham*
el jarabe m *syrup, cough syrup*
el jardín m *garden*
el jarro m *jug*
la jaula f *cage*
el/la jefe/a mf *boss, head, manager*
joven a *young*
el/la joven mf *young man/woman*
la joya f *jewel* joyas *jewels, jewellery*
la joyería f *jewellery, jeweller's shop*
jubilarse vr *to retire*
la judía f *bean*
el/la judío/a mf *Jewish man/woman*
el juego m *game, play*
el jueves m *Thursday*
el/la juez(a) mf *judge*
el/la jugador/a *player*
jugar v *to play*
el jugo m *juice*
el juguete m *toy*
julio m *July*
junio m *June*
junto/a a *together*
junto (a) ad *near, next/close(to)*
justo/a a *just, exactly*
la juventud f *youth*
juzgar v *to judge*

K

el kilo m *kilo*
el kilómetro m *kilometre*

L

la art def *the (fem)*
el labio m *lip*
el lado m *side*
el ladrillo m *brick*
el ladrón m *thief*
el lago m *lake*
la lágrima f *tear*
lamentar v *to regret, be sorry*
la lámpara f *lamp*
la lana f *wool*
la langosta f *lobster, locust*
lanzar v *to throw, launch*
el lápiz m *pencil*
largo/a a *long*
la lástima f *pity, shame*
la lata f *tin, can*
el latín m *Latin*
latinoamericano/a a *Latin American*
el lavabo m *washbasin, washroom*
el lavado m *washing*

la lavadora f *washing machine*
la lavandería f *laundry, launderette*
el lavaplatos m *dishwasher*
lavar v *to wash*
lavarse vr *to get washed*
el lavavajillas m *dishwasher*
la lección f *lesson*
la leche f *milk*
la lechería f *dairy*
la lechuga f *lettuce*
la lectura f *reading*
leer v *to read*
la legumbre f *pulse, vegetable*
lejano/a a *distant*
lejos (de) ad *far, far away(from)*
la lengua f *language, tongue*
las lentes de contacto fpl / la lentilla f *contact lenses/lens*
lento/a a *slow*
el león m *lion*
la letra f *letter*
levantar v *to lift*
levantarse vr *to get up*
la ley f *law*
liberar v *to free, release*
la libra (esterlina) f *pound (sterling)*
libre f *free, available*
la librería f *bookshop, bookcase*
el libro m *book*
el/la licenciado/a mf *graduate*
la licenciatura f *degree*
la liga f *league*
ligero/a a *light, delicate, quick*
el limón m *lemon*
la limonada f *lemonade*
limpiar v *to clean*
la limpieza a seco f *dry cleaning*
limpio/a a *clean*
la línea f *line*
la linterna f *torch, lantern*
la liquidación f *sale*
liso/a a *smooth, straight*
la lista f *list*
listo/a a *ready, clever*
el litro m *litre*
la llamada f *call*
llamar v *to call, phone, knock*
llamarse vr *to be called*
la llave f *key*
el llavero m *key ring*
la llegada f *arrival*
llegar v *to arrive*
llegar a *come to*
llenar *to fill, fill up*
lleno/a a *full*
llevar v *to wear, carry, take*
llevarse vr *to get on with*
llorar v *to cry*
llover v *to rain* llover a cántaros *to rain cats and dogs*
lloviznar v *to drizzle*
la lluvia f *rain*
lluvioso/a a *rainy*
lo art def
loco/a a *mad*
lograr v *to achieve, obtain*
la loncha f *slice*
Londres m *London*
la lonja f *slice*
la lotería f *lottery*
la lucha f *fight, battle, struggle*
luchar v *to fight, struggle*
luego ad *then, after*
luego con *therefore*
el lugar m *place*
el lujo m *luxury*
lujoso/a a *luxurious*
la luna f *moon*
el lunes m *Monday*
la luz f *light*

M

la madera f *wood, timber*
la madrastra f *stepmother*
la madre f *mother*
la madrugada f *early morning*
madrugar v *to get up early*
maduro/a a *mature, ripe*

el/la maestro/a mf
primary teacher, maestro
el magnetofón/magnetofono m
tape recorder
el magnetoscopio m
video recorder
magnífico/a a *magnificent*
mal ad *badly, ill*
la maleta f *suitcase*
el maletero m *car boot*
malhumorado/a a
bad-tempered
malo/a a *bad, wrong, ill,
naughty*
la mamá f *mum, mummy*
la mancha f *stain*
manchar v *to stain*
mandar v *to send/order/be in
charge*
manejar v *to use, handle*
la manera f *way, method*
la manifestación f *demonstration*
manifestar v *to show,
demonstrate*
la mano f *hand*
la manta f *blanket*
el mantel m *tablecloth*
mantener v *to maintain/hold/
keep*
mantenerse vr *to stay, remain*
la mantequilla f *butter*
la manzana f *apple,
block of houses*
el manzano m *apple tree*
mañana ad *tomorrow*
la mañana f *morning*
el maquillaje m *make-up*
maquillarse v *to put on make-up*
la máquina f *machine*
el mar m *sea*
maravilloso/a a *marvellous*
la marca f *make, brand, mark*
marcar v *to dial, score, mark*
marcar una señal *put a sign*
la marcha f *march, progress,
departure*
marcha atrás *reverse*
marcharse v *to leave, go away*
la marea f *tide*
mareado/a a *dizzy, travel-sick*
marearse vr *to feel sick, dizzy*
el mareo m *dizziness, sickness*
el marido m *husband*
el/la marinero/a mf *sailor*
los mariscos mpl *seafood*
marrón a *brown*
el martes m *Tuesday*
marzo m *March*
más a/ad *more*
más allá *further away*
más o menos *more or less*
el matador m *bull-fighter*
matar v *to kill*
la matrícula f *registration,
enrolment, car registration
number*
el matrimonio m *marriage*
mayo m *May*
el/la mayor mf *oldest, eldest*
la mayoría f *the majority*
me pron *me, to me*
me da igual *I don't mind*
me gusta mucho
I like it/him/her a lot
el/la mecánico/a mf *mechanic*
el mechero m *cigarette lighter*
la media pensión f *half board*
mediano/a a *medium,
average*
las medias fpl *tights, stockings*
el medicamento m *medicine*
el/la médico/a mf *doctor*
la medida f *measure,
measurement*
medio/a a *half*
el medio m *middle, centre, way*
medio ambiente *environment*
el mediodía m *midday*
medir v *to measure*
la mejilla f *cheek*
el mejillón m *mussel*

mejor a *best*
mejorar v *to improve*
mejorarse vr *to get better*
el mellizo/a mf *twin*
el melocotón m *peach*
el melón m *melon*
mencionar v *to mention*
menor a *younger, smaller*
el/la menor mf *youngest,
smallest*
menos ad *less*
al menos *at least* menos
cuarto *quarter to*
el mensaje m *message*
mensaje electrónico *email*
mentir v *to lie*
la mentira f *lie*
mentiroso/a a *untruthful, lying*
el menú m *menu*
el mercado m *market*
merecer v *to deserve*
la merienda f *teatime snack*
la mermelada f *jam*
el mes m *month*
la mesa f *table*
meter v *to put in, insert*
el método m *method*
el metro m *metre, underground*
mezclar v *to mix*
mezquino/a a *mean, miserly*
el microondas m *microwave*
el miedo m *fear*
la miel f *honey*
el/la miembro/a mf *member*
mientras conj *while,
meanwhile*
mientras que *while*
el miércoles m *Wednesday*
militar a *military*
la milla f *mile*
el millón m *million*
el/la minero/a mf *miner*
mínimo/a a *minimum, minute*
el/la ministro/a mf *minister*
minusválido/a a *disabled*
mirar v *to look at, look, watch*
la misa f *mass*
mismo/a a *same, very, self*
misterioso/a a *mysterious*
la mitad f *half*
mixto/a a *mixed*
la mochila f *backpack, rucksack*
la moda f *fashion*
el modelo m *model*
el modo m *way, method, type*
mojado/a a *damp, wet, soaked*
mojarse vr *to get wet*
molestar v *to trouble, disturb*
molestarse vr *to get upset,
trouble yourself*
la molestia f *bother, trouble*
la moneda f *coin*
el monedero m *purse*
el/la monitor/a *instructor, coach*
mono/a a *pretty*
el monopatín m *skateboard*
montar v *to ride, put together*
el monte m *mountain, hill*
el montón m *pile, large amount*
el monumento m *monument*
la moqueta f *fitted carpet*
morado/a a *purple*
morder v *to bite*
moreno/a a
dark-haired, brunette, tanned
morir v *to die*
la mosca f *fly*
la mostaza f *mustard*
el mostrador m *counter*
mostrar v *to show*
la moto(cicleta) f *motorbike*
mover v *to move*
móvil a *mobile*
el/la mozo/a mf *waiter/'tress,
porter*
el/la muchacho/a mf *boy/girl*
la muchedumbre f *crowd*
mucho/a a *a lot, many*
la mudanza f *house move*
mudar v *to change*

mudarse de casa *move
house*
el mueble m *piece of furniture*
la muela f *tooth, back tooth*
la muerte f *death*
muerto/a a *dead*
la mujer f *woman, wife*
la multa f *fine*
el mundo m *the world*
la muñeca f *doll, wrist*
el muro m *wall*
el museo m *museum*
muy a *very*

N

nacer v *to be born*
nacido/a a *born*
el nacimiento m *birth*
la nación f *nation*
la nacionalidad f *nationality*
las Naciones Unidas fpl *UN*
nada pron *nothing*
nada ad *not at all*
de nada *don't mention it*
nadar v *to swim*
nadie pron *nobody*
el naipe m *playing card*
la naranja f *orange*
la nariz f *nose*
la nata f *cream*
la natación f *swimming*
la naturaleza f *nature*
la Navidad f *Christmas*
la neblina f *mist*
necesario/a a *necessary*
negar(se) vr *to deny (refuse)*
el negocio m *business, shop*
negro/a a *black*
el neumático m *tyre*
nevar v *to snow*
la nevera f *refrigerator*
ni conj *neither, nor*
¡ni hablar! *no way!*
la niebla f *fog*
el/la nieto/a mf *grandson/
daughter*
la nieve f *snow*
el nilón m *nylon*
la niñez f *childhood*
ninguno/a a *none, no*
el/la niño/a mf *boy, girl*
el nivel m *level*
no ad *no, not* no cuelgue *don't
hang up, please hold*
no hay de qué *don't mention it*
no importa *it doesn't matter*
no me importa *I don't mind*
la noche f *night*
la Nochebuena f *Christmas Eve*
la Nochevieja f *New Year's Eve*
el nombre m *name* nombre de
pila *first name, Christian name*
el nor(d)este m *north-east*
el noroeste m *north-west*
el norte m *north*
la nota f *note, mark, grade*
notar v *to notice*
la noticia f *piece of news*
la novela f *novel*
noveno/a a *ninth*
noviembre m *November*
el/la novio/a mf *fiancé(e), boy/
girlfriend*
la nube f *cloud*
nublado a *cloudy, overcast(sky)*
nuboso a *cloudy*
la nuera f *daughter-in-law*
nuevo/a a *new*
la nuez f *walnut*
el número m *number
(zapatos) shoesize*
nunca ad *never*

O

la o f *o (the letter)*
o/u conj *or* o....o
either......or
obedecer v *to obey*
el objeto m *object, aim*
la obra f *work, deed* obra de
teatro *play, theatrical
production*

el/la obrero/a mf *workman/
woman*
la ocurrencia f *idea*
ocho a *eight*
el ocio m *leisure*
octavo/a a *eighth*
octubre m *October*
ocupado/a a *occupied,
engaged*
ocuparse de v *to look after*
ocurrir v *to happen, occur*
odiar v *to hate*
el oeste m *west*
la oferta f *offer*
la oficina f *office*
ofrecer v *to offer*
el oído m *ear (inner)*
¡Oiga! (v) excl *Listen!
Excuse me!*
oír v *to hear, listen to*
¡Ojalá! excl *I wish! I hope so!*
el ojo m *eye* ¡Ojo! *Look out!*
la ola f *wave*
¡Olé! excl *Hooray!*
oler v *to smell*
el olor m *smell*
olvidar v / olvidarse de vr *to
forget*
la ONU f (Organización de las
Naciones Unidas) *UN*
opinar v *to think, give your
opinion*
la oportunidad f *opportunity*
la orden f *order (command)*
ordenar v *to arrange, order*
la oreja f *ear (outer)*
el orgullo m *pride*
orgulloso/a a *proud*
el origen m *origin*
la orilla f *bank, edge*
el oro m *gold*
la orquesta f *orchestra*
os pron *you, to you*
la oscuridad f *dark, darkness*
oscuro/a a *dark*
el oso m *bear*
la ostra f *oyster*
el otoño m *Autumn*
otro/a a *other, another*
la oveja f *sheep*

P

el/la paciente mf *patient*
pacífico/a a *peaceful*
el padrastro m *stepfather*
el padre m *father*
la paella f *paella (rice dish)*
la paga f *pay, wages,
pocket money*
pagar v *to pay*
la página f *page*
el pago m *payment*
el país m *country*
el paisaje m *landscape*
el pájaro m *bird*
la palabra f *word*
el palacio m *palace*
pálido/a a *pale*
el pan m *bread*
la panadería f *bakery, baker's*
el/la panadero/a mf *baker*
el panecillo m *(bread) roll*
la pantalla f *screen*
el pantalon m / los pantalones
mpl *trousers* pantalón corto/
pantalones cortos *shorts*
el panti/panty m / los pantys
tights
el pañuelo m *handkerchief,
headscarf*
el papá m *daddy*
el Papa m *Pope*
el papel m *paper*
la papelera f *wastepaper
basket/bin*
la papelería f *stationer's,
stationery*
el/la papelero/a mf *stationer*
el paquete m *packet, parcel*
el par m *pair, couple*
para prep *for, in order to,*

so that
el parabrisas m *windscreen*
la parada f *stop*
parada de autobuses *bus-stop*
parado/a a *stopped, still,
unemployed*
el parador m *(state-run) hotel*
el paraguas m *umbrella*
parar v *to stop*
pararse vr *to stop,
come to a stop*
parecer v *to seem, appear,
look like*
me parece *it seems to me*
parecerse a vr *to look like*
parecido/a a *similar*
la pared f *wall*
la pareja f *couple, partner*
el/la pariente/a mf *relative,
relation*
el paro m *unemployment,
stoppage*
el parque m *park*
la parrilla f *grill*
la parte f *part*
el partido m *match/game,
party (political)*
pasado/a a *past, last* pasado
mañana *the day after tomorrow*
el pasado m *the past*
el/la pasajero/a mf *passenger*
pasar v *to pass, spend (time),
happen*
pasar (la) lista *to take the
register*
pasar (por) *to go past, through*
pasar la aspiradora *to vacuum*
pasarlo bien *to have a
good time*
el pasatiempo m *hobby, pastime*
pasear v *to take a walk*
pasearse vr *to go for a walk/
stroll*
el paseo m *walk, stroll*
el pasillo m *corridor*
el paso m *step, way* paso a nivel
level crossing paso de
peatones
pedestrian crossing paso
prohibido *no entry* paso
subterráneo *subway*
la pasta de dientes f *toothpaste*
el pastel m *cake, pie*
la pastelería f *baker's, cake shop*
la pastilla f *tablet, pill*
la pata f *leg (animal/furniture)*
la patada f *kick*
la patata f *potato*
patatas fritas *chips, crisps*
el paté m *paté*
el patín m *skate*
patín de ruedas *roller skate*
el patinaje m *skating*
patinar v *to skate*
el pato m *duck*
el/la patrón/ona mf *employer,
owner, landlord/lady*
la pausa f *pause, break*
el pavo m *turkey*
el/la payaso/a mf *clown*
la paz f *peace*
el peaje m *toll*
el peatón m *pedestrian*
el pecho m *chest*
el pedazo m *piece*
el pedido m *order, request*
pedir v *to order, ask for*
pedir prestado *to borrow*
pegar v *to stick, hit*
pegar fuego *to set fire to*
el peinado m *hairdo*
peinarse vr *to comb your hair*
el peine m *comb*
pelar v *to peel*
la pelea f *quarrel, fight*
pelear v *to quarrel, fight*
la película f *film*
el peligro m *danger*
peligroso/a a *dangerous*
pelirrojo/a a *red-haired*
el pelo m *hair*

---

nouns — **m**: masculine   **f**: feminine   **pl**: plural   **v**: verb   **vr**: reflexive verb   **a**: adjective | *Spanish–English Dictionary* |

la pelota f ball
la peluquería f hairdresser's
la pena f sorrow, shame
la pendiente f slope
el pendiente m earring
pensar v to think
la pensión f guest house
peor a worse, worst
pequeño/a a small, little
la pera f pear
percibir v to perceive, notice
perder v to lose
la pérdida f loss
perdón excl sorry! pardon me
perdonar v to forgive
perezoso/a a lazy
la perfumería f perfume shop
el periódico m newspaper
el/la periodista mf journalist
el periquito m parakeet
permanecer v to stay, remain
el permiso m permission, licence
permitido/a a permitted,
   allowed
permitir v to allow
pero conj but
el/la perro/a mf dog
la persiana f (Venetian) blind
el personaje m celebrity,
   character
el personal m staff, personnel
pertenecer v to belong
la pesadilla f nightmare
pesado/a a heavy, difficult,
   boring
pesar v to weigh
la pesca f fishing
la pescadería f fishmonger's
el pescado m
   fish (dead, for cooking/eating)
el/la pescador/a mf fisherman
pescar v to fish
el peso m weight
el petróleo m oil, petroleum
el pez m fish pez de colores /
   pez dorado goldfish
la picadura f prick, sting, bite
picante a hot, spicy
picar v to sting, bite, prick
picar un billete to clip a ticket
el pico m beak, peak son las dos
   y pico it's just after two
el pie m foot
la piedra f stone, rock
la piel f skin
la pierna f leg
- la pieza f piece
la pila f sink, battery
la píldora f pill
la pimienta f pepper (spice)
el pimiento m pepper (vegetable)
la piña f pineapple
   pinchar v to get a puncture
el pinchazo m puncture
pintado/a a painted
el pintalabios m lipstick
pintar v to paint
el/la pintor/a mf painter
pintoresco/a a picturesque
la pintura f painting, paint
la pipa f pipe, pip, seed
los Pirineos mpl the Pyrenees
pisar v to walk on, tread on
la piscina f swimming pool
el piso m flat, floor
la pista f court, track, piste
   pista de hielo ice rink
   pista de patinar skating rink
la pizarra f blackboard
el placer m pleasure
la plancha f iron, grill
planchar v to iron
plano/a a flat
el plano m plan, map
   planta baja ground floor
la plata f silver
el plátano m banana
el platillo m saucer
el plato m plate, dish, course
   plato combinado
   one course set meal

plato del día dish of the day
la playa f beach
la plaza f square
   plaza de toros bullring
   plaza mayor main square
el plomo m lead
la pluma f feather, pen
la población f population
pobre a poor
la pobreza f poverty
poco/a a little, few
poco ad little poco hecho rare,
   slightly cooked
poco m un poco a little
poder v to be able, can
la policía f the police,
   policewoman
el policía m policeman
el polideportivo m sports centre
el/la político/a mf politician
el pollo m chicken
el polvo m dust
la pomada f ointment, cream
el pomelo m grapefruit
poner v to put
   poner la mesa lay the table
   ponerse vr to become
   ponerse a to begin to ponerse
   la ropa to put clothes on
por prep for, through, by, along
   por ciento percent
el porcentaje m percentage
porque conj because
el portamonedas m purse
portátil a portable
el/la portero/a mf caretaker,
   concierge
la portezuela f small door (train)
el porvenir m future
la posibilidad f possibility
la postal f postcard
el postre m sweet, dessert
potable a drinkable, drinking
practicar v to practise
práctico/a a practical
el prado m meadow, pasture
el precio m price
   preciso/a a necessary, precise
predilecto/a a favourite
preferido/a a favourite
preferir v to prefer
la pregunta f question
preguntar v to ask
   preguntarse vr to wonder
el premio m prize
la prensa f the press,
   newspapers
la preocupación f worry
preocupar v to worry, trouble
   preocuparse vr to worry
prescindir de v to do without
la presentación (oral) f
   presentation
presentar v to present,
   introduce
   presentarse vr (para un
   empleo) to turn up (for a job)
la presión f pressure
prestar v to lend
la primavera f spring
primero/a a first
el/la primo/a mf cousin
la princesa f princess
el príncipe m prince
el principio m beginning
la prioridad f priority
la prisa f hurry
   privado/a a private
el probador m changing room
   probar v to try, test, prove,
   taste
   probarse vr to try on
el problema m problem
procedente (de) a coming
   from
el procesador de textos m
   word processor
producir v to produce,
   producirse vr to take place
el/la profesor/a mf teacher
la profundidad f depth

profundo/a a deep, profound
el programa m programme
el progreso m progress
prohibir v to prohibit, ban
prometer v to promise
el pronóstico m forecast
pronto ad soon, early, quickly
el/la propietario/a mf owner
la propina f tip
propio/a a own
proponer v to propose,
   suggest
proporcionar v to supply
el propósito m purpose
proteger v to protect
la proximidad f proximity,
   closeness
próximo/a a next
el proyecto m project
la prueba f proof, test
publicar v to publish
la publicidad f publicity,
   advertising
el público m public, audience
el pueblo m village, people
el puente m bridge
el/la puerco/a mf pig/sow
el puerro m leek
la puerta f door, gate
el puerto m port
pues conj well, then
el puesto m post, position, job
   puesto que conj since
el pulpo m octopus
la pulsera f bracelet
el puño m fist
el punto m dot, point, spot, place
el pupitre m desk
puro/a a pure

Q

Que pron/conj that, who, which
¡Qué! ad how! ¿Qué? Interrog.
   what?, which?
quebrar v to break
quedar v
   to remain, stay, suit (clothing)
   quedarse vr to arrange, stay
los quehaceres mpl tasks
la queja f complaint
   quejarse vr to complain
la quemadura f burn
   quemar v to burn
querer v to want, love
   querer decir to mean
querido/a a dear
el queso m cheese
quien pron who, whom
la química f chemistry
el/la químico/a mf chemist
   a chemical
la quincena f fortnight, two weeks
quinto/a a fifth
el quiosco m kiosk, news stand
quisiera v
   I/he/she/you would like
quitar v to remove, take away
   quitar el polvo to dust
   quitarse vr to take off (clothes)
quizá(s) ad perhaps

R

el ramo m bunch
el rango m rank
la ranura f groove, slot
rápidamente ad quickly
rápido/a a fast
el rápido m express train
raramente ad rarely
raro/a a strange
el rascacielos m skyscraper
rasgar v to tear, rip
la rata f rat
el ratero m pickpocket
el rato m while, amount of time
el ratón m mouse
el rayo m ray, flash of lightning
la razón f reason
   real a royal
   realizar v to carry out,
   achieve

la rebaja f reduction, sale
las rebajas fpl sales
la rebanada f slice
la rebeca f cardigan
el recado m message, errand
la receta f recipe
recibir v to receive
el recibo m receipt
recientemente ad recently
recoger v to pick up, collect
la recogida f collection
la recompensa f reward
reconocer v to recognize
recordar v to remember
el recreo m break, playtime
recto/a a straight, honest
el recuerdo m souvenir, memory
   recuerdos regards
el recurso m resource
la red f net, network
redondo/a a round
el reembolso m reimbursement
reflexionar v to reflect,
   think about
el refresco m soft drink
regalar v to give (as a present)
el regalo m present, gift
regar v to water, irrigate
la regla f regulation, ruler
regresar v to return
la reina f queen
el Reino Unido m United
   Kingdom
reír(se) v to laugh
relajar v to relax, loosen
   relajarse vr to relax
el relámpago m flash of lightning
el relato m story, account
rellenar v
   to fill up, stuff, fill in (form)
el reloj m watch, clock reloj de
   pulsera wristwatch
la relojería f watchmaker's shop
remar v to row
el remedio m remedy, alternative
el remite m return address
el/la remitente mf sender
rendido/a a exhausted
reñir(se) v to quarrel
reparar v to repair
repartir v to share, divide
repasar v to revise
el reportaje m report, article
resbalar v to slip, skid
rescatar v to save, rescue
el rescate m rescue
resfriado/a a having a cold
respetar v to respect
el respeto m respect
respirar v to breathe
responder v to respond, reply
la respuesta f reply, answer
el resultado m result
el resumen m summary, résumé
retener v to keep, hold
el retraso m delay
el retrovisor m rear-view mirror
la reunión f meeting
   reunirse v to meet, reunite
el revés m back
   al revés backwards
el revisor m ticket collector,
   inspector
la revista f magazine
   revoltoso/a a naughty, unruly
   revolver v to stir
el rey m king
   rezar v to pray
   rico/a a rich, wealthy, delicious
el riesgo m risk
   riguroso/a a severe, harsh,
   tough
el rincón m corner
el río m river
la riqueza f wealth, richness
la risa f laugh
el ritmo m rhythm
   rizado/a a curly
   robar v to rob, steal
el robo m theft, robbery
la roca f rock

rodear v to surround, enclose
la rodilla f knee
rogar v to ask, beg
rojo/a a red
romper/se v/vr to break
roncar v to snore
ronco/a a hoarse, husky
la ronda f round
la ropa f clothes
   ropa interior underwear
la rosa f rose
rosado/a a pink
el rostro m face
roto/a a broken
el rotulador m felt tip pen
rubio/a a blonde, fair-haired
la rueda f wheel
el ruido m noise
ruidoso/a a noisy
la ruta f route

S

el sábado m Saturday
la sábana f sheet
saber v to know
sabio/a a wise, learned
el sabor m flavour, taste
saborear v to taste
el sacacorchos m corkscrew
el sacapuntas m
   pencil sharpener
sacar v to take out, get
el saco m bag, sack
sacudir v to shake
la sal f salt
la sala f room, living room
salado/a a salty, charming
el salario m salary, wage
la salchicha f sausage
la salida f departure, exit
salir (de) v to go out (of/from),
   leave, depart
el salón m lounge, living room
la salsa f sauce
saltar v to jump, jump out
la salud f health ¡Salud! Cheers!
saludar v to greet
el saludo m greeting saludos
   greetings, best wishes
salvaje a wild
salvar v to save
el salvavidas m lifebelt, life jacket
salvo/a a safe
salvo prep except for
la sandía f water melon
la sangre f blood
la sangría f sangria (drink)
sano/a a healthy
santo/a a holy
el/la santo/a mf saint
la sartén f frying pan
el/la sastre/a mf tailor
satisfecho/a a satisfied
se pron to him/her/you/them,
   him/her/your/oneself/
   themselves
   se trata de it's about
el secador de pelo m hairdrier
la secadora f tumble drier
secar v to dry
seco/a a dry
el/la secretario/a mf secretary
la sed f thirst
la seda f silk
seguir v to follow, continue
según prep according to
segundo/a a second
la seguridad f security, safety
seguro/a a safe, certain, sure
el sello m stamp
la selva f jungle, rainforest
el semáforo m traffic lights
la semana f week
semanal a weekly
la señal f signal, sign, mark
las señas fpl address
sencillo/a a simple, single
el sendero m path
el/la señor/a mf man/woman,
   mr/mrs, sir/madam

nouns — **m**: masculine   **f**: feminine   **pl**: plural   **v**: verb   **vr**: reflexive verb   **a**: adjective

la señorita f *miss, young lady*
sensible a *sensitive*
sentarse v *to sit down*
el sentido m *meaning, feeling, sense*
el sentimiento m *feeling, sorrow*
sentir v *to feel*
lo siento *I'm sorry*
separar v *to separate*
se(p)tiembre m *September*
séptimo/a a *seventh*
ser v *to be*
ser de (+ material) *to be made of*
ser de (+ place) *to come from*
la serie f *series, serial*
serio/a a *serious*
el servicio m *service, toilet*
los servicios *the toilets*
la servilleta f *serviette*
servir v *to serve*
se(p)tiembre m *September*
el seto m *fence*
el sexo m *sex*
si conj *if*
sí ad *yes*
sí pron *himself, herself, itself*
la sidra f *cider*
siempre ad *always*
la sierra f *mountain range*
la siesta f *short sleep (after lunch)*
el siglo m *century*
significar v *to mean*
el signo m *sign*
siguiente a *next, following*
silbar v *to whistle*
la silla f *chair*
el sillón m *easy chair, armchair*
la silueta f *silhouette*
la simpatía f *warmth, friendliness*
simpático/a a *nice, friendly*
sin prep *without*
sin plomo *lead free*
el síntoma m *symptom*
el/la sirviente mf *servant*
el sitio m *place, space, room*
situado/a a *situated*
sobrar v *to be left over, remain*
el sobre m *envelope*
sobre prep *on, about, around (time)*
sobre todo *above all*
el/la sobrino/a m *nephew/niece*
la sociedad f *society*
el/la socio/a mf *member*
socorrer v *to help*
el/la socorrista mf *lifeguard*
el socorro m *help, aid*
el sol m *sun*
solamente/sólo ad *only, just*
el/la soldado mf *soldier*
soleado a *sunny*
sólido/a a *solid*
solo/a a *alone*
el solomillo m *sirloin steak*
soltero/a a *single, unmarried*
la sombra f *shadow, shade*
el sombrero m *hat*
soñar (con) v *to dream (about)*
sonar v *to ring, sound*
el sonido m *sound*
sonreír(se) vr *to smile*
la sonrisa f *smile*
la sopa f *soup*
soplar v *to blow, blow out/away*
sordo/a a *deaf*
sorprender v *to surprise*
la sorpresa f *surprise*
el sorteo m *draw, raffle*
la sortija f *ring*
la sospecha f *suspicion*
el sostén m *support, bra*
sostener v *to support, hold*
Sr abb (Señor) *Mr.*
Sra/s abb (Señora) *Mrs.*
Sres abb (Señores) *Messrs*
Srta abb (Señorita) *Miss, Ms.*
suave a *smooth, soft, gentle*
la subida f *rise, increase, ascent*

subir v *to go up, rise*
subir a *get into (a vehicle)*
súbito/a a *sudden*
suceder v *to happen*
sucio/a a *dirty*
la sucursal f *branch (office)*
sudar v *to sweat*
el sudeste m *southeast*
el/la suegro/a mf *father/mother-in-law*
el sueldo m *salary, wage, pay*
el suelo m *floor*
suelto/a a *loose*
el sueño m *dream, sleep* tener sueño *to be sleepy, tired*
la suerte f *luck, chance*
el suéter m *sweater*
sufrir v *to suffer*
sugerir v *to suggest*
sujetar v *to hold, fix*
la suma f *addition, total, sum*
la super f *four-star petrol*
superar v *to surpass, overcome*
el supermercado m *supermarket*
suplementario/a a *supplementary*
suponer v *to imagine, suppose*
el sur m *south*
surfear el Internet v *to surf the net*
el suroeste m *southwest*
el surtido m *selection, range*
sustituir v *to substitute*
el susto m *shock*

T

la Tabacalera f *tobacconist's, stationer's*
el tabaco m *tobacco*
la taberna f *bar, tavern*
la tabla f *plank, board*
tal a *such* tal vez *perhaps*
el Talgo m *inter-city express train*
la talla f *size (clothes)*
el taller m *workshop*
el talonario de cheques *chequebook*
el tamaño m *size*
también ad *also*
el Tamesis m *Thames*
tampoco ad *neither*
tan ad *so, such*
tanto/a a *so much*
tantos/as a *so many*
la tapa f *lid, top, snack* tapas *snacks*
la taquilla f *box office, ticket office*
tarde ad *late*
la tarde f *afternoon, evening*
la tarea f *task* las tareas *homework*
la tarifa f *rate, price*
la tarjeta f *card*
el tarro m *jar, pot*
la tarta f *cake, tart* tarta casera *homemade cake/tart*
la tasa f *rate*
el/la taxista mf *taxi driver*
la taza f *cup*
el tazón m *bowl, mug*
te pron *you, to you*
el té m *tea*
el teatro m *theatre*
el tebeo m *comic*
el techo m *ceiling*
el teclado m *keyboard*
técnico/a a *technical*
el/la técnico/a mf *technician*
el tejado m *roof*
los tejanos mpl *jeans*
la tela f *cloth, material*
telefonear v *to phone*
el teléfono m *telephone*
teléfono móvil *mobile phone*
la telenovela f *soap opera*
el televisor m *television set*
el tema m *theme, subject*
temblar v *to tremble*
la tempestad f *storm*
templado/a a *mild, temperate*

la temporada f *season, time period*
temporal a *temporary*
temprano ad *early*
el/la tendero/a mf *shopkeeper*
tenderse v *to lie down*
el tenedor m *fork*
tener v *to have*
el TER m *inter-city express train*
tercero/a a *third*
terco/a a *stubborn*
terminar v *to finish*
la ternera f *veal*
la terraza f *terrace*
el terremoto m *earthquake*
el terreno m *ground, land*
el/la testigo/a mf *witness*
la tetera f *teapot*
tibio/a a *cool, tepid*
el tiempo m *time, weather*
la tienda f *shop, tent* tienda de campaña *tent*
la tierra f *earth*
tieso/a a *stiff*
el tigre m *tiger*
las tijeras fpl *scissors*
el timbre m *bell (electric), stamp (official)*
tímido/a a *shy, timid*
tinto a *red (wine)*
el tío m *uncle*
típico/a a *typical*
el tipo m *type, kind*
tirar v *to throw, throw away, pull*
tirarse vr *to throw oneself*
el título m *title, qualification*
la tiza f *chalk*
la toalla f *towel*
el tobillo m *ankle*
el tocadiscos m *record player*
el tocador m *dressing table*
tocar v *to play (instrument) / touch*
tocarle a uno *to be someone's turn* (te toca a ti *it's your turn*)
todas fpl *all*
todavía ad *yet, still*
todo/a a *all, every*
tomar v *to take, have*
tomar el sol *to sunbathe*
el tomate m *tomato*
el tono m *tone*
la tontería f *silliness, nonsense*
tonto/a a *silly, stupid*
el tópico m *topic*
torcer v *to turn, twist*
la tormenta f *storm*
el torneo m *tournament, competition*
el tornillo m *screw*
el toro m *bull*
torpe a *slow, dim, clumsy*
la torre f *tower*
la tortilla f *omelette*
la tortuga f *tortoise*
la tos f *cough*
toser v *to cough*
la tostada f *slice of toast*
trabajador/a a *hardworking*
el/la trabajador/a mf *worker*
trabajar v *to work*
el trabajo m *work, job*
traducir v *to translate*
el/la traductor/a mf *translator*
traer v *to bring*
el tráfico m *traffic*
tragar v *to swallow*
la tragedia f *tragedy*
el traje m *suit* (de baño) *swimsuit*
tranquilo/a a *calm, quiet*
transbordar v *to transfer, change*
el transbordo m *change* hacer transbordo *to change (trains etc)*
el/la transeúnte mf *passer-by*
el tranvía m *tram, local train*
el trapo m *rag, cleaning cloth*
el tratamiento de textos m *word processing*

tratar v *to try, treat, deal with*
la travesía f *crossing, voyage*
travieso/a a *naughty*
el trayecto m *journey, route*
el tren m *train*
el triángulo m *triangle*
el trimestre m *term*
triste a *sad*
la trompeta f *trumpet*
tronar v *to thunder*
el trozo m *piece, bit*
la trucha f *trout*
el trueno m *thunder*
tu a *your*
tú pron *you (familiar)*
el tubo m *tube, pipe*
tumbarse vr *to lie down*
el túnel m *tunnel*
el turismo m *tourism*
el/la turista mf *tourist*
tutear v *to use the informal "tú" when talking to someone*

U

ubicado/a a *located, situated*
la UE f (Unión Europea) *EU*
últimamente ad *recently*
último/a a *last, latest, final*
único/a a *only, unique*
la unidad f *unit, unity*
unido/a a *united, close*
el uniforme m *uniform*
la universidad f *university*
un/a art indef mf *a, one*
uno/a pron *one*
unos/as pron pl *some*
la uña f *fingernail*
la urgencia f *urgency, emergency* urgencias *emergency services*
usar v *to use*
usted(es) pron *you s/pl (formal)*
útil a *useful*
utilizar v *to use*
la uva f *grape*

V

la vaca f *cow*
las vacaciones fpl *holidays*
vaciar v *to empty*
vacío/a a *empty*
el vagón m *coach, carriage, wagon*
la vainilla f *vanilla*
la vajilla f *dishes, crockery*
vale excl *ok, fine*
valer v *to be worth, cost*
válido/a a *valid*
valiente a *brave*
el valle m *valley*
el valor m *value*
el vapor m *steam*
los vaqueros mpl *jeans*
variar v *to vary, change*
varios/as a pl *several, various*
el vaso m *glass (drinking)*
la vecindad f *neighbourhood, area*
el/la vecino/a mf *neighbour*
el/la vegetariano/a mf *vegetarian*
el vehículo m *vehicle*
la vela f *candle, sailing*
la velocidad f *speed*
vencer v *to overcome, defeat*
la venda f *bandage*
el/la vendedor/a mf *vendor, seller*
vender v *to sell*
venir v *to come*
la venta f *sale*
la ventaja f *advantage*
la ventana f *window*
la ventanilla f *(vehicle/bank) window, box office*
ver v *to see, watch*
veranear v *to spend summer hols*
el verano m *summer*
la verbena f *fair, festival*
la verdad f *truth* es verdad *it's true*

verdaderamente ad *truly, really*
verdadero/a a *true*
verde a *green*
la verdulería f *greengrocer's shop*
la(s) verdura(s) fpl *vegetables*
la vergüenza f *shame, embarrassment*
la versión f *version*
verter v *to pour, spill*
el vestíbulo m *hall, foyer*
vestido/a a *dressed*
el vestido m *dress*
vestirse vr *to get dressed*
el vestuario m *clothes, wardrobe, dressing room*
el/la veterinario/a mf *vet, veterinary*
la vez f *time, occasion*
la vía f *way, lane (motorway), track*
viajar v *to travel*
el viaje m *journey*
el/la viajero/a mf *traveller*
la víctima f *victim*
la vida f *life*
el videojuego m *video game*
el vidrio m *glass (material)*
viejo/a a *old*
el/la viejo/a mf *old man/woman*
el viento m *wind*
el vientre m *stomach, belly*
el viernes m *Friday* Viernes Santo *Good Friday*
vigilar v *to supervise, guard*
la viña f *vine, vineyard*
el vinagre m *vinegar*
el vino m *wine*
la visibilidad f *visibility*
la visita f *visit*
el/la visitante mf *visitor*
visitar v *to visit*
la víspera f *day before*
la vista f *view, sight*
el/la viudo/a mf *widower/widow*
la vivienda f *home, dwelling*
vivir v *to live*
vivo/a a *alive, lively*
el vocabulario m *vocabulary*
volante a *flying*
el volante m *steering wheel*
volar v *to fly*
volcar v *to knock over, tip out*
el voleibol m *volleyball*
volver v *to return, turn*
volver a + inf *to do again*
volver de *to have just*
volverse vr *to turn round, back*
vomitar v *to vomit, be sick*
vosotros pron pl *you (pl informal)*
la voz f *voice*
el vuelo m *flight*
la vuelta f *return* la vuelta al colegio *return to school* dar una vuelta *go for a spin/stroll*

W

el wáter m *toilet*
el windsurf m *windsurfing*

Y

y conj *and*
y media *half past, and a half*
ya ad *already, yet, now*
el yerno m *son-in-law*
el yogur m *yoghurt*

Z

la zanahoria f *carrot*
la zapatería f *shoeshop*
el/la zapatero/a mf *shoemaker*
la zapatilla f *slipper*
la zapatilla de deporte f *trainer*
el zapato m *shoe*
la zona f *zone, area* zona peatonal *pedestrian precinct*
el zoo m *zoo*
el/la zorro/a mf *fox/vixen*
el zumo m *juice*

---

nouns — **m**: masculine   **f**: feminine   **pl**: plural   **v**: verb   **vr**: reflexive verb   **a**: adjective | Spanish–English Dictionary |

Index